Pilgrim Stories

PILGRIM STORIES

On and Off the Road to Santiago

Nancy Louise Frey

UNIVERSITY OF CALIFORNIA PRESS

Berkeley · *Los Angeles* · *London*

*The publisher gratefully
acknowledges the generous gift
from the Spanish Ministry of Culture
toward the publication of this book.*

University of California Press
Berkeley and Los Angeles, California

University of California Press, Ltd.
London, England

© 1998 by
The Regents of the University of California

Library of Congress Cataloging-in-Publication Data

Frey, Nancy Louise, 1968–
    Pilgrim stories : on and off the road to
Santiago / Nancy Louise Frey.
        p.   cm.
    Includes bibliographical references and index.
    ISBN 0-520-21084-0 (alk. paper)
    ISBN 0-520-21751-9 (pbk.: alk. paper)
        1. Christian pilgrims and pilgrimages—
Spain—Santiago de Compostela.   2. Christian
pilgrims and pilgrimages—Spain—Santiago de
Compostela—Interviews.   3. Frey, Nancy
Louise, 1968–.   4. Santiago de Compostela
(Spain)—Church history—20th century.
I. Title.
BX2321.S3F74   1998
263'.0424611—dc21   98–14153
                                          CIP

Printed in the United States of America
9 8 7 6 5 4 3 2 1

The paper used in this publication is both acid-
free and totally chlorine-free (TCF). It meets the
minimum requirements of American Standard for
Information Sciences—Permanence of Paper for
Printed Library Materials, ANSI Z39.48-1984.

*al
placer
de mi
vida*

Contents

Illustrations

FIGURES

MAPS

Acknowledgments

There are many people who helped to make this book a reality. I am deeply grateful to my teachers, who both inspired and motivated my way: Roy D'Andrade, Alex Bolyanatz (my first teaching assistant), Melford E. Spiro, Tanya M. Luhrmann, Stanley H. Brandes, Alan Dundes, Nelson H. H. Graburn, and Robert N. Bellah. I thank Professors Joaquín Rodríguez Campos (and his family), Nieves Herrero Pérez, and José Antonio Fernández de Rota of Galicia for their encouragement. For their careful readings of the work, I thank William Christian, Jr., and Juan E. Campo; for their inspiration, Judith Adler and Catherine Bell; for her sharp and sensitive copy editor's eye, Sheila Berg; and for his support of the book from the beginning, Doug Abrams Arava. In addition, I am grateful to Tino Martínez for his technical assistance with the photographs.

My friends Ayfer Bartu, Angela Davies, David Kessler, Robyn Kliger, María Massolo, Sara Miller, Ed Molloy, Betsy Ringrose, Luis Sanz, and Serena Van Buskirk offered insights and support.

My gratitude goes to the people of the villages and cities in which I briefly lived for their welcome and good humor: in Roncesvalles, Angel, Jema, Elena, Pili, Pilar, María Asún, Paxti, and the canons of the Real Colegiata; in Belorado, Jacinto García, Agustín Puras, Don Angel, María Jesús, Angelinas, Honorio and Encarna, and Matías and his wife; in Hospital de Orbigo Inmaculada, Raposo and Dolores. I also thank Felix Cariñanos, Jesús Jato and his family, and Marina Otero and Jesús

García for their hospitality while I was in Santiago. Those people with whom I worked as an *hospitalera* deserve special thanks for their patience with my incessant questions: Isabel de Melchor, Marieta Schoone, Beth Lahoski, and Johannes Verhoeven.

I also appreciate the assistance of those whose lives have touched mine via the Camino: Linda Davidson, David Gitlitz, Jonathan Harris, Ioannis Sinanoglou, Barbara Haab, Debbie Salaiz, Joaquín Fernández-Castro, and Elyn Aviva. I owe the members of the Confraternity of St. James in London a hearty thanks, among them, Laurie Dennett, John and Etain Hatfield, Pat Quaife, Joseph May, Marion Marples, Marigold and Maurice Fox, Alison Raju, Sue Morgan, Michael Bartlett, Phinella Henderson, Steve Stuart, Fiona Hedges, Kirby Haye, Stephen Brown, Rosemary Clark, Stephen Badger, Andrew Teeton, and Mary Remnant.

Members of a number of associations also assisted my research: Dirk Aerts (Belgium); Adrien Grand and Joseph Theubet (Switzerland); Mme Jean Debríl (France); Patricia Kennedy (Ireland); Elisabeth Alferink, Herbert Simon, and Konrad Breitrainer (Germany). Within Spain, I thank Angel Luis Barreda; Fernando Imaz (Guipúzcoa); Maribel Roncal and Jesús Tanco (Navarra); Antonio Roa (Estella); Pilar Matute, Antonio Calavia, José Carlos Rodríguez, and María Remedios Malmierca (La Rioja); Jaime Valdivielso (Alava); José Miguel Burgui (Alicante); José Luis López (Astorga); Quim Faroux, Asunción Cuchi, Paco Requena, and Pepa de la Casa Martín (Barcelona); José Luis Nebreda and Alfonso Barcala (Burgos); Domingo Sánchez (Bierzo); Joaquín Miláns del Bosch (Astur-Galaica); Alejandro Uli (Zaragoza); Ferrán Lloret (Sabadell); Xerardo Pardo (Lugo); Juan López-Chávez (Vigo); and Antón Pombo (Santiago). In addition, José Ignacio Díaz, Maite Moreno, and Jaime García Rodríguez (and his staff, Ana López and Antonio Fondo) proved crucial in assisting my research; I thank them heartily.

The original research was made possible through institutional support. My deep gratitude to the Department of Anthropology at the University of California at Berkeley, the Council for European Studies at Columbia University, the Center for German and European Studies at U.C. Berkeley, the Institute of International Education, the Program for Cultural Cooperation Between Spain's Ministry of Culture and United States Universities (University of Minnesota), and the European Communities Studies Association (University of Pittsburgh).

I would like to acknowledge each person who shared a story with me at some time, but I am afraid that this is impossible. Among many more, I thank the following (given in no particular order) who off the road corresponded or spoke with me at length about their experiences: Karl Hallen, Jane and Daniel Potvin, Terry Toner, Ailish Maher, Romain and Renee Degeest, Sara Corredoira, Julio Ruíz, Stefan Schacher, Emilio Bermejo, Olga Ineunza, Alfred Kramer, María Luengo, Roberto de Melchor, Markus Reis, Pepe Izquierdo, Louis Roger, Stefan Ingendoh, Antonio Ferrero, Jesús Ignacio Santos, Ignacio Alonso, María Paz Faraldos, Bernhard Pokorny, Stephan Turnovszky, Audrey and John Timmins, Eduardo Moreno, Marcel Genet, José Pérez, Julian Lord, Iñigo Villacieros, José Miguel, Margit Mühler, María Jesús Recogera, Geurt van de Weg, María Beguiristain, Javier Zulueta, C. Ferte, Samuel and the Maristas from Trinidad de Arre, Mikel Ayestaran, Phil Rees, Jorge Fernández, Isidro Sancho, Silke Maier, Ton and Henny, Sergio Ródenas, Ana Romero, Jorge Moreno, Kaja Montgomery, Joanna Clarke, the brothers Küpper and Newzella, Nino Amor, José Miguel Mosquera, Michael Hartman, Torsten Kopp, Christian Drechsler, Miranda Van Vugt, Stijn Oosterling, Luciana Magalotti, Jesús Cevera, Manolo Tormo, Sophie Blondelle, Ferrán Solsana, Vicente Malabia, Elena Goyanes, César Acero, Isidro Sancho, Jean Teste, Fausto Melo de Souza, Stephen Brown, David Wilks, William Griffiths, Leo Nabben, Lourdes Lluch, Carlos Sagaseta, Massimo Seschleifer, José Klecker, Sandy Lenthall, and Pamela Warnock. In addition, the following people receive my heartfelt thanks for their profound impact on my work: Wilhelm Rinke, Erwin Schneider, Anton Heinrich, Jean Claude Martin, Joan Bueno, and Carmen Winterflood. Howard Nelson enriched the book immeasurably through his careful reading of the text and by allowing me to include three of his poems ("At a small chapel, on a crest"; "For all that they follow the Milky Way"; and "Steering an erratic course"). Andy Breuner provided the base and seed from which the book grew; without him the work probably would not have begun. Mary Pérez and Antonio Placer kindly supported my work and mountains of paper with grace and good humor, for which I thank them profoundly. To my parents, Jane and Charlie Frey, with great love and gratitude for their encouragement. In particular, I thank my mom, a constant beacon and wellspring of love.

And finally, for Jose. There are no words that express the gratitude I feel for his inspiration, patience, critical feedback, and involved support every step of the way. Without him *Pilgrim Stories* would not be.

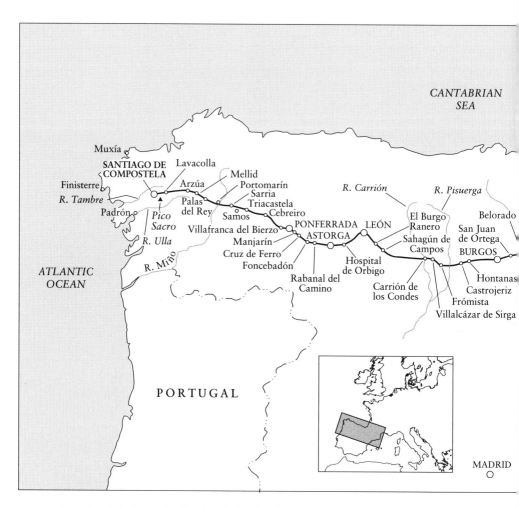

CANTABRIAN
SEA

Muxía

SANTIAGO DE Lavacolla
COMPOSTELA
Finisterre   Mellid
R. Tambre   Arzúa   Portomarín   R. Carrión   R. Pisuerga
    Palas   Sarria
Padrón   Pico   del Rey   Triacastela   Belorado
    Sacro   Samos   Cebreiro   El Burgo
       Villafranca del Bierzo   PONFERRADA   LEÓN   Ranero   San Juan
   R. Ulla   Manjarín   ASTORGA   Sahagún de   de Ortega
      Cruz de Ferro   Campos   BURGOS
ATLANTIC   Foncebadón   Hospital
OCEAN   Rabanal del   de Orbigo   Hontanas
       Camino   Carrión de   Castrojeriz
       los Condes   Frómista
       Villalcázar de Sirga

R. Miño

PORTUGAL

MADRID

The Way of St. James (El Camino de Santiago)

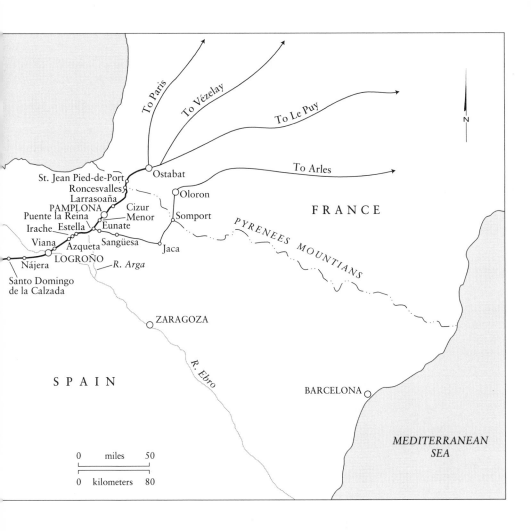

To Paris

To Vézelay

To Le Puy

To Arles

N

St. Jean Pied-de-Port
Roncesvalles
Larrasoaña
PAMPLONA
Puente la Reina
Irache Estella
Viana
Azqueta Sangüesa
LOGROÑO
Nájera
Santo Domingo
de la Calzada

Ostabat

Oloron

Cizur
Menor

Somport

Eunate

Jaca

R. Arga

FRANCE

PYRENEES MOUNTIANS

ZARAGOZA

R. Ebro

SPAIN

BARCELONA

MEDITERRANEAN
SEA

0	miles	50
0	kilometers	80

Arriving at the End

. . . Alice had not a moment to think about stopping herself
before she found herself falling down a very deep well.
                    —*Lewis Carroll*, Alice in Wonderland

From the moment I entered the majestic Plaza del Obradoiro in Santiago
de Compostela, I was surprised to see that far from having disappeared
with the Middle Ages, the pilgrimage was alive and well. I could immediately recognize the modern pilgrims, who represented a mixture of the
present and the past. Their backpacks and bicycles were adorned by the
pilgrim's scallop shell, and many carried walking sticks. They ambled in
the plaza—some alone, others in groups, all ages and nationalities—while
some appeared to know where they were going, others seemed to be in
their own private worlds. Their faces, tanned by many days of sun, reg-
istered a combination of joy, tears, disappointment, and fatigue. They
seemed to be perfectly integrated into the animated scene. Occasionally
a tour bus pulled up and middle-aged men and women got off, visited
the plaza, and then moved toward the cathedral's double staircase. At
the base of the granite stairs three or four women gathered, their arms
laden with silver charms and souvenirs, while former members of the *tu-
nas* (university student singing groups), their long black capes flowing in
the wind, tried to vend their music. In the plaza's center a group of ten
teenagers flopped down to rest on top of their packs and staffs. A pair of
cyclists, with shells tied to their handlebars, stopped in the middle of the
square, looked at the cathedral's baroque facade, and hugged each other.
Passing by them were what appeared to be businessmen and an occasional
black-robed priest or nun. In the air was a combination of church bells
and the sweet sound of a flute reverberating across the stone of ages.

Figure 1.   Plaza del Obradoiro and cathedral, Santiago de Compostela.

As I sat on one of the granite benches that line the plaza taking in this scene, a young woman with a camera approached and asked me to take a photo of her and her boyfriend with the cathedral as the backdrop. I asked if they were pilgrims, noting the shell she wore on a cord around her neck. With a smile they nodded and said that they had begun in Roncesvalles, on the border of Spain and France, and had walked for a month to reach Santiago in the northwest corner of Spain, a journey of 750 kilometers. I was impressed and asked them what it was like to arrive. They replied that they were disappointed the journey was over. They felt strong physically and hoped to come back next year. We spoke for a few more minutes, and then they said they needed to go. I asked them where they were going now. "To the cathedral," they replied. Did I want to come? Finding myself more and more curious about the modern pilgrimage, I agreed. They picked up their backpacks effortlessly (practice, I thought), and as we crossed the plaza, they explained that this was their honeymoon, that they both had made the Camino de Santiago (Road of Saint James) before but wanted to begin the marriage with a strong foundation forged by sharing the natural and human beauty of the Camino. I began to feel a bit confused.

It was noon, and the Pilgrim's Mass was starting. We sat down. The young woman caught someone's eye, and they exchanged a warm smile and small wave. It seemed that at least twenty other pilgrims were at the Mass. The backpacks mounted at the base of one of the massive Romanesque pillars probably belonged to the teenagers who now filled several of the wooden pews instead of the plaza. I recognized older northern Europeans: white hair, polypropylene clothing, bright colors. I found I could not listen to the sermon for the overwhelming impact of what I was seeing and feeling. After the Mass we left by the south entrance to the horse fountain plaza where the young couple rejoined some friends from the trip. With clear regret they said good-bye to their companions from the journey. They had to get the *Compostela* (the cathedral's certificate of completion, they explained) and then rush off to the train station. Both had to be at work the next morning in Barcelona.

I found myself with two other walkers who invited me to join them for a pilgrim's gastronomic tradition: lunch at Casa Manolo where the food was cheap and abundant. As we walked I was surprised at their openness to my questions. They did not seem to mind, and in fact one seemed to need to share his stories of the journey. He had walked out his front door in southern Germany two months previously, feeling an inexplicable loss and hoping that in walking things would become clear. Despite having had the trip of his life he was a bit worried about returning.

His companion, a Basque, felt energized and eager to return to his family and work. I did not have time to ask why, because we arrived and three other friends from the Camino were already in line—two men (one Spanish, the other English) and a Dutch woman.

It was a memorable lunch. Story after story in a mixture of Spanish and English tumbled out of the pilgrims. The Basque man had initially been accompanied by a friend who developed severe tendonitis and had to leave at Burgos, where he met the German. Shared moments and different versions of the same instances caused argument and frequent laughter. They asked about others on the way. What happened to the Frenchman with the donkey? This man, apparently, was also famous for his snoring, which they all recalled ruined a good night's sleep a week earlier in Cebreiro. Two were going to continue to the coast to Finisterre, the medieval end of the earth, the next morning by bus. They did not want to stop yet. I realized that the group had formed by chance; although they had started out alone, they had become friends as they walked. I mostly listened. As I had seen them all at the Pilgrim's Mass I assumed they were Catholic, but one explained that it was an ecumenical road, that one's religious beliefs were irrelevant. I was not a part of this group of "pilgrims," but I could see that I wanted to be. And so it was. The next summer I readied my backpack and took off for the Camino with two American professors and five other students. We also walked 750 kilometers. In 1994 I returned for thirteen months to study and live the pilgrimage for my doctoral dissertation in anthropology.[1]

When faced with the complexity of the contemporary Camino, the categories "pilgrimage" and "pilgrim" seem to lose meaning. Usually the words, especially in English, are associated with a religious journey, faith, or devout seekers, or for Americans, the Thanksgiving Day school plays that re-create the *Mayflower*'s journey. The monopoly on confusion on this point, however, is not limited to the American side of the Atlantic. Before going to Santiago to study a young Italian woman was told that Compostela was similar to the Catholic healing shrine of Lourdes in France. Believing that she would find only "rain and religion," she was surprised by the inaccuracy of this stereotype.[2] Although the Santiago pilgrimage has a religious foundation based in Catholic doctrine regarding sin, its remission and salvation, in its contemporary permutation these religious elements endure, but they also share the same stage with transcendent spirituality, tourism, physical adventure, nostalgia, a place to grieve, and esoteric initiation. The Camino can be (among many other things) a union with nature, a vacation, an escape from the drudgery of the everyday, a spiritual path to the self and humankind, a social reunion, or a personal testing ground. It is "done" and "made" as a pilgrimage, but what does that mean now? The glue that holds these disparate elements together seems to be the shared journey, the Camino de Santiago.[3]

ROAD MAPS TO DISCOVERY

What is now commonly referred to as the Camino de Santiago is really a network of routes, many of Roman origin, extending throughout Europe that have been used regularly by pilgrims since the eleventh century to reach Santiago de Compostela.[4] The various *caminos* are based on other historical pilgrimage roads to Santiago. The *camino inglés* (English way) led British pilgrims arriving by sea at La Coruña south to Santiago, the *camino portugués* (Portuguese way) brought pilgrims north, and the *vía de la plata* (silver way) was used by pilgrims from the south and center of the peninsula to join the *camino francés* (French/Frankish way) at Astorga.

The "Camino" now generally refers to the camino francés because it is and was the most popular for its infrastructure of pilgrims' refuges (*hospitales,* or hospices) and cities as well as monasteries, hermitages, and churches. The early medieval pilgrimage played an important role in the Christian repopulation of the peninsula fostered by the reigning political forces: kings of Navarre, Castile, and Galicia eager for control of lands and ecclesiastical powers seeking to expand reformed monastic orders south of the Pyrenees. The repopulation brought merchants and artisans, particularly Frankish ones, the development of an extensive infrastructure of villages, bridges, roads, and the construction of Romanesque and Gothic churches. Many elements of Spanish medieval art, literature, music, and architecture can be traced to Frankish influences of the same period, and vice versa. Much of this artistic traffic occurred along what was, by the thirteenth century, a well-developed pilgrimage and economic exchange route that touched all of early Europe. This route and the *camino del norte* (north way) along the Cantabrian coast brought pilgrims from the rest of Europe to Santiago. After crossing the Continent by one of the four French routes (Paris, Vézelay, Arles, Le Puy) pilgrims reached the natural frontier created by the Pyrenees.[5]

In the late twentieth century, as in the twelfth century, the camino francés enters Spain at two mountain passes, Roncesvalles and Somport. Both unite at Puente la Reina and continue via the stunning medieval stone bridge as one route that crosses Spain and a richly varied countryside— from the gentle mountains of the Pyrenees to the lush, rolling Navarrese

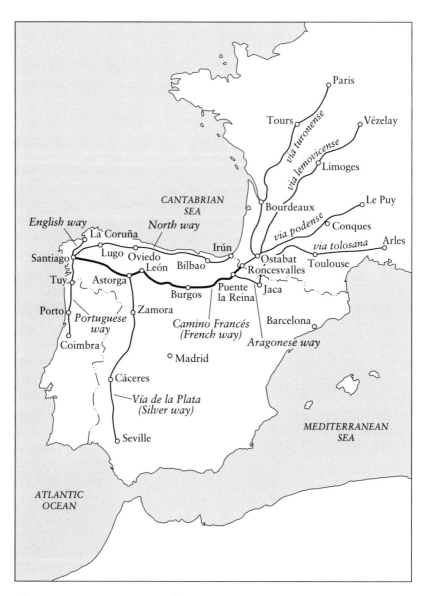

Pilgrimage routes to Santiago in Iberia and France

hills and the bull-running streets of Pamplona to the famous vineyards of La Rioja and the wild forests and ancient dwellings outside of Burgos through the often desolate, high plains of Castilian wheat (the *meseta*) to the slow-rising mountains protecting Galicia and finally through the verdant eucalyptus-lined paths that lead to Santiago's door. The Camino also passes through large urban areas and villages whose formation and history coincide with its development. The pilgrimage routes are predominantly rural, open, and unpaved—just as modern pilgrims wish.

As I learned about the pilgrimage's reanimation, I discovered that these historical facts are important; modern pilgrims often want to travel the same routes as the medieval pilgrims who first ventured to Santiago, and to experience them in the same way. The emphasis placed on the journey and how one reaches the shrine at Santiago struck me as marking an important difference between other popular western European pilgrimage centers such as Fátima in Portugal or Lourdes in France. With these other centers, whose devotion is centered on the Virgin Mary by a Catholic majority, the pilgrims' essential ritual acts occur within the bounded sacred space of the shrine. The pilgrims' mode of transport, or way of arriving, at the shrine is usually secondary or irrelevant. It surprised me that unlike the pilgrims at Fátima or Lourdes, these white, urban, European, middle-class men and women made the pilgrimage—from a week to four months—on foot, bicycle, and horse. Rather than a healing shrine of short-term visits, the contemporary Santiago pilgrimage is not confined to the city itself but consists of a long physical and often internal (spiritual, personal, religious) journey. In many cases making the pilgrimage becomes for participants one of the most important experiences of their lives. Pilgrims want to feel and live the road step by step (or pedal after pedal). Non-Catholics, agnostics, atheists, and even seekers of esoteric knowledge go side by side with Catholics and Protestants.

The Catholic Marian-centered shrines (with devotion focused on the Virgin Mary) also lack the long-term infrastructure and the sense of community that Santiago pilgrims develop by forming part of an informal society whose membership goes back a thousand years and includes such notables as Charlemagne, Saint Francis of Assisi, and King Ferdinand and Queen Isabella of Spain. Marking the popularization and desacralization of the Camino on a wide scale, actress Shirley MacLaine joined the ranks of the famous by making her spiritual journey on foot in 1994 (finding out I was American, Spaniards often remembered her and commented on her presence in their villages). The majority of the Marian-centered shrines (Lourdes in France, Fátima in Portugal, and Medjugorje in Bosnia) are based on miracles or apparitions (Church-confirmed earthly visitations of the Virgin Mary to a seer or seers) that occurred after 1850. The pilgrimage to Santiago is based on a tradition said to reach back to the foundation of Christianity.[6]

Beginning in the 1980s an infrastructure of pilgrim's *refugios* (hospices or refuges), run by *hospitaleros* (volunteer attendants) and based on the medieval model of charity, sprang up on the route, allowing pilgrims to journey knowing that shelter is available and affordable. The routes are marked with bright yellow arrows or scallop shells. Signs along the route explain the pilgrimage's numerous historical sites. Pilgrims also carry a credential, or pilgrim's passport, that is stamped each day and, in Santiago, presented at the cathedral's office of reception for pilgrims to receive the *Compostela*, a document certifying completion of the journey. Before or after the journey pilgrims sometimes join a confraternity of St. James or a Friends of the Camino association, found throughout Europe and with chapters in the United States and Brazil. The pilgrimage may begin with the decision to make the journey, but it rarely ends with arrival in the city.

A PASSAGE TO SPAIN

A perplexing question haunts the pilgrimage: How did the northwestern hinterlands of the Iberian Peninsula become the final resting place of an apostle martyred in Jerusalem? Other than notes from apocryphal texts there is no evidence that James ever set foot in Iberia, yet by the twelfth century the number of pilgrims visiting his tomb rivaled that of Rome and Jerusalem. The answer leads one into a maze of legends, political intrigue, and religious belief in medieval Europe. The pilgrimage's fame rapidly grew after the first millennium, drawing pilgrims from all walks of life and corners of the Christian world eager to be close to one of Christ's inner circle.[7]

Before becoming the fourth apostle of Christ, James the Elder (or the Greater) was a fisherman in Galilee with his brother John (the Evangelist) and his father, Zebedee. One day while they were mending their nets Jesus passed and called them to Him. They left the nets behind, took up their new work with a passion—they were given the nickname Boanerges, or Sons of Thunder, by Jesus—and became especially important among the apostles, appearing at moments crucial in the ministry of Jesus: the Transfiguration and the Agony in the Garden of Gethsemane. Because of their apparently favored position among the apostles, they (or their mother) had the audacity to ask to sit eternally on the right and left side of God and for their impudence received a decisive lesson in humility from Jesus. James's scriptural and mortal end comes swiftly in Acts: Herod Agrippa martyrs him (by beheading) in A.D. 44.[8]

At this point facts dry up and the rich legends begin. There is no mention of Iberia or James's postdeath whereabouts in the Gospels, but according to later texts and eighth- and ninth-century documents, Jesus sent James to proselytize in the west, to the end of the earth—Finisterre.[9] After achieving only marginal success, James returned to Jerusalem, and while en route the Virgin Mary appeared to him along the banks of the Ebro River in Zaragoza, bearing a jasper pillar. This apparition of the Virgin not only provided literal and symbolic support to his mission, it also helped give birth to the popular cult and shrine of the Virgen del Pilar.

After his return to Jerusalem and his subsequent beheading James made his second and, arguably, most important coming to the Iberian Peninsula. His remains (including his head), collected by two faithful disciples, were miraculously returned to the northwestern corner of the peninsula in a stone boat that had neither sail nor oars.[10] The boat, with the disciples and their holy charge, moored on the banks of Iria Flavia near Padrón (16 km from Santiago). It was also in the return that the first miracle associated with his presence in Spain is invoked, linking him to the scallop shell, a key symbol of the pilgrim: "As the stone ship . . . neared the land at Padrón, a horseman riding on the beach was carried by his bolting horse into the waves. Instead of being drowned, however, both horse and rider emerged from the deep covered with scallop shells."[11] James's body was transported inland to the mount that is present-day Santiago de Compostela after having received hard-won permission from Lupa, the local pagan queen (who subsequently converted), to bury the apostle.

Santiago's tomb was forgotten for nearly eight hundred years until one day a religious hermit named Pelayo reported seeing a glowing light or star, which on cautious investigation revealed the apostle's resting place. Compostela is thus said to have received its name from *compostium,* burial ground, or *campus stellae,* starry field.[12] Pelayo went to Bishop Teodomiro, who immediately called an investigation and ordered the construction of a church on the site with the financial support of the Asturian king Alfonso II. Thus began Santiago's patronage of Spain, his miraculous postmartyrdom presence in the Iberian Peninsula, the alignment of Church and civil authority, and the beginning of a thousand-year history of pilgrimage calling the faithful from the farthest reaches of the Continent.[13]

The ninth-century rediscovery of the tomb filled a political-religious

Figure 2.   Santiago's translation from Jerusalem and the legend of the drowning bridegroom on the granite wall of the Plaza de las Platerías, Santiago de Compostela. Note the horseman with a scallop shell (bottom right) and the little fish (left).

need linked to the Reconquest of the peninsula from the Islamic Moors and reflected the importance of sacred relics in the Christian worldview of the eleventh and twelfth centuries. What Santiago was unable to do during his lifetime through nonviolent preaching was rectified in his ninth-century incarnation as Santiago Matamoros, or Caballero (Moorslayer, or Knight). At Clavijo (La Rioja area of Spain) in 844 his legendary appearance to King Ramiro I launched the first decisive counter-Islamic victory. In the dream Santiago told Ramiro, "Our Lord Jesus Christ . . . gave Spain for me to watch over her and protect her from the hands of enemies of the Faith. . . . And so . . . tomorrow will you see me go into battle, *on a white horse, with a white standard and a great shining sword in my hand.*"[14] Thus Santiago Matamoros was born, and his appearance at other crucial Reconquest battles astride a white horse continued to urge the holy drive south.[15] This iconography of Santiago as Moorslayer, found almost exclusively in Spain, played an important role throughout the Reconquest, and it has been a recurrent theme in violent aspects of Spanish politics and piety since.[16] In 997 the Islamic military forces of the mighty Almanzor swept down on the nascent Santiago de Compostela, razed the city, and, according to legend, carried off the church's bells to Córdoba (where they were inverted and used as lamps for the Mezquita). Despite this destructive foray the Moors never established themselves strongly in the Northwest, chilly and isolated behind a natural mountain barrier. Santiago was the ideal symbolic tool, though, to unify and rally Christian forces against the Islamic majority (711–1492) in Iberia.

Belief in the apostle's presence in Compostela bolstered the Christian drive south and the repopulation of the peninsula, which ultimately led to the expulsion of non-Christians from Spain in 1492. Compostela's status as a major pilgrimage center was definitively launched in the tenth and eleventh centuries when the political powers of Aragón, Navarre, and León realized the political expedience of aligning themselves with the French kings and abbots through marriage, military alliances, and monastic reformation. The Benedictine Order of Cluny was the favored religious body in the monastic push south, and the many monasteries located on the route bear witness to its ecclesiastical influence. In addition, the sharp political maneuverings of Compostela's mastermind bishop, Diego Gelmírez, positioned Santiago favorably with Rome.

Another dominant feature of Santiago's multidimensional character and iconography is that of Santiago Peregrino (Saint James the Pilgrim). Uniquely, Santiago appears in the iconography as a pilgrim to his own shrine.[17] He is often depicted wearing a three-cornered hat and a long cape

*Figure 3.   Saint James/Santiago as Moorslayer/Matamoros (left) and Pilgrim/
Peregrino (right).*

laden with pilgrim shells and carrying a staff with a gourd for drinking
and a small pouch. The pilgrimage flourished within a religious worldview that regarded it as a means to achieve salvation of the soul and remission of sin through penitential acts (sometimes through physical sacrifices).[18] During the first centuries of the second millennium it was believed
that through touching and seeing sacred relics, or earthly remains, of holy
people and things they were in contact with (beginning hierarchically with
Christ and extending to the Virgin Mary and the apostles and finally the
saints), including hair, hands, feet, and, of course, the whole body, the pilgrim could transfer part of the sacred to himself. The faithful sought to
bring themselves closer to the divine through physical contact with the
relics. The Catholic church encouraged this belief by instituting penitential pilgrimages and granting indulgences to those who visited sacred
places. In effect, one could be assured a place in the afterlife if money,
time to journey, and fortitude were plentiful. This worldview was reinforced by Romanesque art, nicknamed the Bible in Stone for its didactic
success with a largely illiterate population. The sculptures and frescoes
both inside and outside the churches graphically depicted the horrors
awaiting the sinful, the promise for the good, scenes (primarily) from the

New Testament, and so on. Romanesque art (and later, Gothic art) helped to promote the cult of the saints and is found extensively along the pilgrimage roads throughout Europe (which were fundamental in its expansion and in making it the first international Christian art style). The confirmation of the presence of one of Christ's most important apostles in Galicia made Santiago de Compostela and the hundreds of churches along or near the route with their own relics new important destinations for medieval pilgrims and an important alternative to Rome and Jerusalem, the latter closed to pilgrims in 1087 by Muslim occupation.

The early popularization of the Camino, thanks to papal support from Rome, was cemented through authority vested in the written word. Success came quickly for those pushing to increase Santiago's prestige: Pope Calixto II conferred the coveted Jubilee, or Holy Year, status in 1122 to the shrine, allowing pilgrims to receive plenary indulgences.[19] A key factor in the cult's early spread throughout the Christian world was the twelfth-century appearance of the *Liber Sancti Jacobi* (Book of Saint James), whose letter of introduction, attributed to Pope Calixto II, also makes it the *Codex Calixtinus*. This remarkable text consists of five chapters, or books, that provide a wealth of detail on the history, music, and liturgy of the cult of Saint James, the translation story, and a polemical account linking Charlemagne's campaigns to the Reconquest and his success to the apostle's influence. Curiously, the twenty-two miracles attributed to Santiago in the second chapter take place away from the shrine, before or during the journey to Compostela—an indication of the importance of the road since its founding.[20] The final chapter, the Pilgrim's Guide, is one of the first guidebooks of the Christian West, generally attributed to Aimery Picaud, a cleric from Parthenay-le-Víeux in the Poitou. The guide gives detailed descriptions of the hospices, relics and reliquaries, landscapes, routes, rivers, and peoples of the way as well as a primer of the Basque language and vivid examples of twelfth-century Frankish chauvinism. The purpose of the *Liber* seemed to be a combination of proving the authenticity of Santiago's presence in Galicia, bolstering the importance of Compostela as a pilgrimage destination, and linking the French Cluny to the promotion of the pilgrimage.[21]

The journey to Santiago in the tenth through the thirteenth century was not easy, but nonetheless the pilgrimage flourished. The roads were dangerous and wild; besides disease and animals such as wolves, bears, and boars, the pilgrim had plenty of thieves to contend with. Traveling in large groups, unlike today, pilgrims sought safety in numbers. Unless they were wealthy, they carried little and relied on the religious charity or alms of hospices and monasteries to maintain themselves as they attempted to cross the north. All classes of people went to Santiago, but the majority were sick, old, and poor. The medieval pilgrims, like their contemporary counterparts, went to Santiago for a variety of motives, which were subject to change over time. Though it is hard to discern motivations across the centuries among the illiterate majority, devotion to Saint James (including prayer and hope for future health and betterment) was probably the most prevalent motive. Penitents were sent to atone for minor sins and serious crimes. Civil sanctions could also be paid through the journey. And some pilgrims went for the adventure, out of curiosity, or to free themselves from rigid social norms.[22] Others capitalized on the economic benefits to be gained from the pilgrimage's growing status as a well-traveled road. Death was an anticipated outcome of the journey, but one that ensured safe passage to the heavenly Jerusalem. In leaving home the pilgrim set off on a long journey with an uncertain return, often leaving kith and kin behind. In spite of the hazards millions of pilgrims flocked to Compostela believing and hoping in the efficacy of Santiago and his shrine of stone. Then, as now, it was inevitably an adventure.

After the Protestant Reformation of the sixteenth century pilgrimages to Santiago declined significantly. A number of entertaining pilgrims' accounts survive from the fourteenth to seventeenth centuries, indicating that pilgrims braved the way despite the Spanish Inquisition and, later, the wars in the Pyrenees and southern France.[23] Writings critical of the pilgrimage began to surface, and pilgrims became mistrusted.[24] To make matters worse, the saint's relics were lost (hidden) in 1589 with the threat of Sir Francis Drake's arrival on the coast; they were found during the 1879 excavations in the cathedral. And in the seventeenth century Santiago's status as the patron saint of Spain was threatened to be replaced by the mystic nun Saint Teresa of Avila. In the nineteenth century the numbers of pilgrims arriving in Santiago again dwindled significantly but never completely ceased. The general decline continued into the twentieth century until after World War II, when attention began to focus on rebuilding Europe through a collective past.[25]

REANIMATING SANTIAGO

In 1986 the late Father Elías Valiña Sampedro, a man deeply devoted to the pilgrimage, commented that the resurgence of the Camino "was a European social phenomenon that had been put into motion which nobody could detain."[26] And so it is. The reanimation of the Camino[27] began at a political moment in European history serving well the interests of Church, state, and the individual. The breaking down of political and social borders on a pan-European scale helped to facilitate this process. The relative peace in Western Europe since the late 1940s, the increased mobility of middle-class Europeans seeking leisure opportunities, and the continuous transnational publicity of the Camino brought it literally to the front doors of many Europeans.

Despite a decline in church attendance across Europe since the 1960s, an aging membership in religious orders, and a general secularization of public society, a noted resurgence of interest in alternative spiritual and religious movements also influenced the pilgrimage's reanimation. "A growing number of people are on a 'pilgrimage for spirituality'" notes the author of a best-selling guide to reading the Bible. Not only are metaphorical pilgrimages popular, but an increased interest in travel to European pilgrimage centers is noted and even confusing to religious leaders: "The chase for material goods has left them with more toys and less satisfaction, the culture assaults their sensibility and politics seems stale. So they are looking for something more for themselves and their families—something they hope to find in a new inner life."[28]

The grassroots work of the Friends of the Camino associations, return pilgrims, energetic and historically minded people along the Camino, astute politicians, and academics of medieval studies have also helped to launch the Camino definitively into the cultural and political limelight. Within an ethos of political and cultural nostalgia individuals in greater numbers began to take up the call of the Santiago pilgrim and head west with the sun to Santiago de Compostela. What fin-de-siècle pilgrims find in the image of Santiago Peregrino goes beyond the obvious political overlay and leads us to a more personal view of what moves people to journey, like their ancestors, to Santiago. In the medieval pilgrimage and pilgrim modern pilgrims find a direct link to the past, an authenticity based on sacrifice, endurance, and austerity imagined to have been lived by the medieval pilgrim, and a community of souls united by the rhythm of their feet as the second millennium comes to a close.

ORGANIZATION OF THIS BOOK

In my initial introduction to the Camino in 1992 the pilgrimage's reanimation as a personal experience and social phenomenon of visible import intrigued me. The issues that shaped my subsequent research into pilgrims' lives and the pilgrimage's aftermath began to unfold during this first encounter with the Camino and its participants. What are modern pilgrims saying about the world by walking and cycling? What kind of dialectical relationship is there between the development of the inner and outer journey across space and time? What happens when pilgrims go home? I knew from my own experience that going home is not always easy. I wanted to find out in a general way what others experienced. Why has the pilgrimage and the idea of being a pilgrim become popular once again for both the nonreligious and the devout?

Chapters 1 through 4 focus on the contemporary Camino within Spain and the pilgrims who course its ways. Through contact with nature, the routes, and others pilgrims often open themselves to potential personal and social transformation. These experiences of the journey influence the participant's sense of becoming a pilgrim. It becomes apparent that the journey becomes meaningful through movement and contact with the natural landscapes and people along the way. Chapters 5 through 7 focus on the physical journey's end and what happens to pilgrims as they reach Santiago de Compostela. Once there pilgrims begin to make the transition back to daily life within the city but sometimes opt to continue to other sites associated with the pilgrimage. Endings are made on various physical, psychological, and spiritual levels both during and after reaching Santiago. Instead of ending in Santiago, like most accounts, the focus shifts in chapter 8 to the journey home. How do participants understand their experiences? And how do these experiences continue to influence their daily lives, if at all?

CHAPTER I

PILGRIMS TO SANTIAGO

In the general sense a pilgrim is anyone who is out of his
own country; in a limited sense pilgrim means only one who
travels to or returns from the house of St. James. . . . They
are called *palmeros* who journey across the sea to that Holy
Land, whence they often bring back palms; they are called
pilgrims who journey to the house of Galicia, because the
tomb of St. James is farther away from his home country
than that of any other apostle.
                    —*Dante,* La Nuova Vita

Dante suggested in the thirteenth century that distance traveled and foreignness made one a Santiago pilgrim. Today there are many types of
pilgrims,[1] many ways of going, and many ways to interpret what it means
to be a pilgrim to "the house of Saint James." Rather than the length
of the journey, the central factor in pilgrims' categories is how one makes
the journey. In general terms the division is between human- and motor-
powered travel; between those who walk, bicycle, use a pack animal, or
go by horseback and those who make the journey seated in a car, bus,
or airplane.

THE POLEMICS OF MOVEMENT: AN ANECDOTE

I was sitting outside the curious eight-sided twelfth-century church in Eunate, Navarre, resting my legs and warming my back after the morning
walk when I saw a red figure approaching in the distance. From the slow
gait, large pack, and unmistakable red rain suit, I recognized a German
pilgrim I had met the day before. We exchanged smiles as he lowered his
bag to the ground. Luckily the church was open, and we entered the cool,
dark space talking about the various legends associated with its unusual
shape, inexplicable name, and lost history. As we sat down on one of the

wooden pews against the wall, a group of about twenty-five Germans in their late fifties loudly filed in and took seats in the small shrine. I was quite surprised to recognize their leader, an active member of a German Friends of the Camino association whom I had interviewed in Cologne the month before. After he delivered a lecture on the church, the group sang several hymns and ended with a prayer. Meanwhile my reticent pilgrim friend suddenly turned loquacious and made critical remarks about the group: because they traveled by bus, they didn't understand the pilgrimage, they thought they were pilgrims but weren't, their religious practice seemed hypocritical and disrespectful, and so on. Finally they looked at us with some curiosity and then got on the bus and left. We warmed ourselves in the sun for a while and then put on our packs and continued on the dirt road.

Walkers and cyclists see a world of difference between pilgrims who travel under their own power and those who use some other form of transport to get to Santiago. Like this German walking pilgrim, most pilgrims of the former category usually consider those who go by bus to be tourists, that is, inauthentic. The latter, they argue, do not understand what it means to be connected to the road and, as another put it, to go the "human speed." Even if one is religiously motivated, pilgrim status is reserved for those who get to Santiago by foot and pedal. Pilgrims use their bodies and the ways they move to make a statement about themselves and their society. One's movements and ways of traveling the Camino contribute to its consecration or desecration as a sacred space. Cars and buses (in the walkers' view) tarnish the essence of the road.[2]

Motorized coach pilgrimages organized by parishes or cultural groups represent the majority of pilgrims who go to Santiago to visit the cathedral, to pray at the tomb of Saint James, to attend Mass, or to present an offering at the altar.[3] Bus groups come from all over Europe, Japan, the United States, and Latin America; and participants tend to be Catholic. For example, in the United States the Catholic Travel Center organizes worldwide tours and pilgrimages and Eucharist Congress groups from their offices in Van Nuys, California, and Rome, Italy. Their itineraries for 1993 included package tours to Santiago, Lourdes, and Barcelona or Lisbon, Fátima, and Santiago. Similar patterns of short-term, organized and informal motorized pilgrimages are found at most of the major European Christian pilgrimage centers and are "the most characteristic modern pilgrimage . . . blended with tourism, [involving] a major journey, usually by modern means of transportation, to a national or international shrine."[4]

Figure 4.   A Swiss man and a Spanish woman walking, with the village of Villamayor and the Castle of Monjardín (Navarre) in the background.

Pilgrims who go by car usually attempt to follow the Camino as closely as possible and use guidebooks to find their way and locate monuments, churches, and bridges, and so on, associated with the pilgrimage. These may be repeat pilgrims traveling with family members who are not able or do not wish to walk or those who would simply prefer to get to Santiago without the physical effort. A novel group of car pilgrims formed in 1994: the Friends of the Seat 600, a small car famous throughout Spain in the 1960s and 1970s, drive in caravan to Santiago, attend Mass in the cathedral, and make a floral offering at Santiago's altar.

NON- AND SEMIMOTORIZED PILGRIMAGES

Pilgrims who go to Santiago on foot, by bicycle, by horse, or with a pack animal fall into the nonmotorized category. Those who do the same but rely on a support vehicle to transport heavy equipment (cooking gear, tents, books, extra supplies) are in the semimotorized group. Support-car pilgrims walk or cycle to the designated evening stopping place, where they are joined by the support vehicle. Sometimes the drivers and walkers rotate, or one person drives ahead and then hitchhikes back to the starting point. Increasingly in the mid-1990s some foot pilgrims take taxis or buses for portions of the journey that are considered less scenic or when they are tired or pressed for time.

Within these groups there are further subdivisions: full-time, part-time, and weekend pilgrims. Full-time pilgrims, who make up the majority, begin at one point on the route (e.g., Roncesvalles, Burgos, or León) or at their homes (in Spain, France, Belgium, etc.) and travel without stopping to Santiago. Part-time pilgrims get to Santiago in stages, and the journey may take a number of years through short-term (one-week or two-week) trips. The cumulative distance and time may be the same or longer than that of full-time pilgrims. Part-time pilgrims usually explain that time constraints prohibit them from making the continuous journey, though some, believing that pilgrimage is a process that requires the passage of time to bear the fruit of insight, choose to make the journey in stages. A Dutch woman I met in the pilgrim's refuge of Estella, in her seventh year of two-week stages to Compostela, believed that the pilgrimage was a journey of leaving and returning home, of walking and subsequent reflection. Each year she began renewed and eager to explore ideas from the previous year. She felt like a full-time pilgrim both on and off the road and even criticized those who make the journey without pause because they are unable to absorb and understand all it offers in the moment. She suggested that they often remain pilgrims only while they are on the road, and the effects of the journey are thus diminished.

Weekend pilgrims are usually members of associations dedicated to the pilgrimage and its routes which organize walking excursions on various Jacobean paths. A portion of the Camino is selected, and the participants drive or are bused to the starting point and then walk the section. Despite the limited time and length of their journeys, weekend pilgrims believe they too are undertaking a pilgrimage ("All roads lead to Santiago, no?"). For example, while I was working as an *hospitalera* in Roncesvalles I attended the daily Mass in which the long-distance pilgrims are invited to approach the altar and are given an eight-hundred-year-old pilgrim's blessing by one of the canons of the Real Colegiata (a type of monastery in the small village). One day a group of nearly fifty Spanish weekend pilgrims (from the Burgos Friends of the Camino Association) arrived by bus to begin a two-day stint the next morning. As usual, the priest called the pilgrims forward and, to his surprise, the whole group went to the altar with the long-distance foot and bicycle pilgrims. He perceived this to be a grave misunderstanding of the pilgrimage but nonetheless gave them the blessing, illustrating the multiple interpretations of the modern pilgrim.

Large-scale weekend pilgrimages, which link elements of *romerías* (local pilgrimages associated with the celebration of a saint's feast day),[5] began to be made to Santiago in the early 1990s. These are often community events announced in local and regional newspapers. For example, in 1996 this article appeared: "Within the program organized by the Friends of the Camino de Santiago, 100 people from Lugo walked in pilgrimage between Portomarín and Palas [Galicia]."[6] This was the first 23-kilometer day of the group's foot journey to Santiago that they were making on weekends from January to March. The day also included a cultural visit and a group dinner, the typical atmosphere of a romería.[7]

MOTIVES

These general divisions say very little about why people travel to Santiago or who they are. Different values and styles of life motivate the journeys of motorized and nonmotorized pilgrims. The restaurant Américain in the French village St. Jean Pied-de-Port is run by a Spanish woman from Santander who lived for fifteen years in Bakersfield, California. By chance we struck up a conversation in English, and she asked me what I was doing in St. Jean. This led naturally to the Camino.

MARÍA: I've been to Santiago [1993].

N.L.F.:   How did you get there?

MARÍA: (A laugh) I went by bus and we walked parts to get the . . . the . . . I don't know the word in English, indulge . . .

N.L.F.:   *Indulgencia,* indulgence.

MARÍA: Yes, that's it, *indulgencia.*

N.L.F.:   How long did it take you? (I was thinking the answer would be a week or so.)

MARÍA: Almost the whole day. We stopped and picked up more people on the way from Santander. Four days in total.

N.L.F.:   And what did you do in Santiago?

MARÍA: It was not the cathedral but the Plaza de Obradoiro that impressed me. There are other cathedrals in Spain more beautiful, but just being there was impressive. I felt power in the church as well, but it was too short a visit.

María's bus pilgrimage from her diocese during the 1993 Holy Year, taped on home video, is fairly typical of the many organized excursions (especially Spanish) to Santiago motivated by devotional practice in which the special emphasis is on going to the cathedral in Holy Years and the group social element. Her family and friends participated, and it was a

normal extension of other types of social activities with a religious overlay within her natal Catholic, working-class community. Frequently three-
or four-day coach trips to Santiago combine religious and cultural
tourism and may include visits to other historic and religious monuments,
lectures, masses at select churches, gastronomic offerings, and possibly
a weekend on the Galician coast. Spain's National Social Security Institute (Instituto Nacional de Serguridad Social, or Inserso) organizes,
among various other activities, inexpensive trips within Spain for retired
people. It ran numerous trips to Santiago during the 1993 Holy Year
which brought thousands of retired people to visit the apostle Saint James
and the Galician coast.

The wish to earn the special indulgences associated with Holy Years
(*ganar el jubileo*) also motivates large numbers of organized Catholic pilgrimages. There have been 115 Holy Years (which occur when July 25
falls on a Sunday) since their institution in 1122 by Pope Calixto II, and
they occur in a cyclical pattern of every 6-5-6-11 years. For example, the
1993 Holy Year was preceded by the 1982 celebration. The next and last
Holy Year of the twentieth century, in 1999, also marks the end of the
second millennium. During a Holy Year a plenary indulgence (a remission of sin based in Catholic doctrine) is conferred on those who do the
following: (1) visit the cathedral, recite a prayer, and pray for the inten-
tions of the Church and (2) confess (fifteen days before or after) and take
communion.[8]

How one arrives at the cathedral, whether motorized or nonmotorized, makes no difference on a doctrinal level for the receipt of indulgences. Nonetheless some people are not sure about how the system functions and believe that only pilgrims who walk or cycle (for the greater
physical effort) may receive an indulgence. An increase in pilgrims and
communions during Holy Years is common. The largest increase is in
the motorized category, though for the 1993 Holy Year an unprecedented
100,000 out of 6 to 8 million total visitors either walked a minimum of
100 kilometers or biked 200 kilometers to Santiago to receive the *Compostela*. These distances, established arbitrarily by the Church in the
1980s, represent an idea of pilgrimage based on suffering and sacrifice
(time and physical effort).

Local bus pilgrimages to Santiago and those from beyond Galicia are
often distinct. Among the many Galician pilgrims, who often go on pilgrimages organized by the diocese, one commonly hears "Haiche que estar a ben co Apóstolo" (One has to be in good standing with the apostle). The cult of the saints is strong among rural, elderly Galicians who

want to keep all the saints "content," above all Saint James. This sense of being on the apostle's "good side" motivates devotional practices and encourages the visit to Santiago.

Like the German bus pilgrims at Eunate who made a religious and educational stop, the bus pilgrimage is often culturally oriented toward Spain and the rituals of the Camino, culled from centuries of pilgrims' travels, both along the way and in Santiago. Bus pilgrims may identify with the image of the "authentic" walking pilgrim through buying souvenirs associated with the pilgrimage (e.g., the pilgrim's staff and scallop shell) while in Santiago. In this milieu the walking and cycling pilgrims often become objects of attraction themselves, a curiosity representing sacrifice and action that the average visitor would not make. Coach pilgrims, identified stereotypically as Japanese, may ask walking pilgrims to pose for a photo.

Pilgrims who travel by motorized means may also want to participate in these rites and even look on with envy at the foot and cycle pilgrims. Walking a one-kilometer stretch from the bus down the "old way" (as did María's bus group from Santander) may be integrated into the itinerary so that participants can get a feel of the road. Or bus groups commonly walk the last 6 kilometers from the last high point, Monte del Gozo, before reaching Santiago. "It made all of us excited to arrive in Compostela like pilgrims," said one man, as his four-day bus pilgrimage group from San Sebastián walked into the monumental city.[9]

There is a famous *milladoiro* (pile of rocks used to mark a crossroads or route) at the top of an important summit, Monte Irago, which used to mark the boundary between the Maragatería and the Bierzo (León). The Romans called the area the Mountains of Mercury. Crowning the milladoiro is the simple yet impressive La Cruz de Ferro (The Iron Cross). On top of a twenty-foot-high oak beam a small iron cross rises up to the sky. According to legend all passing travelers were to add rocks to the base of the cross. Today, many pilgrims follow this practice by tossing stones onto the pile. Some pilgrims suggest that the weight of the rock carried symbolically represents the level of internal burden or sin that one bears. Thus pilgrims arrive with stones that often have their own stories: where they are found, what they mean to the owner, the size. Most rocks bear no markings of their owner, but others are painted with bright colors or have names, dates, or messages etched or written on the surface. Some stones are brought from the hometowns of pilgrims already knowledgeable about the tradition while others are gathered twenty feet from the base of the cross. The more elaborately marked stones are quickly

Figure 5. La Cruz de Ferro/The Iron Cross (Monte Irago, León).

Figure 6.   Detail of the Iron Cross. Note the ex-votos and stones with writing at the base.

removed, by whom I do not know. In the mid-1990s La Cruz de Ferro has become an informal shrine. Its base is adorned with flowers, pilgrims' shells, messages, *ex-votos,* and so on.

The tossing of the stone is generally a ritual of the foot or bicycle pilgrim who fulfills a "tradition" or relieves both literal and symbolic weights by adding to the pile. A Dutch foot pilgrim laughed as he told me about seeing car pilgrims stop at the base of the cross, get out, and throw rocks on the pile and then continue driving. Another Dutch pilgrim on a two-week van excursion with fifteen others offered a different interpretation when he came by the Hospital de Orbigo pilgrims' refuge, where I was working as an hospitalera. He asked if I would stamp his diary with the refuge's seal. Curious as usual, I asked him about his group. He told me that they combined walking and driving the pilgrimage, stayed in cheap hotels, and also participated in Camino rituals. He explained that when they got to the area of the cross they would pick up stones and walk up the road and deposit them and then continue by van. He felt connected to the road, the pilgrimage, and the pilgrims through this act.

This type of behavior seemed laughable to the Dutch walker because it contrasted sharply with values that motivated his journey. He went on vacation because work was a sedentary, mental exercise and now, with his son, he wanted both a physical and a mental challenge. In fact, he did not think that the Camino was tough enough, so he went with detailed survey maps. In contrast, I often heard nonpilgrims ask scornfully, "Why don't they just take the bus?" From the outsider's perspective it appears to be dangerous to walk or cycle on the road, which is hot and dirty and leaves one vulnerable to speeding trucks and cars. It does not make sense to them that people would choose to walk (or cycle or go on horseback) to Santiago, but they do. Pilgrimage, like all human movement, is patterned according to societal norms, lifestyles, class values, fashion, and cultural ideals. The questions become how and why certain modes of transport are used, what they mean to those whose use them, and who the people are who use them.

Foot and cycle pilgrims tend to call those who go by bus and car tourists, and themselves, pilgrims. To be labeled a tourist is pejorative and to be avoided. As one anthropologist remarks, "Speakers of English tend to understand tourism as a superficial and frivolous phenomenon, while pilgrimage is seen to be something genuine, authentic, serious, and legitimate."[10] The term "pilgrimage" signifies a religious journey made out of faith or devotion. Bus and foot or bicycle pilgrims also make the journey for a wide assortment of religious, cultural, sport, and personal reasons. Among both groups there are individuals who go to Santiago for strictly religious reasons, but the vast majority have multiple reasons for getting to Santiago. Therefore, when bus pilgrims are labeled "tourists" by foot or bicycle pilgrims it is not a pejorative statement about their motives but about their movement choices. Tourists, understood to be frivolous, superficial people, travel en masse by bus, car, or plane. Pilgrims, understood to be genuine, authentic, serious people, walk and cycle.

Both human-powered and motorized pilgrims are moving toward Santiago, but the meanings those movements have for participants differ. The link between "modern forms of travel glossed as 'tourism' [and] modern and earlier styles of travel glossed as 'religious' is . . . human *mobility,* deliberately shaped with expressive and communicative, rather than simply instrumental, purposes in mind."[11] It is not just devotion (an instrumental purpose) that drives pilgrims to walk and cycle to Santiago, but in choosing to go in a nonmodern way pilgrims make statements (expressive and communicative purposes) about their society and their values. Broadly speaking, these values include an appreciation of nature and physical effort, a rejection of materialism, an interest in or a nostalgia for the past (especially the medieval), a search for inner meaning, an attraction to meaningful human relationships, and solitude. For example, at age twenty-six, Susan (nominally Protestant) decided to leave her job as a kindergarten teacher, move out of her apartment, put her belongings in storage, and fulfill a lifelong dream: to walk from her Swiss homeland to Portugal using the Camino de Santiago. She was fed up with the recent turns her life had taken (intimate relationships, lack of self-esteem) and hoped that four months of walking would put things in perspective. She remarked, "To compare the pilgrimage with other travels, I think the main difference is that the pilgrimage changed me as a person, made me more confident, made me accept and love myself more and open me up to new ideas and patterns. It was an inner and outer way. Other travels are mostly outer ways, . . . to educate yourself, see new things, culture, people, environment. But I've never heard of anybody saying, 'I'm going on three weeks holiday to search for something more, to answer some questions'—as you do as a pilgrim."

Becoming a pilgrim to Santiago does not necessarily mean making a religious journey, but it does often signify for cyclists and walkers an inner and an outer journey, a means of finding transformation. Some pilgrims wish to give their leisure time meaning, to take a much-needed break from the rat race, and they are attracted to the possibility of adventure, of finding a link to the past and a way to connect meaningfully with themselves, others, and the land, to feel their bodies, and to use all of their senses, to see every blade of grass rather than pass rapidly through a meaningless countryside, to live with less, to relax for a while. They want a space to pray, think, or meditate. From the perspective of the road these things seem impossible to attain from behind the window in the air-conditioned bus.[12]

The composition of the Camino is fluid, like a river with tributaries entering and leaving the main flow. Consequently it is difficult to gauge the actual number of pilgrims on the camino francés, and statistics often misrepresent the numbers of those who walk and cycle to Santiago. The population is ever changing from the "beginning" in Roncesvalles to the "end" in Santiago. Part-time pilgrims may begin in Roncesvalles or from home in Aachen, Germany, but not get to Santiago until three or more years later. At any given moment there may be pilgrims beginning and ending at the same point. Despite this ebb and flow the greatest confluence of pilgrims (especially Spanish and Galician) begins after León and in Galicia. For example, the Spanish Federation of Associations of Friends of the Camino de Santiago calculated that about 30,000 people made part or all of the pilgrimage in 1996 (based on the number of credentials issued), whereas the Pilgrim's Office in Santiago reported a total of 23,218 people (based on the number of *Compostelas* issued). The 7,000-person difference is largely due to the factors of ebb and flow.

Statistics on pilgrims are kept with some vigor at several points along the road. These data provide a general picture of participants and the complicated nature of motives and illustrate how bureaucracy manages to work its way into pilgrims' experiences. In the mid-1980s Don Javier Navarro of the Real Colegiata in Roncesvalles took an interest in cataloging the pilgrims and pilgrimages to Santiago. He (and the office for pilgrims at the Colegiata) still collects information through a printed questionnaire, as an Anglican pilgrim, David, from England discovered in 1994. A man who played soccer for forty years and ran seven marathons, David demonstrates how motives are often layered and varied. "On the morning of the 16th we were blessed by the Abbot (?) of the monastery. Our Pilgrim Passports were stamped, and we had to fill in a form with questions such as whether we were Catholic or Protestant. 'Both,' I whispered to John. Why were we undertaking the Pilgrimage—for religious, spiritual or cultural reasons? 'All three,' I wrote."[13] Other pilgrims with whom I spoke after they filled out the forms found themselves at a loss as well on the motivation question. They often listed more than one, not liking to be "boxed." Some said they put down a religious or spiritual motive because the attendant appeared to be a priest and they did not want to offend him.

The form requests basic information about the journey. On arrival at some refuges pilgrims give the following information to the attendant: name, age, nationality, mode of travel, and starting point. Refuges usually ask only name and country. In some refuges, for example, Burgos and Rabanal, the data are more systematically collected and tabulated. At times pilgrims resent the collection of information because they do not want to be statistics—which is what many are seeking to escape.

Both the Pilgrim's Office in Santiago and the Spanish Federation of Associations of Friends try to keep a statistical rein on the pilgrimage.[14] Data collected by the cathedral's Pilgrim's Office reflect quite well those who end the journey in Santiago and receive the *Compostela* and includes information on numbers of participants, points of origin, and other personal data (age, sex, mode, and motivation). Most, but not all, pilgrims go to the office on arrival in Santiago. In 1993 and 1994 the federation began to send questionnaires to pilgrims who were issued credentials once they returned home. Besides the large difference in number of estimated pilgrims and issues related to religious motivations of participants, the two surveys correspond fairly well.

According to these data in 1996 between 23,218 and 30,000 pilgrims made it to Santiago: 71 percent walked, 28 percent cycled, and less than 1 percent (56 of 23,218) went on horseback. Sixty-five percent were men and 35 percent were women. The average age is thirty. Pilgrims tend to have a high level of education—they are students, teachers, white-collar workers, priests, and technicians—and come from urban areas. The majority—70 percent—are Spanish, but the remaining 30 percent (6,710) come from sixty-three countries, including Argentina, Croatia, Japan, and Poland. The largest numbers of non-Spanish pilgrims are from France, Germany, Holland, Belgium, and Italy—in that order. I can count the number of pilgrims of color I have seen in five years on one hand (one, a Catholic missionary from Tanzania in residence in Spain, and several Japanese men). While 70 percent of pilgrims are Catholic (by birth but not necessarily in practice), the pilgrimage is ecumenical in spirit. Less than half of those who profess to believe in God (84 percent) practice their religion. This rough sketch indicates that the majority of pilgrims are urban, educated, and middle-class. Removing the 45 percent who are students (many are Spanish and make the journey during July and August) makes the average pilgrim a bit more mature, a bit more middle-

class, and a bit more foreign.[15] Thus depending on when you go, the
Camino and its character is always changing.

A curious aspect of the reanimation is the overwhelming preponder-
ance of male pilgrims. This can be attributed to the adventure and the
physical aspects of the journey, differences in male and female leisure,
and a lack of social sanction in Europe (until the 1970s) and especially
Spain (until the 1980s) for women to develop professional and athletic
lives. Many men boast about the number of kilometers they are able to
travel each day. Instead of the 20- or 30-kilometer average, some walk
40 to 60 kilometers per day. Cyclists may use racing bikes to cover 100
kilometers per day or more. Until the generation born in the 1960s and
1970s, men have been more frequently socialized to express themselves
through physical activity. Women have not had the freedom to leave the
family and home to strike out on an independent physical journey, though
more and more women in their late forties and fifties have begun to do
so—and report feeling greatly empowered by it. Among young people
the percentage difference between male and female pilgrims is significantly
less, and the numbers will probably begin to equalize in the coming years.

When I asked walking and cycling pilgrims to describe who was on
the road with them they rarely, if ever, mentioned bus or car pilgrims.
Instead they named various foot and cycle subgroups. The following description was given to me by Angela, an Englishwoman in her thirties
who walked the pilgrimage in 1992 with another woman over a period
of ten weeks from France. Since then she has begun historical research
on the Camino and considers among her best friends others who made
the Camino (not necessarily with her). Angela, who views the Camino
as a "positive form of escapism," based her groupings on both life cycle
and motives. Although this was the first time she had consciously made
such divisions, she rapidly produced the following, beginning with life
cycle: (1) young people, who don't know exactly who they are or why
they are there but think that making the Camino is a good way "to have
fun" and spend summer vacation; (2) older people (i.e., those who range
in age from the late twenties to the fifties), who have some idea of who
they are and welcome the chance to see what the Camino can offer them
and who are serious in intent; (3) retired people, who make the way to
mark this break.

Angela suggested the following divisions according to motive: (1)
sports fanatics, especially cyclists, who travel keeping their heads down,
and power walkers, mostly men, whose interest is solely in making as
many kilometers as possible; (2) people at a crisis point who need to make

a decision; (3) those who made the journey for religious reasons (Angela commented that she didn't see many but knew they were there); (4) people such as historians who are making the way for professional reasons (she added, "Like you."); (5) and self-promoters, who "want to write a book about their experience."

Angela, like many pilgrims, was quick to mark the difference between religious and spiritual motives, generally understood by pilgrims to be the difference between orthodoxy and personal devotion. Some pilgrims were adamant about the difference; others, usually practicing Catholics, found it difficult when asked to distinguish one from the other. I listened to a young Spanish woman from Barcelona and a retired man in his sixties from San Sebastián debate this point one afternoon in a refuge. He argued that one cannot separate spirituality from religion, that the Church and its rituals are necessary for a fulfilling spirituality. She countered by saying that she believed in Jesus and his teachings but that she related to him on a personal level through prayer and contact with nature. For example, she explained, during Mass the previous day the priest was not saying anything that helped her reach Jesus. She concluded, "I don't need intermediaries. I just sat back, closed my eyes, and began to pray." The man could not understand any of this and insisted that spirituality comes from the Church.

Both argued the difference from a Catholic perspective, but a spiritual orientation often exists completely outside of a specific religious orientation. One theologian who writes on the use of the labyrinth as a kinetic tool for spiritual awakening suggests, "'Religion is for those who are scared to death of hell. Spirituality is for those who have been there.' A division has emerged in Western culture. We have confused religion with spirituality, the container with the process. Religion is the outward form, the 'container,' specifically the liturgy and all the acts of worship that teach, praise, and give thanks to God. Spirituality is the inward activity of growth and maturation that happens in each of us."[16]

When pilgrims speak of the Camino as a spiritual journey there is no shared definition, but it is generally related to this idea of the uncontained, nonstructural, personalized, individual, and direct relationship one has to ultimate reality. The outward activity of walking or cycling is twinned to the "inward activity of growth and maturity." As the young woman from Barcelona said, on the Camino one can access one's religious feelings without intermediaries. Among some pilgrims this is simply called the inner journey. A religious journey, then, relates to faith in God and the practice of rituals (going to Mass, praying the Rosary) and contemplation of liturgy associated with a particular religious (Catholic, Protestant, Anglican) tradition. From the Catholic viewpoint a specific goal of the Christian pilgrimage is a movement toward conversion or toward God. Frequent reference is made to the New Testament passage in John 14 in which Christ, after the Last Supper, responds to Thomas's fear of losing the way without Jesus by stating, "I am the Way, the Truth, and the Life." Santiago is the end and the goal of the physical journey; transformation comes through interpreting one's suffering and the unexpected in relation to the message of Jesus—the Camino is a metaphor for life—and the solidarity among pilgrims is a model of the Christian community. Once this movement toward belief and conversion occurs, from the official Catholic point of view, the Camino does not end but begins its next important phase, the mission: spreading the "word" or the "good news" among one's family and community.

Among religious motives are the fulfillment of *promesas* (vows, promises), a crisis and renewal of faith, the receipt of indulgences, reflection and meditation, prayer for others, expiation of one's own or others' sins, giving thanks to Santiago, a request for intercession, or a demonstration or testimony of faith (a way "to suffer for the greater glory of God," as one American evangelical Catholic put it). Some make the pilgrimage for those who cannot: one man went to Santiago because his parents, both invalids, asked him to go in their name. A few go after having become priests or ministers or as part of the process of dedicating their lives to a religious commitment. A vow to make a pilgrimage to Santiago is often made in a moment of crisis such as the loss of employment, personal or familial illness, suffering, or despair. In one dramatic case, an Englishman promised a friend, six hours before he died of cancer, to make the pilgrimage to Santiago for him. I met a Belgian man and his brother cycling to Santiago. They had no interest in the Camino per se, but in a desperate moment one of the brothers suddenly thought of Saint James and vowed that he would make the journey if his Spanish wife was cured of an illness. She did get well, and he made the pilgrimage from his wife's village in Castile without knowing anything about the Camino and its recent reanimation. A petitioner may vow to make the pilgrimage several times. Pilgrims are often reluctant to discuss their vows, even when questioned.

Most walking group pilgrimages with a religious orientation attract young people, are organized by a parish and led by a priest, and focus on spiritual development, catechism, and learning to give a religious interpretation to things felt, seen, and experienced. The significant number of young Spanish walkers and cyclists is related to the Camino's active promotion by Catholic youth groups (and nonreligious Boy and Girl Scout troops). The groups are clearly visible: they range in number from eight to sixty, members often wear the same color neck bandannas to promote group solidarity, and they may have support vehicles. The day is often broken into periods of walking and reflection on specific liturgical themes such as humility, suffering, brotherhood, charity, and austerity. Some groups are more rigid than others in structure and teachings, reflecting the wide range of interpretations of Catholicism in Europe. Believing that making the Camino is a positive, even necessary, alternative to contemporary consumer society, Father José Miguel Burgui has led many groups of young people on foot to Compostela. He claims that in the hard, austere journey pilgrims learn valuable lessons of life.[17] In the same vein a Valencian priest, two seminary students, and various youths between the ages of seventeen and thirty walked from Roncesvalles in August 1996 to focus on prayer and *reflexión cristiana* (Christian reflection); and a seventy-three-year-old Italian priest celebrated his fifty years doing God's work with twenty members of his Turinese parish by cycling to Santiago. Before returning to Italy the latter group went south to Portugal to visit Fátima.

Spiritual motives are more vaguely defined personal searches or inner journeys of transformation. An emphasis on "personal" or "transcendent"[18] spirituality and a rejection of religious orthodoxy form part of the modern ethos in Euro-American society, from which many contemporary pilgrims come.[19] Also part of this ethos is an orientation toward creative personal alternatives and a reinfusion in religious practice of the magical with its "rejection of rationalism, established orthodoxies, and technology."[20] One religious commentator posits, "I wonder if we're witnessing something that, if it isn't exactly new under the sun, may be happening on an unprecedented scale: the rejection of religion itself, which tends to ground itself in communal contexts . . . in favor of privatized spiritualities that have little context but the self."[21] A famous sociological study of American society finds that this type of individualized creative religiosity is typified by "Sheilaism"—a noncommunal, "privatized" yet "diverse" form of religious expression.[22] Privatized religious movements are certainly not limited to the United States. Angela, the Englishwoman who has been involved with the Camino since the mid-1980s, with a specific interest in its historical, pre-Christian roots and syncretic elements, remarked to me that she practiced her own "DIY" religion. I asked her to elaborate: "Oh, DIY, do-it-yourself. I make up my own." Both DIY and Sheilaism exemplify well these individualized spiritualities.

For someone who wants time to reflect, a road to wander feels uncomfortable with organized religion; or for someone who is disen-
chanted by the Church, the Camino provides a space to create alternatives. A twenty-six-year-old pharmacy student from Madrid explained
his decision to walk the Camino thus: "I had left my girlfriend, I had
doubts, and I needed answers. I like to walk, and I love the north of
Spain." Guy, a French psychologist in his early forties who walked to
Santiago to and from Le Puy, said, "It's this real dissatisfaction [with
life] which gives birth to the desire to start on the Camino." The sense
of dissatisfaction can have many different roots. A twenty-nine-year-
old Sorbonne student from Monaco said, "I walked the second time to
destroy the failure of the first." He had not been able to finish the
Camino the year before because of personal and physical problems,
which left him distraught, and he needed to finish what had been left
undone.

The emphasis on the spiritual shares the stage with a wide variety of
esoteric, cultic, or individualized religious practices characteristic of Western religious and New Age movements.[23] The classic work of this genre
is Juan Pedro Morín and Jaime Cobreros's *El Camino Iniciático de Santiago* (The Initiatory Way of Santiago). It is a guidebook to spiritual awakening via the camino francés. Believing that modern society is fundamentally corrupt, the authors suggest that it is essential to turn one's gaze
back to the medieval wise (alchemists, builders of cathedrals) who left
secret knowledge in the form of signs and figures, and in the structural
forms of the stone buildings along the Camino. Initiation occurs through
a combination of the discovery of these signs and a spiritual awakening
while making the Camino, which is divided into experiential or spiritual
parts: Somport/Roncesvalles to Burgos, universal spirituality; Burgos
to Astorga, symbolic death; Cruz de Ferro to Noya/Finisterre, spiritual
resurrection.

Esoterics may also try to reach "a new plane of consciousness," according to one guide, via other routes linked indirectly to the Camino.
Some pilgrims are sensitive not only to signs but also to tellurian points,
or sites believed to possess accumulated energies. One young German
woman stated, "The Way contains a certain kind of energy, the energy
of all the people who walked it and the energy they left while walking."
Some pilgrims search for pre-Christian or Celtic influences, even the legendary Atlantis. Others do the Camino as if it were a game board on
which the *juego de la oca,* or game of the goose, is played. They are the
pawns that move over the landscapes, escaping hazards and moving

ahead toward a distant goal by finding mysterious etymological links that repeatedly occur between *oca* (goose) and place-names of the Camino.

The search may also be linked to following the Camino de las Estrellas, the Road of the Stars (also known as the Vía Láctea, the Milky Way), which is said to parallel the physical, terrestrial Camino in the nighttime sky. Some pilgrims believe that the Milky Way "is a celestial reflection of the earthly path taken by medieval pilgrims which later became the Way of St. James." The stars of the Milky Way can also be interpreted as a path of dead souls; the light they produce helps the lost wandering soul to find its way to paradise once believed to exist off the end of the earth.[24] One pilgrim explained, "It is the true and ancient path of spiritual death and rebirth. . . . By staying within a certain latitude—the latitude of the Milky Way—and trying to pass through places with names of mystical birds and animals."[25] The popular linking of the Milky Way to the Camino was largely influenced by the legend of Charlemagne's dream found in the apocryphal fourth book of the *Codex Calixtinus.* As the emperor sleeps "he see the Milky Way . . . [and] the Apostle Santiago appears to him and explains to the astonished monarch the significance of the road of stars: it is the road to the saint's tomb presently impassable for being overrun by the infidels."[26] The dream continues with Santiago urging the emperor to open the road with his help, which Charlemagne does, then continuing west and becoming the legendary first pilgrim to Santiago.

Some pilgrims claim to be modern-day Templars, knights of the religiomilitary Order of the Temple (Jerusalem) that formed in 1118 to protect pilgrims on the way to the Holy Land after the first Crusade. These orders were shrouded in mystery and said to be the holders of never revealed esoteric knowledge that is believed to be encoded in their castles, temples, and churches.[27] Spaniards in their twenties and early thirties, Brazilians (thanks to Paulo Coelho's best-seller describing his own esoteric, initiatory journey), and non-Catholic Europeans (ages 25 to 45) tend to be attracted to these movements.[28]

Being devoutly Catholic (or any other denomination) does not necessarily preclude a belief in tellurian points, in the Camino's "energy," or in other esoteric elements of the road. There is often an eclectic commingling of beliefs associated with the pilgrimage. I was surprised by the experience of one practicing Catholic woman, who frequently uses religious metaphors in her discourse: "The well-informed pilgrim should experience two energy points: the Hermitage of Santiago in Monte Irago near La Cruz de Ferro and the Hermitage of San Marcos in Monte del Gozo. Spending the night under its eaves is like taking another step deeper into the Camino." For her, there is no conflict between Catholicism and belief in tellurian points.

"Those of the distant past were devout Catholics, but today's pilgrims . . . seem more interested in adventure and solitude," commented an American journalist after three days en route to Santiago.[29] This is an accurate statement as many pilgrims find themselves on the Camino for what lies between the adventure and the solitude; search through travel, that is, going on the physical road to find the road within. A thirty-three-year-old female physical therapist from Madrid was motivated to walk to Santiago because, she said, "It was going to be an adventure, sport, nature, something different with my vacation—something healthy and historical." Pilgrims walk (20–30 km/day) and cycle (60–80 km/day) on a wide variety of surfaces: national highway, paved and unpaved access roads, dirt, stones of all shapes and sizes, or one-way single-track paths. Avid hikers and even novices sometimes may be attracted to the Camino by a love of the outdoors and walking in beautiful places. Depending on the season in which the pilgrimage is made, the pilgrim may encounter a month of breathless Spanish sun in July or August, travel fourteen days in October with pounding, ceaseless rain, or brave the uphill challenge of a silent and snowy mountain pass in December. Over the course of the long journey it is possible to move with the seasons—to watch the bloom of spring through the early mountains, then observe the formation of Riojan grapes and possibly the golden turn of Castilian wheat in early summer. In late summer and fall blackberries and nut and fruit trees are found on some parts of the way. Life and nature are experienced and lived in their cycles, in a way that other means of travel simply do not afford. This same sense of the cycle and rhythm of life can be found in the ubiquitous play of storks, whose bell-tower nests and impressive steps into flight accompany the pilgrim through much of the summer's journey. Day after day the kilometers slowly mount, from village to city to countryside in a constant westerly direction, following their long shadows in the morning and ending with the setting of the sun.

Many pilgrims walk and cycle alone to Santiago. The value of the group (versus the individual) experience in southern European societies motivates many Italian and especially Spanish pilgrims between the ages of fifteen and twenty-five to go in groups of five to fifteen. Unlike many Euro-American teens who are encouraged to be independent and value solitude, for many Spaniards being alone can signify social rejection or a lack of solidarity. Outdoor activities tend to be oriented toward friendship and group building rather than competition and personal character

Figure 7.   Spanish bicycle pilgrims on a Galician corredoira *(stone path).*

building. Large groups of friends who make the pilgrimage together during summer vacations reflect a new trend in Spanish leisure oriented toward appreciation of nature and physical activity. For example, in August 1996 fourteen technical engineering majors from Madrid (between the ages of twenty and twenty-six) made it to Santiago. And nine "adventurers" between the ages of twenty-one and forty made their third annual Camino by Línea Recta (Straight Line; i.e., they created their own route) basing their pilgrimage on sport, challenge, and interest in the outdoors. Very rarely in five years of study did I meet or hear about a group of four or more non-Spanish friends who made the pilgrimage together, unless it was an organized religious, educational, or youth group. Euro-Americans, in general, want to make the pilgrimage alone or with a friend or spouse, and while enjoying new international contacts and the camaraderie of the way, they revel in the solitude and the chance to be independent and "away from it all."

Other pilgrims use the Camino as a testing or meeting ground for a relationship or to celebrate anniversaries and honeymoons. A young couple from Madrid (ages twenty-two and twenty-five) decided to spend their honeymoon walking 500 kilometers from Burgos to Santiago. Despite being encouraged to go to Hawaii (and having already made the pilgrimage two and three times, respectively), they chose the Camino for the contact with nature and the feeling of being "relaxed and tranquil." They commented further, "The Camino is like a catharsis, it becomes something intimate and personal, where all the steps make sense. . . . It brings you closer to God . . . and you realize that the things that seem important in daily life really aren't."[30] It is common, especially in the summer, to see families on the road taking advantage of the healthy, open environment to find extended "quality time" through the shared journey. Instead of the regular summer vacation to the beach many families "make the Camino." Occasionally one hears the remarkable story of parents who decide to take a year off from work and journey with their children. Such was the case of a Belgian couple (he an artist and she a functionary) who walked with two daughters (ages six and nine) and two donkeys from their home. Leaving on May 1, 1997, they arrived seven months later, in late November, after a long, hard journey.

Pilgrims also claim historical and cultural motives. One can see the famous monuments of the Camino in a unique way and hear bells whose ringing has called thousands of faithful for centuries. A middle-aged Dutch couple expressed this well:

> Is there a more beautiful goal than this unknown city in northern Spain, where all of Christianity journeyed a thousand years ago? Add to this that there are a great many historical and cultural monuments preserved along the routes to Santiago. The Romanesque churches that we travel to see are treasure chambers where we too, in imitation of medieval pilgrims, go to gape in wonder. To feel something of what the beggars and wretches and the punished and the sick and the plague-ridden from far before our time lived through—albeit that we in our time can never do so fully, in that we cannot share their fears and dreams, and above all that we lack their childlike and blind faith—that is what we wish. Bound with your own past and that of our entire European culture and savoring this solidarity sparsely—each day a little piece—building it up further in your innermost self.[31]

An American pilgrim called it awe-inspiring to "walk in the shadows of the past" through unexpectedly encountering two-thousand-year-old Roman remains (bridges, road, ruins) and art and architecture ranging from Visigothic and baroque to Mudéjar and even an example of Spain's modernist master Gaudí (Astorga) along the Camino. Two of Europe's finest Gothic cathedrals (León and Burgos) as well as some of the earliest examples of Romanesque sculpture and architecture are found along the road. Each day's journey becomes a field trip through a continuous museum, through the vagaries of Iberia's (and Europe's) history, politics,

*Figure 8.   Walking on a muddy track in the forest near Roncesvalles (Navarre).
Note the scallop shells and walking sticks.*

Figure 9.   Treading a 2,000-year-old Roman road (Navarre).

and religious devotion. It is impressive to imagine oneself crossing the same plains outside of Burgos as did El Cid or crossing the same mountains as did Charlemagne and Napoleon to reach Roncesvalles and Spanish territory.

In addition to the physical remains of the pilgrimage's glorious history, bits of the rich folklore continue to inspire in the form of song, legend, and proverb. A particularly popular legend is the miracle of the Hanged Innocent and, associated with it, the bizarre tradition of keeping a pair of live white chickens in a glass henhouse in the Santo Domingo de la Calzada cathedral. Many versions of the legend are recorded over the last centuries and relate, more or less, the story of a pilgrim to Santiago who is falsely accused of theft and ordered to the gallows and hanged but remains alive because of his innocence and the saint's support. He is freed when the local judge, who has just sat down to eat a pair of roasted chickens, announces that the cock will crow if the young man is innocent. And so it was. This became a very popular legend throughout Europe, and Santo Domingo became irrevocably linked to it—keeping a hen and a cock (which are rotated regularly) and its spirit alive. Bakeries in the town sell "hanged pilgrim" pastries, numerous shops vend pins of the legend, and some contemporary pilgrims, much like their medieval forebears, hope to be in the right place when the cock crows (for good luck) or when one of the white feathers floats out of the cage.[32]

In the Camino there is often a "sentimental longing for feelings and things of the past"—a sense of nostalgia—[33] particularly for the medieval past. In 1982, as in the 1990s, a central motivator was "to walk in the footsteps of one's ancestors."[34] This trend is not unique to the Camino but is part of a postindustrial, postmaterialist society in which the past feels more authentic than the modern present. As the historian Patrick Geary states, "'Medieval civilization' is an extremely imprecise designation, obscuring rather than defining a wide variety of distinct cultural and social traditions that appeared across Europe over a period of a thousand years."[35] "Medieval" is used very imprecisely by modern pilgrims, linking their experiences to a past encompassing a long historical period. Getting closer to one's cultural and personal roots by returning to sites important in the past also influences the desire to walk the road—to perhaps form part of and to create history through one's actions. Many pilgrims want to follow the "old routes," even if it means a longer journey or a detour. When the old road has been paved over or lost in a field of wheat, the idea of old way is conflated with the unpaved and rural. In general the less asphalt seen and smelled by walkers, the better.

Some pilgrims make the Camino to advance causes—religious, altruistic, political, or personal. Cause pilgrims, especially the English, make altruistic pilgrimages by raising money for a charitable cause through sponsorship of kilometers walked or cycled.[36] In February 1997 seven members of the Spanish Protección Civil (civil protection) made 154 kilometers of the Camino, from the Galician border town Cebreiro, to protest the Basque terrorist group ETA's kidnapping and sequestering of two people for political reasons.[37] It is a powerful statement that a person makes in a world in which the individual often feels impotent to influence even local events. The simple act of walking or cycling has made an enormous difference to various causes; it has raised money to fight disease, raised consciousness, and perhaps demonstrated that despite what seem to be insurmountable odds an individual, through determination and with a simple human act, can change the world.

People even make the Camino as a way to appear in the *Guiness Book of World Records*. In a well-publicized media event in September 1996 two Germans, a dentist and a journalist, attempted to beat the record for walking without eating, covering the Camino from St. Jean Pied-de-Port to Santiago in fourteen days. It is not clear whether they arrived.[38]

The vast majority of modern pilgrims go to Santiago because they want to. However, the medieval penitential pilgrimage exists in modern form in the Belgian and Dutch juvenile penal systems.[39] Since 1982, in conjunction with the Belgian Ministry of Justice, a nonprofit group called Oikoten (from the etymological root meaning "home") has used the Camino de Santiago as a path of rehabilitation for young social reprobates. The program was inspired by an American documentary film of the early 1980s, *Caravan of the Last Chance,* detailing a six-month trip by troubled youths through the Nevada desert. In an attempt to reintegrate these young people into society, Oikoten (among other organizations now also in Germany and forming in Spain) sends one to two young people with one or more monitors on a four-month version of the pilgrimage for reflection and repentance. The motto of the group and these "getting away" projects is "Away from home, Away from the home country, By one's own means, Relying on one's own strength."

The goal is to help these youths navigate the trials of life through contact with nature, physical activity, and learning self-reliance. The hope is that new understandings garnered along the way will inspire "inward activity of growth and maturity" and translate to the home environment.

Figure 10.   *Nuestra Señora de la Trinidad de Arre (Navarre), currently a Marist seminary and a pilgrims' refuge.*

A brochure on the project emphasizes the separation of the individual from known social relations and society to "experience themselves and others in a new way. . . . After the project the young person returns home with another story. He/she will have grown both in the eyes of the contemporaries . . . and of the family. . . . We hope that in this manner the vicious circle can be broken."[40]

INNER WORLDS AND THE WALKING WOUNDED

Pilgrims' diaries are helpful in providing insight into their inner worlds.[41] In discussing their journals pilgrims suggested that even though they are private, there are often experiences and feelings too personal to be committed to paper. Sometimes deeper layers may be revealed unexpectedly, as Angela told me when our conversation shifted to the doors that the Camino can open—to the self, to other worlds and possibilities, to people, and so on. The idea of being connected through one's bodily action to the past, to a community of people, moving over the same lands in common purpose, is very affecting for many. In my interview with Angela she became emotional when she spoke about this aspect of the pilgrimage: "It was something I was very aware of . . . walking in footsteps and wanting to . . . Who was I doing it for? Everyone who couldn't do it, who'd died or couldn't. I did it for them. I realized when I began that people I never knew started and couldn't finish . . . [she began to cry and paused] I feel very emotional about that and I don't know why." Ostensibly her pilgrimage represented a long-term interest in part based on historical reasons, but clearly it became something much larger and deeper for her, as it does for many people.

Motives also change over the course of the Camino. A Basque chef went on the Camino as a gastronomic odyssey, another Basque man explained to me, but by the time he reached Santiago his motives had become more spiritually oriented. He was so moved that he went back to Roncesvalles to ask if he could alter the form he had filled out to reflect his new sense of purpose. With this complicated amalgam of motives and categories, it is not surprising that the meanings of the pilgrimage and being a pilgrim are contested.

Motives address the question, Why am I going? But this question does not address another level of understanding, that of inner orientations: In what state do I arrive at the Camino? A striking difference exists between Lourdes or Fátima, where thousands of sick gather in prayer and hope, and Santiago. Pilgrims at Lourdes may make extraordinary physical sacrifices within the shrine space, walking on their knees in acts of supplication, devotion, thanks, or hope for intercession. The shrines are organized to accommodate thousands of international visitors gathered to worship at Stations of the Cross and group prayers and masses. To the disappointment of some religious pilgrims, this atmosphere does not exist in Santiago. The underlying assumption among most people who know nothing about the modern pilgrimage is that the goal is Santiago and that religious devotion motivates the journey. The goal, however, is often the road itself, not the city. Unlike many pilgrims to Marian shrines, those who walk and cycle to Santiago often are not motivated by the pains of the suffering body but by the pains of the suffering soul.

Perhaps the most eloquent expression of this depth of the inner world and layered quality of motives comes from George, an Englishman in his fifties recently retired from the Civil Service. After returning from one of several trips to the Camino as a part-time pilgrim, he reflected, "I do enjoy the company of fellow pilgrims and sometimes ask myself why. I think we're a society of solitaries. Couples are the exception rather than the rule; all of us know what it is to be alone, whether by choice or necessity, and—this is true, I find, especially of my French pilgrim friends— we've all been wounded . . . the walking wounded.[42] Everyone, as you get to know them, has a story to tell."

The journey of the Camino can reveal wounds—loss, failure, fear, shame, addiction—left festering from daily life. Experiences along the way often act as the catalyst that allows them to be exposed. It has been, and appears to continue to be, a road for hopes and miracles of fulfillment of a different order. Some pilgrims, acknowledging this themselves, refer to the Camino as *la ruta de la terapia,* the therapy route.

The pilgrims' inner orientations often relate to issues of transition, loss, rupture, or marginality. Many are making a life-cycle transition—from youth to adulthood, from midlife reflection and crisis to retirement. More serious wounds—or "critical life gaps," as one pilgrim put it—also draw pilgrims to the Camino. One man ran from Bordeaux, France, to Santiago to relieve the grief he felt after the loss of his son. Another Frenchman found himself walking the Camino after he lost a successful job, his home, and then his wife. He was devastated, had nowhere to turn, and, to the shock of his friends, began to walk to Santiago as his final recourse.

Pilgrims frequently have a difficult time explaining why they are making the pilgrimage: "I knew what I was fleeing from, not what I was seeking."[43] Such pilgrims are simply drawn to the Camino and feel that it comes at just the right time in their lives. For some, as George explained, "the wound may be undeclared, sensed but not identified. [They] need the therapeutic action, the opening up, the courage given by the way, to be expressed and faced." I met an American woman from New Mexico cycling for the third time in 1995, this time with her teenage daughters. She described reaching Logroño (three days into the first trip) in 1990 and, with some trouble, finding shelter at a convent. When the nuns opened the door and let her in, she began to cry, cathartically. Throughout the trip she had bouts of weeping that she could not explain, until she began to sense its source. In Santiago the priest told her this was normal, and I also found this to be true. While it will not determine outcomes, making the pilgrimage can help the participant on a personal level to "rework the past" and possibly "move toward a renewed future."[44]

Some pilgrims feel alone or marginalized in their home environment, and the Camino provides a testing ground or an opportunity for change, a center and goal not so easily found in "real life." Going to or going on the Camino as a stranger (pilgrim), a marginal figure, heading toward a known center on a well-marked path with many other like-minded individuals, often gives pilgrims the reorientation they seek in their own lives. The sense of belonging the Camino affords, amid a daily life of estrangement, is expressed well by Jane, a thirty-three-year-old Irishwoman teaching English in Spain and Portugal: "As a person who for various reasons feels an outsider, for example, among my family, in the place where I was born and grew up, in many work situations, in my way of viewing the world, here in Spain, etc., etc., etc., I realized the importance of choosing an ambience that doesn't make you feel strange, left out. I felt at home on the Camino, the kind of people I met." In pilgrimage one can find a place, a home, and a center.

CHAPTER 2

JOURNEY SHAPING

Give me my scallop-shell of quiet,
My staff of faith to walk upon,
My scrip of joy, immortal diet,
My bottle of salvation,
My gown of glory, hope's true gage,
And thus I'll take my pilgrimage.
                    —*Sir Walter Raleigh*

The pilgrimage does not begin with the first step or ride down the trail. Pilgrims begin to shape their journeys well before they leave the front door. The physical movement of arriving at the Camino is anticipated by some kind of internal movement—a decision, an impulse, an unexplained prompting, a long-held desire finally realized, a promise seeking fulfillment, a hope for change. The internal space is in some way already in flux before the journey begins—anticipatory, eager, confused, exhausted, open. Using myself as an example, I knew after my first visit to Santiago in 1992 that I wanted to return. I spent the next year researching, imagining the trip, but not thinking about it as a pilgrimage, a religious journey. Graduate school was mentally and emotionally draining, and going away gave me something to look forward to. Besides my attraction to the theme and the prospect of getting to know parts of Spain more intimately, the physical challenge also excited me, especially after a sedentary academic year. I dreaded the time away from my husband. We had not been separated for more than five weeks since we met as teenagers, and this would be a separation of nine and a half weeks.

After the decision to go is made preparation takes a number of forms, and pilgrims make a series of choices before beginning that influence the experience as well as reveal implicit assumptions. While some plan and prepare the journey for years—researching routes, speaking with friends who have made the pilgrimage, deciding when and who they will go with and what they will carry—others may find themselves unexpectedly on the way to their starting point several days or a month after first hear-ing about it. Still others may prepare spiritually by acquiring a letter of presentation or recommendation from their parish priest or minister or receiving a benediction. One Spanish spiritual guide suggests asking friends and family to pray for one's journey and opening the soul with prayer several weeks before beginning. Moreover, this author suggests that one's "spiritual equipment" ought to include "faith in oneself and those around you, hope that your ways of being are susceptible to change, love towards yourself, others and nature, being strongly motivated to make a true pilgrimage, being ready to let down all of your defense mech-anisms, and having a good sense of humor."[1] Part-time and repeat pil-grims prepare differently than those going for the first time. As many is-sues of the first-time journey are now irrelevant, the focus is on refining or improving the previous experience. The vast majority of repeat pil-grims express a desire to have more time with which to make the pil-grimage. Others decide to change variables such as routes, companions, seasons, and mode of going.

Fifty-year-old Daniel, an Anglican priest, decided to make a pilgrim-age as a time for renewal during a sabbatical. He wanted to integrate both Christian Celtic and medieval models of pilgrimage to create his own long, solo journey by bicycle. He explained in a letter,

> I went to Holy Island in Northumberland, the cradle of Celtic Christianity in the north of England. I have been to the Christian centre many times. . . . Medieval ideas of pilgrimage involve a destination, for example, Rome or Jerusalem. Well and good. But the earlier and Celtic idea was that one just set off and you prayed that God would guide you to who knows where or how. I decided to combine the best of these two well-tried patterns of pil-grimage. . . . Then came the idea of terminating with an ancient place of pilgrimage—Santiago. My middle name is James. It was my father's name. I felt, five years after his death, it would be part of my healing through grief. What happened in between starting and finishing points was up to God.

In shaping his journey Daniel drew on different patterns of Christian pilgrimage to create a passage meaningful to him. He wanted a desti-nation but wanted to wander to it. He also decided to begin in Africa because of its strong allure as the "dark continent," as he put it, which allowed him a more profound "stepping out" of his own self, society, and Western culture in general, thus powerfully becoming the stranger. Moreover, the journey was in part a continuation of a mourning process taking him symbolically back to himself and to his father. This type of eclectic journey making with a layering of motives is common among contemporary pilgrims, who draw on personal experience and knowledge as well as current and past models of pilgrimage in planning their journeys.[2]

On the pragmatic level journeys are often shaped by vacation times and season, though some pilgrims receive special leaves from work or actually quit their jobs. Pilgrimages are not limited to any particular time of year, but the greatest numbers of pilgrims arrive in Santiago between the months of May and October, peaking in the summer months of July and August. This can be explained by the correspondence of this period with European vacation months, ease of travel, and the fact that the saint's day falls on July 25. Though it is not always a motive for going to Santiago, the days around July 25 draw larger numbers of visitors.

Probably the single most important decision pilgrims make before going is movement choice. Will I bear all the weight on two feet, move more rapidly on bicycle, or, in the rare instance, use a pack animal or a horse? In addition, other questions are often contemplated. Will I make a long, slow journey or a rapid, spontaneous one? Will I travel alone or with others? Do I want to read about the pilgrimage before going or let the experiences sweep over me? Will I try to visit churches and monuments or just walk? What do I need for thirty days or a week? Books—the Bible or a favorite poet, perhaps Rilke? The Rosary to pray with? Music? A Walkman? A camera? Will these be distractions? Many of these decisions are made beforehand or are improvised during the pilgrimage as the pilgrim gets caught up in the movement of the way, the flow of other pilgrims, the rhythm of life coursing above and under the road.

Someone interested in going on the Camino may also turn to one of the many Friends of the Camino associations for information on routes, accesses, the credential, or lodging. They may be advised to prepare on mental, physical, spiritual, and practical levels. The Confraternity of St. James in England holds workshops for the practical pilgrim in which those who are thinking about making the journey hear presentations and receive advice from former pilgrims. Pilgrims are given information about what to expect, the necessity of physical training, and tips on clothing and equipment, guidebooks, seasons, routes, dealing with wild dogs, refuges and infrastructure, and so on. Some pilgrims in attendance were not planning to make the journey for several years hence but wanted to begin informing themselves. I attended a much less formal workshop held biweekly in San Sebastián, Spain, by Friends of Guipúzcoa.

Although pilgrims are usually advised to prepare their bodies for walking with a full backpack or rucksack and to break in their boots or shoes to prevent pain, horrendous blisters, strained muscles, and the like, some pilgrims arrive completely unprepared. In Rabanal, where I was an hospitalera, a group of seventeen teenagers from the Canary Islands straggled into the refuge one hot July afternoon. It was their second day of a weeklong trip, and they felt rushed to get to Santiago. I was almost moved to tears. Almost all of them had two or three blisters that we treated, and the sole of one boy's foot had to be stitched because a blister had caused a two-inch tear in the skin. Determined to reach Santiago together, they traveled by bus to the Galician border to continue their journey.

The extent of preparation is highly individual, but in general Spanish pilgrims make the journey more spontaneously. A Spanish man who runs an information center laughed incredulously while telling an anecdote about receiving a telephone call from some potential German pilgrims wanting to know the average daily temperatures on the Castilian meseta during the summer and the exact distances between village water fountains. This type of hyperorganization is generally much more characteristic of northern European pilgrims, who also are known for their detailed computer-printed day-by-day itineraries for the anticipated journey. These itineraries often fail to account for blisters, unseasonably wet weather, or illness. I was questioned by both British and German potential pilgrims about whether they could make reservations in the pilgrims' refuges, which are run on a strictly first-come, first-served basis. Many people initially plan their pilgrimages as if they were a vacation, perhaps speaking to habit but also to anxiety about the unexpected and a need to control the environment.

During the predeparture period pilgrims begin to develop ideas about what to expect from the pilgrimage, what pilgrims are, what they do, how they behave, what makes them different from tourists (i.e., authentic). David, the English pilgrim who was surprised by the survey in Roncesvalles, explains why his journey took shape as it did: "We intended to walk the pilgrimage in a month, for this was considered good going. This was part of the discipline of the pilgrimage. It was a challenge, an adventure involving a certain amount of discomfort. A proper pilgrim, for instance, should eat in simple and unpretentious bars or restaurants and enjoy the food and wine of the region. No motorised transport; one should carry one's own rucksack the whole way, and no staying in hotels or pensions when there's a Refugio in the town or village. . . . As I've said they are free, but only to genuine pilgrims."[3]

David understood that being a genuine, or "proper," pilgrim involved conforming to some basic rules: the length of time (at least a month); discomfort (pain is good and normal); austere behavior and discipline (simple, low-key yet appreciative, frugal); self-sufficiency (always carrying one's own weight and relying on one's own strength). When I met another English pilgrim, a man in his forties, in Santiago, he touched his scraggly beard and commented self-consciously on his two-week growth. He had not brought a razor with him, imagining pilgrims to be old men with long, flowing beards. It was the first time he had gone unshaven since adolescence. He was quite surprised to find that indeed many men did shave. In part, being a pilgrim is an attitude—doing things differently than in daily life. Like most pilgrims both David and the other man probably picked up these ideas from listening to others or reading about others' journeys or from their personal preconceptions. These "rules" are not usually written anywhere but are implicit—"things that you just know as you go."

Many American pilgrims, for example, have been inspired to go to Santiago by magazine or newspaper articles, such as a commonly referred to 1994 *Smithsonian* piece.[4] A fifty-eight-year-old American woman from Virginia, Stephanie, who "had never hiked, backpacked, or camped" (or heard of Santiago) and who lived a self-described "Mrs. Cleaver life"[5] read this article by chance and "felt '*led*' to think deeply about making the pilgrimage." She continued, "The author described a British woman who walked by herself—was refreshed by the genuine human kindness . . . on the way; pared down to bare essentials . . . doing with so little; who grew in the days she walked and meditated alone. I wanted to do that!" Such articles often play an important role in sparking one's interest, and the desire may be tucked away until opportunity knocks (a year in Stephanie's case).

Early readings influence how pilgrims understand what the Camino is and their decisions but do not necessarily determine them. Stephanie had expectations about the kind of people she would meet, the physical challenge, and the possibility of transformation. Long before setting out pilgrims imagine that the Camino has the potential to influence their lives on many levels. "I hope that the Camino serves me—like it does everyone else—to find God, to find others, and to find myself," wrote a Spanish woman before setting off her first day.[6] Others, who read, for exam-

ple, Coelho's *The Pilgrimage,* are predisposed to the esoteric element believed to be in the route and look for its traces or their own spiritual initiation. Others garner expectations regarding hospitality and may be disappointed if they do not receive it. Or how one decides to make the
journey may be based on replicating the past. For example, Rob Neillands, an English travel writer, decided to cycle because he said, "[it was]
as close as I could get to the horse, and it provided me with plenty of
that essential pilgrim essence, good honest sweat."[7]

Not only do pilgrims learn about the Camino from reading and the
media, they also hear about it from friends who have made the journey
and, in rare cases, travel agents. A Swiss hospitalera was astonished by
the story two Swiss pilgrims, a husband and wife, told her when they arrived on foot at the refuge in Belorado. Both were unemployed yet wanted
a vacation that was within their means. The couple went to Zurich's
tourism office, explained their situation, and were advised to make the
Camino de Santiago, which, of course, they did.[8] I am also aware of doctors in both Brazil and Spain who recommend to some of their patients
that they make the Camino to reduce stress and improve their health.
Thus participants rarely arrive at the Camino without preconceived ideas
of how the journey will be.

SETTING OFF

Before getting to the starting point pilgrims may feel nervous or fearful
or even begin to doubt the journey: What am I doing here? Can I make
it physically? Was this just a foolish whim? Suddenly the clash between
the hopes and putting the backpack or the cycling bags together gives
the trip and its consequences a new reality. Anxton, the Basque man who
first cycled, remembered his nervousness before setting out on foot:
"When the moment arrived to say goodbye to my family, my nervousness hit me hard—Have I forgotten something that I was advised to take?
I repacked my backpack and everything looked okay."[9] Most leave home
without an official ceremony, but some pilgrims may receive a Church
blessing. The Alicante Friends of the Camino gives a blessing in two parts,
an interpretation based on the historical pilgrimage. The pilgrim, his or
her friends and family, other members of the association, and a priest
go to a church, hermitage, or chapel, give the new pilgrim the symbols
of the way—shell, staff, pouch, pilgrim's credential—and then bestow
the blessing. Afterward they share a meal before the pilgrim begins the
journey.

Once the decision is made to walk or cycle, where does one begin the journey? Santiago is the only fixed endpoint on the Camino, and pilgrims may begin wherever they like. Often personal reasons draw pilgrims to certain places; for example, Daniel began in Africa, crossed to southern Spain, and cycled north through Seville. Time often dictates the starting point. David, the Englishman who began in Roncesvalles, wanted to walk a month like a proper pilgrim. Stephanie, the American woman, had only two weeks and went from León. Other factors relate to the current fashion of making the "whole" Camino. It is common to hear pilgrims say, "I did the whole thing," meaning that they began the journey on the Spanish-French border (from Roncesvalles or St. Jean Pied-de-Port) and walked the camino francés to Santiago. The whole, though, is an arbitrary designation new to the late-twentieth-century pilgrimage. It takes between twenty-two and thirty days to walk this originally 750-kilometer distance and about ten days to two weeks on bicycle. Pilgrims of the Middle Ages simply left from their homes and joined one of the established pilgrimage routes to Santiago. Most of today's pilgrims believe that at least a monthlong journey, over this portion of the Camino, is essential for an authentic experience. Thus when I saw that people took taxis from Pamplona to Roncesvalles (a trip of forty minutes and $50) or made long bus, car, train, or airplane journeys from Galicia, Seville, the United States, Brazil, or Germany to reach the "starting point," it was clear that the idea of the "whole way" was an important aspect of feeling like a true pilgrim.

Also, being in certain places that are important to the pilgrimage's history links some pilgrims to what they believe is real about the Camino and will make their experience more meaningful. The fame of many places of the way reveals little about their character. I had heard so much about Roncesvalles before becoming an hospitalera there that I was shocked to discover there was no train directly to or even within miles of the tiny village. Moreover, the bus arrived only several times a week. Many people remark on how moving it is to arrive at Roncesvalles because of its historical association with the *Chanson de Roland,* its pilgrim's hospital, and its two (reconstructed) Gothic churches. A Spanish man from Madrid wrote in the refuge's testimonial book, "Today I begin my pilgrimage. Yesterday, as soon as I got to Roncesvalles, I felt like a Pilgrim. I want to live the day, feel, touch, see the most basic and the smallest— not only in the Camino but when I get back to Madrid."[10]

For many, Roncesvalles becomes a marker of entry to the pilgrimage, going back to the roots, where millions of people passed through-

*Figure 11.   Ready to go at Roncesvalles. An English pilgrim and a Belgian pilgrim
stand next to the plaque that commemorates the battle from the epic* Chanson de
Roland.

out the ages. There is also an eight-hundred-year-old pilgrim's blessing
read at the evening Mass, which can help to set the tone of the journey
even for those pilgrims who are not religious. Part of it reads: "The door
is open to all, sick or well / Not only Catholics, but pagans also / To
Jews, heretics, idlers, the vain / And, as I shall briefly note, the good and
the worldly, too." For one English pilgrim, William, who was coming
over the pass from France, it was very important to get to this Mass.
He said, "I scrambled down [from the hills above] just in time and the
psalm they sang at Vespers was 'He keeps my eyes from tears and my
feet from stumbling.'" For him, a practicing Catholic and avid pilgrim,
this arrival and psalm helped to begin his journey in Spain in a meaningful way. For those who may feel a need for a blessing for their journey, the Mass can provide, often unexpectedly, a sense of departure and
consecration.

Decisions regarding season and speed of the journey, perceived austerity, and expenditure of money also may be related to a developing
sense of what it means to be a pilgrim. One longtime repeat pilgrim, Alison, wrote on the "Winter Pilgrim" for the English confraternity's bul-

letin and commented on how season and being a pilgrim are related to authenticity:

> I was surprised when I walked from Paris to Santiago via the Arles route between the end of September and the beginning of January by the number of people I met along the way who made the same two observations: "You'll earn a lot of merit by doing the *Camino* in winter" and "you ought to do it in the summer; it's better." Ensuing conversation revealed that "merit" resulted from increasing the hardship of what was seen to be an already very arduous undertaking by doing it in cold and possibly inclement weather. "Better," on the other hand, was usually equated with "warmer," though it could also mean that there would be more pilgrims on the *Camino,* not infrequently *"para hablar"* [to speak with]. (The idea that I might in fact enjoy the silence all around was apparently difficult to imagine.) There seemed to be, then, in some people's minds at least, if not actually a "right" then certainly a preferable time to walk to Santiago, though—interestingly—nobody I met mentioned arriving for St. James's Day.[11]

As one sociologist of travel puts it, the "meaning(s) of any given form of travel . . . are best regarded as *plural, contested,* and subject to *change* over time."[12] Pilgrimage (a form of travel) and being a pilgrim (a type of traveler) are no exception. Some pilgrims tend to lose sight of this and are often very self-critical and demanding of themselves and others. Alison focused on the season of travel and ended her article by encouraging pilgrims to "steer well away from the idea that there might be a 'proper' or 'right' time, or even a 'season' at all during which to walk, cycle or ride the pilgrim road to Santiago."[13]

SIGNS OF THE PILGRIM

One of the first words that non-Spanish participants in the Camino learn is *peregrino.* In fact, in most conversations that take place in English among pilgrims of any nationality, the Spanish term "peregrino" is often used instead of "pilgrim." Just as pilgrims learn small bits of language or information as they go, they also learn bit by bit what it means to be a pilgrim.

While working as an hospitalera in Hospital de Orbigo in August 1994, I met a Dutch couple in their late forties who were walking to Santiago. Both schoolteachers on summer leave, they wrote on their return home four months later: "We saw the Camino as sport, as a cultural event, and the religious aspect was a plus. . . . *Naturally on the Camino you can't escape being called a "peregrino," you take the profits of a peregrino and in a way you become a pilgrim.* I think this is different from having a religious goal. . . . When we got to Santiago I knew that the meaning of it was changed, and now I'm telling everybody it was a pilgrimage we did make" (my emphasis).

How is it that pilgrims are noticed so quickly? Santiago pilgrims are known for the scallop shell, the backpack, and the walking staff. These accoutrements visibly mark the participant as a pilgrim and link him or her to the past, to the road, and to a community of pilgrims.[14]

SCALLOP SHELL

Modern pilgrims often wear the scallop shell (*la concha de venera*) on a long cord around the neck or sew it to the hat or to the backpack to clearly identify one's status as a pilgrim. Cyclists often attach the shell somewhere to the bicycle, perhaps on the handlebars or on the panniers. Rather large (up to four inches in diameter) shells may be displayed, or a more discreet shell or even scallop jewelry may be worn. Pilgrims may also wear a pin from a Friends association, which often has the pilgrim or the shell as a logo.

The scallop shell's link to the pilgrimage has early roots in the history of the Camino. According to legend one of Santiago's early miracles was his salvation of a drowning bridegroom/horseman who resurfaced covered in shells, which were abundant along the Galician coast. The word *scallop* (*venera*) is etymologically linked to Venus and by association, birth and regeneration. The scallop has consistently appeared in the iconography of the Santiago pilgrim since the twelfth century and was supposed to be "symbolic of the good works the pilgrim is expected to perform: it reminds him of the spread out fingers of the back of his hand."[15] Rather than beginning with the shell, twelfth- to fifteenth-century pilgrims generally received it on arriving in Santiago as a marker of their status and the journey's completion.[16] Legend also suggests that pilgrims returning to France introduced the scallop into French cuisine, accounting for the dish coquilles Saint-Jacques.

The shell's acquisition often plays a role in the participant's growing sense of being a pilgrim. When I worked in Roncesvalles newcomers preparing to begin the pilgrimage occasionally asked me where to purchase the shell. Buying these shells (real shells printed with the red cross of Santiago) at the local tourism shop became an important step in identifying oneself with the role of the pilgrim. When I made the pilgrimage in 1993 the leaders of my group provided us with shells at the beginning of the journey to adorn our bags. Feeling a great deal of resistance to this tradition, I slipped mine into my pocket. Several weeks later I found

Figure 12.   Two German cyclists wear the scallop shell.

myself stitching the shell to my bag, an acquiescence to my original rejection induced by my slow identification as pilgrim, not just researcher
along for the ride.

While not all pilgrims choose to wear the shell, the majority do, partly
because of pressure to conform to tradition. If a pilgrim does not choose
to begin the journey with a shell, for whatever reason, it is quite common for nonpilgrims along the route to point out the lack to the pilgrim and either offer one or suggest that one ought to be acquired. Susan, the young Swiss pilgrim who saw pilgrimage as both an inner and
an outer way, received her shell on the second day, outside of Lake Constance, from a former pilgrim she met by chance. He had made the pilgrimage twice by bicycle and wanted to give her advice and guidebooks.
He quickly went home and returned with maps and a scallop shell,
which, he told her, was important to have because she was a pilgrim. A
Spanish cyclist also told me how after receiving the shell from a villager
who stopped him, he noticed that he received many more honks of encouragement on the highway and a general increase in the acknowledgment of his status as a pilgrim. In this way other pilgrims or nonpilgrims not only give help on the Camino but help in the process of
becoming a pilgrim.

WALKING STICK OR STAFF

Walking pilgrims frequently use a staff or a walking stick (*bordón*). As
with the shells, pilgrims often learn from other pilgrims, from guidebooks,
and from villagers along the road that an important part of the experience is to carry the staff because it is "traditional": it protects, it is what
pilgrims do, and so on. As with the scallop shell, a reference is made to
the staff in the *Codex Calixtinus,* as a pilgrim's "third foot."[17] Medieval
pilgrims used the walking staff for protection against the dangerous animals of the Camino (wolves and dogs) as well as for physical support
in the difficult portions of the road. There are many interpretations of
the staff's significance—from a phallic symbol to a representation of the
Ascension and to the Cross of the Crucifixion.[18]

These interpretations of the staff say little about what it can mean
personally or about the layered quality of the journey and the development of an inner and an outer way. Barbara Haab, a Swiss pilgrim and
researcher, described the staff thus: "[It helped] me with every step to centre myself, and, in coming to my own centre, to become conscious of myself as a link between Heaven and Earth."[19] The staff created a pathway,

Figure 13. A French pilgrim rests on his staff (Castile). Note the scallop shell pin in his hat.

and it also created a protected space by preventing the sky from pressing down. Some Brazilians said it is like "a magic wand." Others see the staff as a companion and a helper. Or it can even be an instrument that creates a rhythmic beat, keeping the pace of the march. Guy, the French psychologist in his mid-forties, described how his group created a voiceless communication through the rhythm of their tapping sticks while they walked in the dawn, waiting for the sun to rise. Carrying a staff formed part of his group membership. By contrast, one young Canadian woman told me, "I tried carrying a stick, but it never meant anything to me. I wanted to make the Camino without any help."

The staff often narrates the pilgrim's story. Some may be elaborately carved. Pilgrims sometimes carve as they go; moments of the journey become represented on the surface of the stick. Other staffs are completely functional. Walking sticks range from waist to head high (or even higher). Some pilgrims, especially those who hike in the Alps, use ski poles, which fold easily, in the most difficult parts of the way. And a few others take along umbrellas to serve as both sun protection and handy support. Sticks are often waved at dogs to keep them at bay.

Each walking stick is its own world, just as each owner has his or her own story. Several staffs surprised me for their ingenuity. In one refuge I saw a twisted, waist-high staff with an intriguing lizard with a red stone in its mouth glued to the side of its undulating surface. I asked its Swiss owner about its history. He first found the staff while walking and was attracted to its curving shape. Then he came across the dead lizard in the road. The staff was like a snake and the lizard, a dragon—the dragon of Saint George depicted in the art of the way— he explained. "We should acknowledge and recognize the dragon that is in all of us, and the red stone is the treasure or the power that it can give us."

Another man from Barcelona, on his second pilgrimage in 1993, claimed that his intricately carved staff "is a story beginning with Santiago." Sure enough, there was the saint at the top and below, written in English, "I am the Way." The intricate, fine carvings continued down the shaft. Many people had asked him if he was a professional carver. His reply: "No, I'm just Christian and it comes from my faith." The religious moments and symbols of his journey became engraved on his walking stick.

Betsy, an American woman from Colorado, told me how her staff and the carvings became a "map of the process" for her. When she reached a small Navarrese village, Pablito, a man famous among pilgrims of the

1990s, gave her one of the last four sticks of nine hundred that he had made for pilgrims.[20] She felt very honored. It was of hazelnut—"One of my favorite nuts," she said—well balanced, long, and straight. It was "like it should be," she commented. "Higher than you." She carried a bandanna on top of the stick—"like a flag"—which had been with her since a trip to South America eight years previously. Several times she was stopped by rural Spaniards, taken for a witch, and asked if she were casting spells (*hechizando*) with her staff. In Astorga a middle-class Spanish woman jumped when she saw her and then smiled and said, "I thought you were a witch (*bruja*) and casting spells with your stick." People also commented on its beauty and height—over six feet (she herself was 5′9″ or 5′10″)—or asked her where she had got it and wanted to look at the carvings. After receiving it Betsy began to carve personally significant symbols: Egyptian stars, trees, the moon, the lotus. These symbols related to her own feelings of transformation. Others were associated with certain places or experiences on the road. For example, one time when she was angry she drew a lightning rod–shaped snake with its mouth open, which frightened some. On another occasion, after sitting for a long time underneath a tree (the only living thing for miles around) on the Spanish meseta, she carved an acorn. The tree and the experience became another place on the "map" of her staff.

BACKPACK OR RUCKSACK

Even if a pilgrim chooses not to wear a scallop shell or carry a walking stick, walking with a pack or cycling on the camino francés marks one as a pilgrim. Pilgrims setting out from Le Puy were stunned to be asked, "Vous faites le Chemin de Saint Jacques?" (Are you making the Camino de Santiago?) The feeling of having one's goal recognized from nearly a thousand miles away shocked these pilgrims and made them question their own motives. It put their actions into context as part of a much larger ritual whole and community whose membership goes back centuries. One is obviously a transient stranger and often an object of attraction.

With such recognition there may also be a growing sense of one's status as a special being or a stranger and as somehow distinct from the people one's passing in the cities and villages (and from tourists). When I asked an Englishman when he first felt like a pilgrim, he replied that as he stepped off the boat from Plymouth to Bilbao to begin his journey, a man on the dock, recognizing him as a pilgrim for his backpack, crossed himself. Although he thought this quite an odd experience, it was one of the moments when he most felt like a pilgrim, a role he felt at times he was playing as a fraud. In contrast, a villager in Belorado told me that before the large influx of pilgrims in the 1990s they were often taken to be vagabonds or thieves. Slowly, over time, villagers began to associate the scallop shell with pilgrims to Santiago (the shell is not necessarily part of the Spanish "collective memory"). George, the English pilgrim who spoke to me of the walking wounded, commented that he found this suspicious attitude also among French villagers, for example, on the Vézelay route where "the symbols have been forgotten." In fact, pilgrims who travel routes in Spain other than the camino francés often find that villagers have no frame of reference for what they are doing and that they are taken to be tourists, not pilgrims.

Besides the role the backpack plays as a marker of one's status as a transient, independent traveler, it also has personal meaning and influences the transition from walker to pilgrim. The pack can represent the self and the "weight" that one carries in life or, for a devout Spanish Catholic man, the Cross and the weight of one's sins.[21] The desire to go "lightly" in life becomes translated to the Camino through the backpack. Some pilgrims arrive heavily loaded (up to 20 kilograms), in anticipation of every possible disaster or wanting the extra weight to make the journey more difficult for personal reasons. Americans and Germans tend to be cited as the most heavily weighted, but in 1997 I met a very cheerful young Frenchman who carried an eighty-pound leather backpack. To bear the load he used a harness strap between his legs and claimed that he was a mountain climber in training. These pilgrims frequently find themselves at the post office sending the unnecessary items home. Emptying the backpack helps to reduce one's needs to a bare minimum. One Italian woman for whom I sent home a box of things two weeks after she began explained, "To be a pilgrim means to have some kind of detachment toward possessions, work, life—I know I was not a tourist or a walker and from time to time I felt like a pilgrim but *con ¡DINERO!* [with money]." Ideally, for her, the pilgrim's bag is so light that even money is unnecessary. She was using as her model an anonymous nineteenth-century Russian pilgrim who carried "a knapsack with some dried bread in it on his back, and in his breast pocket a Bible."[22] While most do carry money, there are some, often French pilgrims, who go without and count on the generosity of others. One Frenchman from a very wealthy family felt burdened by his background. A young Frenchwoman was considering entering a religious order. Often this way of going is seen as the ideal. The pack's contents become the metaphorical baggage that one carries in life. One pilgrim who found his credit card the heaviest item in his pack, which got lighter and lighter, never could discard the plastic money.

The above comments are equally valid for the cyclist, who must carry all the weight attached to the bicycle. Although the weight is distributed over the wheels, the effort one makes on a bicycle is substantial and it is desirable to have no superfluous items.

A pilgrim's identity is socially conferred as well as personally created. One could walk or bicycle without the symbols of the pilgrim, but many want to identify themselves in relation to others, to the Camino, and to their role as pilgrim. It is an acquired status that gives the bearer a great deal of freedom and even power. It is much more advantageous to the participant to be considered a pilgrim than a tourist. The pilgrim, especially in Spain, is often treated with generous hospitality for simply being a pilgrim. It is not uncommon for those who go alone or in very small groups to be offered a fresh beverage or a snack by someone who recognizes the shell or the staff. It is not likely that a tourist would be invited into the home of a villager. Sometimes this sense of feeling special leads to unwarranted expectations and hubris regarding what the Camino "owes" to the pilgrim.

A symbol often has power because it represents many things to many different people. The meanings of symbols are fluid and subject to change over time. Within the same period the same symbol can have many meanings—official, subversive, or personal. Part of the success of the pilgrimage is the elasticity of the symbols associated with it, which appear to remain constant yet are interpreted differently. Pilgrims and villagers can agree on the "meaningfulness of the symbols" without having to agree on their specific content, which allows them to be shared yet contested.[23] Although in most cases the treatment of pilgrims is positive, they may also be shunned or laughed at by those outside their world. Pilgrims are objects of interest for tourists not because they arrive in Santiago on their knees but because of the significance of the scallop, the staff, and the pack (and the long journey). Not only do the symbols communicate a message—"I am a pilgrim to Santiago"—they also become part of the pilgrim's journey and story.[24]

PILGRIMAGE AND SACRIFICE

The pilgrimage begins to take shape through the preparation and relationship one has to its symbols. In this process meanings of the journey begin to emerge. Meanings continue to emerge through interaction with others, the road, and reflection, as I discovered one day while walking the pilgrimage again in 1995, alone. I experienced this self-questioning when the concept of pilgrimage and sacrifice surfaced over a cup of coffee. A woman, Micaela, invited me in to rest as I passed through her small village in Navarre. I accepted her generous hospitality, and at one point she commented to me, "¡Qué sacrificio es hacer el Camino!" (What a sacrifice it is to make the Camino!). She went on to discuss what a noble activity it was to leave your home, take to the road, and journey all that way to Compostela alone. I could not help but contradict Micaela in my mind. Yes, perhaps for some it is a sacrifice, but the majority of the participants make the pilgrimage because it is the process, not the arrival at the goal, that is most significant in the experience. However, it was hard to tell this woman that for me it was not a sacrifice. Rather it was, as it is for many others, personally rewarding, a journey of self-exploration, human contact, visual and physical pleasure, catharsis, voluntary and self-imposed hardship. I began to wonder if she invited me in simply because she believed I was making a sacrifice. Suddenly I found myself in a bind. I wanted her to think that she had helped someone who was making a sacrifice. I wanted to fulfill her idea of the modern traditional pilgrim, the authentic pilgrim, and not shatter that image. I wondered, as I drank coffee in her small parlor that was covered with macramé and a few photos of herself and pilgrims, What right do I have to be here?

We met on the corner in the village. I just happened to catch the fruit and vegetable man on his rounds. As I heard the beep of the truck signaling his arrival, I noticed two middle-aged women waiting with their shopping bags. I suddenly heard, "¿Peregrina?" Although I wore no symbols of the pilgrimage—no scallop shell or walking staff—my backpack was a telltale sign. I turned with a smile to the women and responded in the affirmative, and we began a bit of conversation. She then told me to come to the first house of the village. She wanted to invite me in.

I found out that she had been born in the hamlet of twenty-one souls and had always lived alone there. She told me that the population today was about the same as when she was a child. Village life was quiet, and most of the few young people had gone to the city. But then the pilgrims began to appear in a constant flow from one side of the village to the other, breaking the daily rhythm of life. Curiosities. Lonely-looking men bearing the great weight of the backpack. They arrive at such unlikely hours walking in the heat. Why not stop one and find out who he is? I imagined her reasoning. Give them a bit of hospitality, and they give me a bit of their story, a bit of life in the otherwise monotonous routine of waiting for the fruit delivery man to come.

When I met Micaela she had a rubber stamp with the village's seal that she offered to mark in my pilgrim's passport. She had carved out a place for herself in the community of pilgrims and, as happens with many of the villagers who take an interest in the pilgrims who constantly pass through, a name. I do not mean to imply that her acts of generosity come from a vain interest in being famous in the Camino's gossip network. Rather I had the impression that her belief in being a good Catholic motivated her acts of kindness. At the same time I could see how her life was enhanced through this voluntary act of hospitality.

Suddenly whether the Camino was a sacrifice for me became less important. Sacrifice is how Micaela understood what she gave to pilgrims. By believing that they were making a sacrifice, she was able to rationalize what would normally be strange behavior on her part: inviting unknown single men and women into her house and giving them coffee or a meal.

The pilgrimage expands the options for creative identity shaping not only among pilgrims but also among the many who populate the way. In essence, authenticity is not always conferred or questioned on an institutional level but rather through a whole series of interactions that take place over time on the Camino. Exchanges do not always take place on the crude level of the dollar. Micaela and I both had roles created by the reanimation of the pilgrimage: she was a helper on the way, and I was a pilgrim. When she planted the question of sacrifice, she also applied a subtle form of pressure. She was defining what a pilgrim is: one who makes a sacrifice. If one is not making a sacrifice, does this mean that one is not a pilgrim, that one should accept Christian hospitality only if one is making a sacrifice? It may force pilgrims to reflect on their own experiences: Why am I here? What does it mean to be a pilgrim? Is it ethical to accept charity from someone who apparently can ill afford it?

People who live along the Camino help to keep pilgrims on the way. They remind pilgrims of their goal and destination: I will nourish you so that you can keep going, so that you can carry my own petition to the saint, a journey I cannot make. For Micaela, it would be a sacrifice. At the same time her acts, like the pilgrims', are voluntary. No one compels her to invite pilgrims into her home. Her performance takes place within the context of her daily life and the pilgrim's performance, within the context of his or her spiritual/ritual/vacation life.

PILGRIM AS SPIRITUAL MESSENGER

As I left Micaela, hoisting my backpack, I told her I would happily take her prayers to Saint James. Those who live along the Camino's boundaries may ask the pilgrim to carry petitions, money, or prayers to the apostle in Santiago. It can be thought-provoking and even confusing when the agnostic pilgrim, who considers the journey to be merely "a long walk through Spain," is asked to fulfill the role of spiritual messenger. If one is not of a Catholic tradition or knows little about Santiago and the pilgrimage, being asked to "give a hug to the apostle" seems odd.[25] To assume responsibility for the spiritual wishes of another may also cause pilgrims to ponder their role and their privileged position. It grants authenticity and meaning to the journey, which might previously have been vague. The journey is given meaning beyond one's own narrow world: I bear the hopes, fears, or gratitude of another. It is no longer the journey of one but of all those the pilgrim meets along the road who share kindness and therefore the journey. In these ways one begins to see oneself more and more as a pilgrim and as part of a larger community of pilgrims and villagers. One Frenchman commented that in participating in these ways, pilgrims become part of the Church without even realizing it.

Even when one is not asked to carry a petition, the villagers with whom pilgrims stop and speak along the way play a large role in fostering the sense of being a pilgrim. Old men and women (especially in Navarre, Aragón, and La Rioja) enjoying the afternoon sun may talk with pilgrims, and although thousands of pilgrims have passed through in the last few years, many often feel special. The older person may ask, Are you a pilgrim? Where did you begin? Are you alone? The pilgrim responds, and the villager exclaims in awe, "Walking! [or Biking!] All the way?" In this manner both claiming the pilgrim's identity and having the importance of the act reinforced by others play a vital role in the conversion process of walker or cyclist to pilgrim.

The pilgrim's journey comes to have meaning not only through the symbols but also through interactions with people along the Camino. People are also places, pauses in movement. The abstract space of the Camino is transformed into place through contacts and events. That village is not just another village in Navarre I walked through but intimately connected to Micaela's story, our meeting and the meanings it came to have for me, which is one way that space comes to be meaningful.[26]

THE PILGRIM'S CREDENTIAL

Given its current popularity it is not surprising that organizations try to control the Camino and its expansion. As David Chidester and Edward T. Linenthal suggest, "A sacred space is not merely discovered, or founded, or constructed, it is claimed, owned and operated by people advancing specific interests."[27] On the political level the moves to control the Camino include the development of an elaborate infrastructure, funded by ecclesiastic, public, and private sources, that consists of marking of routes, construction and maintenance of refuges, preservation of monuments, information centers, pamphlets and brochures, and resurrection of the "traditional hospitality of the Camino" (according to a government-funded brochure). The hospitality takes the form of volunteer hospitaleros, based loosely on medieval models of Christian charity given by religious orders to the sick, the poor, and pilgrims. Although there is no charge to be a pilgrim, except for basic living expenses such as food and personal needs, to participate in the Camino's infrastructure the pilgrim must carry a credential and ideally make donations in the pilgrims' refuges. Some refuges charge a nominal fee of between $2 and $4 per night.

The pilgrim's credential is distributed through the Church and its institutions (parish, confraternity, etc.) and organizations authorized by the Church (e.g., associations linked to the Spanish Federation, some refuges). The credential is only for those who go on foot, bicycle, or horseback and who "desire to make the pilgrimage in a Christian sense, even though it may only be a general searching." Its purpose is to identify the pilgrim, and it has two practical applications: access to the infrastructure of the Camino and to the *Compostela,* the certificate awarded by the Church to the pilgrim after having completed the pilgrimage with a religious motive—"devotionis affectu, voti vel pietatis causa," that is, religious devotion or for a pious cause. Technically, to receive a credential to begin the pilgrimage the participant should present a letter of accreditation from his or her local parish priest to one of the approved distribution locations. In some places where credentials are conferred there is some rigor, but the vast majority of places approve the pilgrim's request without questioning the motive for the journey. The credential also reminds those who bear it that being a pilgrim signifies collaboration, humility, and gracious acceptance of generosity received.

The credential does have a history in the pilgrimage, but rather dif-

Figure 14.   An Italian couple show both sides of their pilgrim's credential, which is full of stamps on reaching Santiago.

ferent from today. In the post-eleventh-century period pilgrims carried a document from a religious authority accrediting their mission. While these were formulaic in nature, there was no systematized document as exists today, and its purpose was to prevent "false" pilgrims (*coquillards*) from taking advantage of the system of hospitality. Currently the credential adds a novel and purposeful tone to making the journey. The pilgrim is instructed to get one stamp a day on the credential. Stamps (ink, not paper) are acquired at refuges, churches, city halls, or even local bars. Since the late 1980s the burgeoning production and historical re-creation of local stamps mirrors the reanimation of the Camino. There is no control on stamps, and anyone can produce and use one. For some pilgrims, the process of getting stamps turns into an important subactivity during the day, and in the end the credential becomes an important souvenir of the journey. For the people who do the stamping, it can provide a means of interchange between locals and pilgrims.

Depending on where one begins, the process of receiving the credential may immediately expose the pilgrim to the power of social forces and gatekeepers. These experiences often play an important part in the emergence of the pilgrimage's meaning. In an emblematic first-day experience for those beginning in St. Jean Pied-de-Port, pilgrims must pass through the doors of a long-term, often disagreeable French gatekeeper who runs the pilgrim's office from her cramped office/kitchen located in the shadow of the medieval citadel. During field research I heard various stories from disgruntled pilgrims about how this gatekeeper had tested their status as pilgrims. According to them her judgments are harsh; she may deny pilgrims a stamp or the credential because they arrive at her office in street clothing, because their mode of going does not seem credible, or because they lack accreditation. Being denied the stamp or credential by her has led to personal doubt, frustration, and even tears. For the authentic pilgrim (according to her), however, her smile lights the room and a bottle of refreshing light wine might appear.

In an interview the gatekeeper told me that there were many inauthentic pilgrims, for example, those who were trying to take advantage of the system by using it as vacation. On another occasion, when I was in her office, a young Italian man arrived to begin the pilgrimage the next day. He came without a letter of presentation from his parish. She sent him away and told him the only way he could have a stamp was if he were to get a fax from his priest certifying his religious motive. He was surprised and disgruntled, not having easy access to a fax machine and not feeling it was necessary to justify his pilgrimage to her. He left the next day without consenting to her requirements and was given a credential on arriving in Roncesvalles. Ironically, the gatekeeper encourages technological intervention yet requires a particular authentic mentality that is opposed to technology. In this encounter it is clear how discontinuities in definitions of pilgrims and pilgrims' behavior among participants reveal a level of unresolved tension regarding the changing nature of pilgrimage and leisure activities in Western European society. The gatekeeper's behavior is at times an embarrassment to other local French Jacobean associations. To ease her work and give a warmer welcome to pilgrims in this important transition point, in the mid-1990s Les Amis de St.-Jacques des Pyrenées Atlantiques (the Friends of St. James–Atlantic Pyrenees) opened another pilgrims' office in St. Jean staffed by volunteers.

Another facet of this anecdote that merits discussion is the juxtaposition of the "borderless Europe" idea encouraged by the European Union and the pilgrim's passport. In theory the Eurocitizen is supposed to move freely. The idea of the pilgrim's passport or credential poses an interesting contrast as a controlling process. Pilgrims walking over the border of France and Spain may have more difficulty getting their pilgrim's credential stamped than their regular passport, which is not checked at all. The normalization of all credentials used in Spain has been a goal of the

Spanish Federation of Associations of Friends of the Camino.[28] Although the credential or passport may be issued by the local or national confraternity or Friends association and used before reaching the border, once in Spain the pilgrims are sometimes requested, by more officious gatekeepers, to use the official credential to participate in the refuge infrastructure. It is a subtle form of power linking pilgrims to society in a bureaucratic way even though pilgrims may feel as if they are outside society while on the Camino.

CHAPTER 3

LEARNING NEW RHYTHMS

As I walked through the wilderness of this world . . .
  —*Bunyan*, The Pilgrim's Progress

I began *to walk*. From this moment, when my heart leapt with joy, my discoveries began. *Landscapes* and marvelous skies, plants, flowers, trees with
an incredible combination of *colors*, majestic flights of *birds*, enchanting *people*
with a word of encouragement, a piece of fruit, or a glass of water who told
me the stories of their villages, and *diverse pilgrims* of different ages, professions, nationalities, social classes, and beliefs, etc. . . . They gave the best of
themselves to others with a display of affection, *solidarity*, and respect so that
each day would be special. I experienced *confirmations of my self* and of my
physical deterioration that *made me suffer* a great deal. I realized that I needed
to take better care of myself and do some kind of regular exercise. I learned
about my capacity to *overcome pain and difficulties*. On many occasions I
overstepped my physical and psychological limitations, believing that I could
do it all, but of course I couldn't. I also discovered how well I deal with *solitude* and being by myself, how well I adapt to *new circumstances*, how unim-
portant *materialistic things* are, how much easier it is to walk when one carries little weight in life. . . . I also learned *to love a healthy life* and how good
I felt *in nature*, as part of it. I found myself living exclusively *in the present*,
in the moment, living without news or daily life and even in another stage of
the century or *another world* where the well-being, the enjoyment, the *energy*, the *freedom*, and the walking are all that matter. Still, as the days pass,
when I think or speak about the Camino, new discoveries arise.

The above is an excerpt from a letter I received from Marina, a thirty-
three-year-old physical therapist from Madrid, three months after she
completed the pilgrimage in summer 1994. Marina and I met at the refuge
in Belorado one hot August afternoon when she arrived two weeks af-

ter beginning her walk. Our first encounter occurred when, in my role as hospitalera, I stamped her pilgrim's credential as she signed in at the refuge. Catholic by birth but nonpracticing, like many modern pilgrims, Marina originally made the Camino as an alternative to the dreary rhythm of daily urban life and to experience a vacation that did not entail the beach and hangovers. She wanted leisure with meaning, and believed she could find it on the Camino. Giving up the stresses of bourgeois life and replacing them with physical activity, with nature, with hardship, with solitude, with the unanticipated and novel, with less, with a new sense of time, place, and the past, and with a goal allowed her to discover herself and others in new ways. It was a physical and psychological—external and internal—process that developed over time and place through contact, private rumination, and movement.

When pilgrims begin to walk several things usually begin to happen to their perceptions of the world which continue over the course of the journey: they develop a changing sense of time, a heightening of their senses, and a new awareness of their bodies and the landscape. Marina begins her statement with "I began to walk," immediately linking basic human movement with joy and discovery. The walking reveals a world of natural beauty existing out of ordinary time. In this moment preparation and chance meet. No matter how much one prepares physically, mentally, and spiritually one cannot prepare for the unanticipated that the Way presents. Launching oneself into the unknown is an important first step into one's role as a pilgrim. A young German man expressed it this way: "In the experience of walking, each step is a thought. You can't escape yourself."

TIME, PLACE, MOVEMENT, PERCEPTION

In a world where the passing of time is marked by changes in the sun, fatigue, the position of one's shadow, or hunger, linear time often gives way to circular time. Both of these types of time exist and influence pilgrims on the Camino: one follows the linear goal, yet most movements are circular as one moves slowly along the Camino from place to place. Wim, a fifty-year-old mental health professional, walked to Santiago from his home in the Netherlands, leaving behind his wife and family to take some desperately needed time to reassess his life. Reflecting on how time is affected by the journey, he commented, "I miss the experience that time and distance are no longer relevant things. You just continue, day after day after day and mile after mile and that brings you somewhere. Back home time is an essential thing, and it was great to feel that I had all the time in the world. I could live day by day for an almost endless period." Participants are usually accustomed to routines based on meetings, appointments, classes, and getting from one place to the next quickly. Some describe beginning the journey at a rapid pace and then slowing down, realizing that there is no rush to get to any particular place.[1]

Pilgrims become aware of their bodies, and in becoming attuned to different rhythms, some begin to guide their movements by them (hunger: I'll stop to rest when I eat; fatigue: I'll walk until I'm tired; cycle of the day: I'll start early to avoid the heat). Pilgrims report experiencing a strong sense of the "here and now." Anxton, the Basque who walked from Roncesvalles, explained, "There's time for everything: to pray, to visit churches, monuments, convents, to speak with the village priest, with the farmers and the shepherds who tell you their problems, with the old folks . . . and the children."[2] The outside world is distant. One may enter a bar and see television images of sporting events, bullfights, or international tragedy flash by, but it is described as a sideshow to a conversation, a meal, or a refreshing glass of water or beer on a hot afternoon. This "out of time" quality exists in sharp contrast to normal life, which is programmed by work, societal norms, and the daily planner. As one pilgrim reported, "There is no destination to which I am rushing. There is only this earth that I touch in so many ways."[3] Normal time (daily life) is inverted while walking or cycling to Santiago.

With these new sensations of time there is often a breaking down of the usual rituals that guide and structure home life. The Camino gives pilgrims opportunities to break habits (*romper esquemas*), as some Spanish say, and to experiment with new confidence. Non-Spanish pilgrims are hard-pressed to find an evening meal before 8:30 P.M., compelling the pilgrim to adapt to different hours or give up cherished cultural habits and possibly learn to listen to their bodies rather than to the clock. For Spaniards, the idea of eating when one is hungry instead of at *la hora de comer* (the hour of eating, between 2:00 and 3:00 P.M.) is revolutionary. It is much easier to live in the moment and be the owner of one's time while walking or cycling to Santiago. The Camino, pilgrims claim, is where one finds "freedom," whereas society constrains.

But time does press on participants. The going is bracketed by the inevitable return. Most arrive with a fixed amount of time in which to make the Camino. The people I met had a minimum of one week and a maximum of seven months to make the pilgrimage. Most pilgrims have two weeks or a month for the journey. The pressure to stick to a routine may conflict with the pilgrim's new sense of living in the moment. Guidebooks may encourage pilgrims to be aware of time and maintain a program of rising early, walking in the morning, and visiting in the afternoon. Refuges also compel pilgrims to maintain specific hours with nighttime curfews and morning closures. Some throw away their itineraries on entering the rhythm of the journey; others find it difficult to compromise.

This conflict is illustrated by Anton, an older German businessman, who felt he missed an important opportunity by maintaining his rush to arrive rather than experience the slow pleasure in getting there. While walking through a rural, verdant region between Castile-León and Galicia, he arrived at a hamlet that appeared to be from another time and place. Many farmers there use oxen rather than tractors, the road is unpaved, and the women are dressed in black. As he walked past a small stone house an old woman signaled to him to stop and rest for a while. He paused but continued his journey, feeling the need to keep going. He passed the hamlet's boundaries and suddenly felt a pang of regret. He stopped and then turned around. But when he returned ten minutes later, to his surprise he could find no one in the hamlet. He knocked on the woman's door, but there was no answer. His regret deepened; the opportunity the Camino had given him was lost. From this experience he felt more committed to honor the moment rather than anticipate the end, an end that like Santiago (or death) will always be there whether he rushes to it or not.

Moving more slowly and getting into the rhythm of the "human speed" in which "each step is a thought" can also affect one's sense of place and experience of the natural landscapes.[4] At first the Camino is a big space in the mind's eye—perhaps bits of historical knowledge or friends' anecdotes liven the picture—but it comes to be a series of personal places and stories through walking and cycling. I found this to be true with my experience with Micaela and her question about sacrifice; that village will always be intimately linked in my mind to the combination of events that occurred there. Lee, a Catholic American who has also lived for long periods in Germany and has been a Dominican priest, a professor of political science, and a subsistence farmer, explains,

> After several hours, I begin to feel something new, something never before experienced. I strongly sense, with my whole self, that I am moving from one place to another. . . . I am not passing *through* space, as one does in a car or airplane. I feel I am in a place; actually, in an infinite number of places. I am not in an undifferentiated space—what one feels in many modern places that, really, are non-places; they are simply repetitions of concepts—the concept

of hospital space, shopping mall space, airport space. . . . Here, with each step, I am always in place, in some place, going to the next place, one centimeter or half a meter farther on. . . . And all my senses seem to be more open. . . . It's as if I'm plowing through infinitely different perceptions, for with every step I *am* in a different place, and each place has its own unique character.[5]

Lee felt this "radically different sensation" his second day of walking. To be in a place, rather than passing through what was for him meaningless space, is directly linked to a growing awareness of his senses. It is his "being" in the world that is different too: he feels each step, is aware of himself in the new places and how he affects and is affected by those steps. The discovery of this sensation of place is in part based on how he moves, what he perceives, and what he touches. The roads are not just flat or bumpy, the hills green, or the birds singing. While walking it is possible to see individual blades of grass, feel every stone in the road (maybe painfully), and note how the senses are heightened. Details are vivid: "The scenery changes constantly, with every step. Underfoot, I feel a different combination of pebbles and rocks each time my foot hits the ground. Not only do I never step in the same place twice, but I never feel the same kind of surface twice. The variations of hardness, softness, and sharpness are never the same. If I look up, the cloud formations are always new. If I gaze around me, the scene is ever unique."[6] Landscape, then, is not just a neutral backdrop but a multidimensional concept related to the understanding of space and movement and the creation of stories meaningful to the pilgrim.[7] As the pilgrim journeys over the vaguely conceptualized Camino the steps and encounters are like the stamps in the credential: at first there is a blank, structural frame, which is then filled slowly, day by day. A pause, a thought, a stamp, a cup of coffee becomes part of a memory, and the vaguely conceived-of whole— the Camino—takes on a new set of meanings. At journey's end the spaces have been filled and marked with personal experiences. Pilgrims express concern about losing the novelty of the unknown spaces, creating routine, when they repeat the pilgrimage. Many find, though, that the landscape is not the only knowable space or variable; each time the encounters with people, the self, seasons, refuges, and companions are different.

Pilgrims often divide the spaces of the Camino into three zones: the Pyrenees; the meseta of Castile and León; and a return to the mountains in Galicia. These spaces, far from value-free, are marked by the personal meanings pilgrims attribute to them. Some religiously motivated pilgrims and Catholic catechism groups use the Camino's geography as a metaphor for understanding and applying the liturgy to one's religious life. The author of one spiritual guide, a Spanish repeat pilgrim who found his own religious renewal through the Camino breaks up the Camino into four geographic and thematic parts. The first, the Pardon, is Navarre and La Rioja with its "juice of mashed grapes" ("to go down to our interior, step on and crush our life far from God, and enjoy the wine of reconciliation with the Father"). The Castilian meseta (the Life of Christ) forms the next portion, where the lessons of austerity, hardness, and humility are learned from the environment, which is characterized by the same traits. The third phase is the portion from León to El Bierzo (the Passion of Christ), where the meseta ends and one climbs several important passes (the Cruz de Ferro and Cebreiro, where the Holy Grail is believed to be located, representing the miracle of transubstantiation), reminding the pilgrim of the Eucharist miracle, solitude, and the meaning of the Cross. And finally, the fourth part, Galicia, marks the Joy of Christ, where the ups and downs of the journey are understood in terms of the Resurrection, joy, and ascension of Christ to heaven.[8]

Alternatively, Barbara Haab, understanding the pilgrimage as a journey of initiation, divides the Camino into parallel geographic and experiential phases. Rather than understand transformation in terms of a direct relationship to God and liturgy associated with the Catholic church, her model focuses on pilgrims oriented toward spiritual and personal change. There is what she calls an "initiatory structure of the Way," and she links both spaces (e.g., the meseta) and places (e.g., the cathedral in León) to internal processes of spiritual transformation.[9] She suggests, for example, that the Castilian meseta is often the site of crisis, sickness, catharsis, or purification for pilgrims as the blazing sun and wide-open landscape act to alter their perceptions. Both views impose a structure of transformation and experience onto the geography of the Camino, but their conclusions lead to different ends: the first ends in Santiago with greater personal faith in the Church and the apostle; Haab understands the experience of walking and space to lead one to a personal initiation of spiritual understanding not necessarily linked to any specific faith or creed.[10]

While both of these models are valid for some pilgrims, I found that perceptions of place and how they influence pilgrims' emotional states vary greatly. One area of the Camino that tends to receive frequent experiential interpretation and appears to affect pilgrims strongly is the meseta, a 200-kilometer stretch roughly between Burgos and León. It is dry and scorching hot in the summer, with a low population density. Pilgrims often describe feeling very alone as they walk through this zone. For some, this is a positive experience; for others, it is disconcerting or challenging. Some experience illness, vulnerability, increased fatigue, and, Haab reports, crisis.[11] One of the characteristics of the meseta is its horizon, which appears to never end. One English pilgrim described feeling "frustration" and psychologically undone by the meseta, which is so unlike his English countryside: "When we were 2,000 feet up in the barrenness of the Meseta, with nothing in sight, when the horizon extended more widely and in greater depth than in England, where hedges, trees, telegraph poles, barns, and farms give one a sense of distance, a feeling of proportion, . . . towards the end of the day, drenched in perspiration and consumed by heat, one is afraid to look ahead for a limit to the distance, as it never seems to come."[12] His normal frames of reference—barns, curving paths—are lost in this new geographic space. His sense of perception is altered, and the ability to gauge distance falters. For him, accustomed to a sense of limit on the horizon, the loss of the border creates great discomfort and an eagerness to move beyond.

Lee, the American man moved by his new sense of place while walking, comments on this same zone in a different way: "Seeing the horizon at all times, I come to know what it is to live with a horizon—an experience lost to most modern people. . . . On the *camino*, I need never think of restricting myself; I can act with total abandon. This is the first place . . . that I can freely move without pain, for I do not exceed any limits. . . . With the horizon always 'out there,' seemingly so distant, I know it is near; I am within its comforting embrace. Before the day is over, I know I will touch it."[13]

The meseta lends itself to further spatial/experiential interpretations. A nonpracticing Italian Catholic woman commented, "I want to be in a space where there is no guilt but serenity and silence, like the meseta. The physical space of the Camino created a space in my own mind and heart." This woman wants to replicate in daily life the way she felt on the meseta, or to feel the meseta internally. One of the most powerful memories I have of the Camino was a moonlit night on the meseta, walking with two other pilgrims through a sea of wheat cut through by a white dirt road. Suddenly we decided to enter the wheat, and we laid down on our backs, completely enveloped by the ripening stalks. The only light was from the moon and the stars, the only sound the warm breeze flowing through the waving wheat. I could have been anywhere or nowhere. In that moment I felt far away from everything and completely free, alone, and happy.

A Basque man who worked at a refuge on the meseta reported that

Figure 15.   On foot in the meseta (Castile).

people often arrived shaken emotionally by the limitless horizon. On this particular route one can see a single tree on the horizon for miles before reaching it. For many pilgrims, the tree comes to symbolize hope as they slowly get closer and closer to it. This hospitalero came to use the tree as a symbol in his own work as a heating repairman in overwhelming moments: "Step by step, like reaching the oak, you'll always get there one step at a time." This is the same oak that became part of the American psychologist's staff when she carved the acorn after sitting under the tree. It becomes possible to see how "spaces are intimately related to the formation of biographies and social relationships," as the experience of different places along the way come to be personalized and part of the pilgrim's experience in a unique way.[14] There is no single way to interpret any one place along the Camino because each person's life-world differs. Pilgrims may experience the same places as particularly meaningful, yet the experiences therein or the personal meanings or the stories attached to them vary from person to person.

Frequently the growing sense of place and the journey's stories through movement lead to a deepening perception of landscapes and the impacts they have on the psyche and the body. Thomas Merton suggests, "The geographical pilgrimage is the symbolic acting out of an inner journey.

The inner journey is the interpolation of the meanings and signs of the outer pilgrimage. One can have one without the other. It is best to have both."[15] The two journeys go hand in hand—at times parallel to each other. At first, in her letter, Ana *sees* the birds, the trees, and the people, and then she begins to *feel* more deeply connected: in union with nature, in solidarity with people. There is a sense of being one with the land or part of creation. In reflecting on his experiences while walking one Spanish priest found himself overwhelmed by both changes in time and, in particular, his sense of connection to the earth: "I was part of the earth. She was my mother. I'm from the country, and I know that the rural can inspire fear, but for me it was the opposite; it was converted into a large house. I couldn't distinguish between what was me and what was the nature around me. I was one with all part of creation, not knowing in moments if I was God or only part of God. Was I the tree or the tree me? I couldn't distinguish between the sound of the church bell and the ringing within myself." This loss of self or creation of a greater self in the environment, the feeling of becoming one and joining with all and not knowing where your body ends and the other begins, affects many. For some, it is expressed as a magical or mystical moment when heaven and earth unite via the person. Time appears to stop, the world becomes whole, and you know that you are connected to something much greater and inchoate. Interpreting this experience in religious terms, a Spanish priest from Madrid explains, "It provokes a clear sensation of transcendence that in our religious experience we understand as the love and grace of God."[16] Religiously oriented pilgrims may come to see the hand of God in all that surrounds the Camino, and each aspect of the Camino can be interpreted with God in mind: a fountain is God's grace; a mountain or rock can be the strength of one's faith.[17] Someone posted the following poem of transcendent union (attributed to Saint Augustine) on the wall in the common room of the refuge in Roncesvalles.

We are the walking breath
We are the spirit of the earth
We are alive and walking
Where we are is beautiful.
I am an acorn, the shell, the seed
God is within me, and God is the tree
I am unfolding the way I should be
Sown in the soil of God's hand
Sown in the soil of God's land
If the past and the future are real
Where are they?

Figure 16.   Pilgrims walking through León.

These sensations are often associated with mystical experiences, but they are not always put into religious terms by pilgrims, who also call this spiritual union the here and now and well-being with nature.[18]

In looking at Dutch and Belgian pilgrims' written accounts of their journeys, Paul Post found that the theme of union and creation is common. He suggests that this sense of union with nature can be translated into an "outdoor liturgy" (such as "meeting god in the Cathedral of nature," as a Spanish priest put it) in which a symbolic language based on Christian metaphors is used (truth, Way, light, hope). Post writes, "We read digressions which . . . verbalise the contrast with the bourgeois existence left behind and sometimes lead to discussions of our estrangement from nature, about nature and the attribution of meaning, milieu, and quality of life coupled with living in harmony with nature."[19]

Estrangement may also be induced when one comes in contact with signs of urban life, which contrast sharply with the experience or union in nature. The major cities (Pamplona, Logroño, Burgos, León, Ponferrada, and Santiago) often shock pilgrims accustomed to the out-of-time quality of the Spanish countryside. Often a sense of disorientation is experienced as the lonely dirt path gives way to the din and speed of the paved streets of the impersonal city. Haab found that there are parts of the Camino "that coincid[e] with a main road, where cars and lorries roar ceaselessly past you, often so close that you have to jump into the ditch to avoid being run over. You feel despair and anger, and sorrow for all that our civilisation 'runs over.' All the dead creatures on the roadside, from butterflies, lizards and snakes, to birds, dogs and cats!"[20] The sense of union with nature found in the Camino, in contrast to the estrangement of daily urban life, coupled with the experience of time as distinct also lead some to reflect on one's mortality.

WALKING WITH THE DEAD

Walter Starkie, a mid-twentieth-century pilgrim, wrote, "A reflective pilgrim on the road to Santiago always makes a double journey when he tries to collect his memories—the backward journey through Time and the forward journey through Space. Every step the pilgrim makes today along the road through France and northern Spain evokes memories of those who passed that way century after century."[21] With the change in linear, directional time, pilgrims often sense that time blends and folds together: past, present, and future coexist. Pilgrims commonly experience themselves with pilgrims of the past as they walk, rest, take shelter, drink at a fountain, cross a bridge, pray in church. Many pilgrims in previous centuries died on the way to Santiago, and some modern pilgrims feel their presence strongly. Lee said, "I suspect that it is because I am continually in touch with the *camino* that I am on such familiar terms with the dead, that I feel them so near to me. It is only through the richly sensible and lowly experience of tramping on this soil that I can hope to move familiarly among those who have walked before me, some of whose bodies lie beneath my feet."[22] Again, it is the feeling nature of the experience, the walking, and the bending of time that take the pilgrim to different dimensions. The common human experience of walking gives one the sense of a shared journey.

Not only are past pilgrims invoked and felt in the present, but there is also a sense of those who will come in the future. One described this as "future memory." George, the English pilgrim who described the walking wounded, turned this idea into poetry:

> At a small chapel, on a crest
> Where two pilgrim roads meet,
> And where thousands once came—
> Utter silence.
> But rest, and cool water,
> Bread, and cheese, and fruit in season,
> Simple sacramental things,
> Which link us to our forebears,
> And to others for whom we too,
> One day, will be among those
> Who have gone before.

Many pilgrims describe carrying the spirit of those from the past and those who have yet to come, and at the same time they feel themselves becoming part of a living history and a larger community based on the common journey. They feel linked through bodily action and through living, at least temporarily, a life reduced to basics (excluding, of course, the hot showers, the excellent shoes, the sturdy backpack, the telephone booths, emergency services, etc.).

The dead with whom pilgrims walk may be other pilgrims or may be those brought forth from their own past. The dead may be anonymous people who could not make the journey themselves and for whom the pilgrim now journeys. While journeying through this different time and place pilgrims find that long-forgotten memories surface; memories of family members and friends, childhood places, secrets or painful circumstances. These new perceptions often take people to internal places not before visited. The days consist of many hours of walking and cycling. In these long moments, which may be experienced alone or in the companionship of other pilgrims, people are confronted with empty time, a concept distant from the lives of most of these urban dwellers. Into these quiet moments may spill unexplained tears. A man from Navarre who had been a pilgrim told me one day that he entered one of the churches in Estella and found a Frenchwoman on her knees before the altar, weeping. Although they did not know each other she wept in his arms yet could not tell him what loss she mourned. These outpourings are described as cathartic, and the catalyst that sets them in motion often mysterious to the pilgrim. The catalyst may be spatial (having distance, perspective, and free time), personal (another pilgrim), or experiential (walking in the meseta).

One's dream life may be affected. Moments from the past and carefully guarded secrets may unexpectedly surface, to be worked out during the long hours of walking or cycling, amid the solitude of the way and the crunching stones underfoot. I met a Frenchman from Burgundy in his early seventies who walked alone yet frequently found himself walking with the dead. He had been in World War II and had seen many people die, he explained after crossing the border between Navarre and La Rioja in Logroño. His eyes filled with tears as he said, "I've been lucky. Today I walked with a German." Then he lifted his chin and pointed to a deep, two-inch-long scar "that came from a German gun in the war." He repeated that he had been lucky: "God has given me this experience. I don't feel alone out here. I feel the presence of all of those who died and can't be here now. The pain of it all, it is very, very hard." His profound grief was being relived through the journey, and in a way he was healed by walking with the child of one who had once been the enemy. He was able to create a new relationship to his past through these unexpected encounters with the dead and the living. Past and present commingled. A Spanish couple, making the pilgrimage repeatedly as a vow for their deceased son, also believe strongly that the pilgrimage must be made on foot and historically re-created. The woman said, "[Each day the Camino] was like a big cemetery, and I spent every second remembering the dead pilgrims." I began to wonder if their focus on the past was an attempt to resurrect both the Camino and their son—that his loss not be tarnished, forgotten, and made meaningless by those who do not understand.

For some, walking with the dead also means becoming aware of one's own mortality. Like many in the Middle Ages, pilgrims still die en route to Santiago. Most are older men, such as a German cyclist who had a heart attack in the mountains of El Bierzo while cycling to Santiago. His final resting place is marked by an iron bicycle. Another man's shoes were bronzed and a monument placed by the Camino when he made his final steps while on the last day of the pilgrimage in Galicia. And in 1996 a Dutch man suffered a heart attack in the refuge near the end of the pilgrimage, his wife waiting for him in Santiago with his return ticket home. Often pilgrims leave flowers, small crosses, and bits of cloth as symbols of solidarity with those who did not make it.

A few pilgrims have met tragic ends on the Camino: near Nájera in La Rioja a plaque remembers a woman hit by a car while cycling, and near Arzúa in Galicia a young priest met his fate the same way while walking with teenagers from his parish. An English pilgrim in his seventies left a more transient mark of his passing. During the summer of 1996 he had planned to walk from Santiago to Finisterre with a friend, a Catalan woman with whom he walked the vía de la plata from Seville a previous summer. She wrote me in October 1996: "He died before the summer. His ashes are in the Chapel of the Holy Spirit in Roncesvalles (some) and in various other points of the Camino that he especially liked. The last ashes are at the Monte del Gozo (what remains of it), in the new 'vista point' at the foot of the cross I made with my staff. It didn't make sense to continue to Finisterre." His last wish, to be scattered to the winds of the Camino, illustrates how deeply some people feel linked to the Camino in life and in death. The Catholic church comments on deaths among pilgrims: "Within the sadness of the separation, to die walking to Santiago is a Christian comfort." The Church grants an automatic plenary indulgence, and in Santiago a mass is offered in the person's memory.

The Camino often reminds one of life's transience. While Jane, the Irishwoman who found home in the Camino, was walking one day she "found a beautiful bouquet of fresh flowers." She said, "I picked it up, wondering what to do with it. It was too big for pressing, too awkward to carry and then I came across the tombstone and my problem was solved." She had reached the monument to the cyclist and decided in that moment as she placed the bouquet below the iron bicycle that she "did not want to spend the last days or months of [her] life dying in bed." This became an important encounter with her own mortality and how she wanted to meet it—like the cyclist, living life to the fullest until the last breath.

Feeling out of time and place influences how pilgrims see themselves and others. On the Camino pilgrims generally use only first names and

Figure 17. A German pilgrim's death is remembered with this monument at El Acebo (León).

often find themselves distant geographically and emotionally from home. That a diplomat walks with a field hand and a teacher with a policeman and a graduate student is very appealing among pilgrims. Feeling one-self anonymous and equal can be remarkably liberating for many. One Spanish priest remarked to me that in his first days on the Camino he found great relief in being treated as a person first and not immediately identified by his profession. He began to share and express himself more, whereas he normally listens and gives counsel. For non-Spaniards the liminality may in part entail being compelled to communicate in broken Spanish or with gestures, getting accustomed to a new rhythm of life, not just that of the Camino but of Spain in general. For one young Spanish woman the opposite occurred. In the summer of 1994 she found herself surrounded by foreigners speaking English and was relieved after several days to meet another Spanish companion.

What the Camino appears to provide for many people relates to the idea of how movement can be art: the Camino is like a canvas into which the participant paints himself or herself. The scenes change as the pilgrim moves forward through time and place, evolving and potentially transforming. From the perspective of many pilgrims, new rhythms are related to slowing down, appreciating the minute and particular, learning to rely on senses other than those of sight, wanting to feel themselves connected to the road and the natural landscapes, and taking what comes. One French pilgrim suggested that, after feeling the influence of time and place in this way, "it is no longer possible to look at one's own reality with the same eyes." With the shift in spatial and temporal reality comes the application to one's own life and a possible reassessment of how things will be. New perspectives lead to alterations in the developing portrait of the Camino.

CHAPTER 4

LANDSCAPES OF DISCOVERY

Caminante, son tus huellas
el camino, y nada más;
caminate, no hay camino,
se hace camino al andar.
                —*Machado,*
        Poesías Completas

Before beginning the pilgrimage some participants believe they will find "something"—God, friendship, themselves, others—while on the road. Some people look to the symbols to find meaning, some look to the road or to certain kinds of experiences; others look to faith, to the authentic pilgrim, or to solitude. The meanings that the journey comes to have usually appear to emerge over time and space—forward, backward, inward—through movement.[1] Pilgrims' stories are not only about moving through the landscapes but also about odd encounters, refuges, and people and pilgrims they meet during the journey. The Camino, which begins as an abstract space, comes to be an accumulation of internalized places made up of stories, sensations, and changes in perception. As one longtime pilgrim stated, "For most of us who have walked it, it has created a place in our souls which we visit when, in other worlds and other circumstances, we cannot put on our boots and backpacks and begin another day on the Road to Santiago."[2] Linda made her first walk to Santiago in the 1970s. Since then she has dedicated much of her professional academic life to the Camino and has introduced other American students to the pilgrimage, including me. In the creation of that "place in our souls" the pilgrim may reveal hitherto unknown personal potential, experience a reorientation of values, have new visions of the self and others, and develop road maps for present and future actions.[3]

ON THE ROAD

Rural and urban northern Spain is diverse socially and culturally. Pilgrims traveling in the summer are bound to encounter the cycle of festivals celebrated with vibrant colors, costumes, processions, fanfare, and music. Some pilgrims join in; others feel disoriented by the "noise" and "commotion" that inevitably occur day and night. Pilgrims also encounter the distinct accents of Castilian Spanish as well as the Basque and Gallego languages within the four autonomous communities—Navarre, La Rioja, Castile and León, Galicia—through which the camino francés passes. Pilgrims are multinational, but the lingua franca is English. Some pilgrims speak as many as four languages and easily shift from one to the other. Northern Spain is also famous for its rich and varied gastronomy; the wines, breads, and local specialties change as frequently as the landscapes. A woman on bicycle commented, "We took it slowly, meandering along. . . . We ate impromptu picnics of goat's cheese and crusty *paisano* bread on the cool shady banks of rivers and bargain *peregrino* feasts in welcoming local restaurants."[4] Pilgrims also find a range of architectural styles—two-story whitewashed homes in Navarre, adobe in the meseta, stone in Galicia.

Experiences of disorientation resulting from a lack of knowledge of Spanish culture can lead to greater cultural or personal understanding. One retired Dutchman, who walked alone to Santiago after dreaming of doing so for many years, experienced much more than he originally imagined when he was "almost run over by bulls in Sahagún"—a story he shared with me by letter six months after returning home. He entered Sahagún, in the meseta of León, in the midst of a celebration; the streets were fenced off but lined with many people, and he could not figure out why. He wrote, "All of a sudden I hear someone shouting: Watch out, Roy, the bulls are coming!" Some pilgrims he had met the day before helped him over the fence "just in time" as the bulls came running down the street. He added, "We had a lot of fun with the story later!" This momentarily frightening experience became an important anecdote of his "Camino adventure." In this way the random meseta village or town became enlivened and personalized. This anecdote also gave him the opportunity to make a cultural critique: "I didn't like the bull thing. The standard of respect for animals is not too high in Spain. But there are a lot of Spanish people who oppose bullfighting." It explains the foreignness he feels in Spain, shows the solidarity that exists among pilgrims, and is a social commentary that he balances by recognizing differences

Figure 18. A shepherd near Sahagún (León).

among Spaniards. While pilgrims feel themselves part of a larger community, they also retain a sense of national identity.

Pilgrims share and build their stories and friendships with one another through active discussion of specific places and people who live along the pilgrimage route. Despite the often greater resources found in the city, many pilgrims speak of the human contact and generosity among the (usually) nonurban people as leaving the greatest impression. What pilgrims often do not realize is that this treatment may stem from an interpretation of Christian hospitality that sees in the figure of the pilgrim a potential Christ figure (from Matt. 10:42—giving to the apostles guarantees a reward—or Matt. 25:35—"I was hungry and you gave me meat, I was thirsty and you gave me drink, I was a stranger and you took me in"). Some who live along the route, such as Pablo and Micaela, dedicate part of their lives to pilgrims and the maintenance of the Camino. Many of these people are known up and down the Camino among participants and would-be participants by their first names: Santiago, the energetic mayor of Larrasoaña; Maribel, the refuge owner of Cizur Menor; Felisa at the outskirts of Logroño; Father José María of San Juan de Ortega; the healer Jato and his family of Villafranca del Bierzo; Father José Ignacio of Santo Domingo de la Calzada; Tomás, the esoteric Templar of Manjarín; Pablito, the generous restaurant owner of Villalcázar del Camino; and on and on. Running refuges, helping pilgrims find their walking sticks, inviting others to rest or share a meal, curing ailments, and marking trails with yellow arrows are just a few examples of their involvement.

One of the most popular anecdotes in pilgrims' stories about people of the way and refuges centers on Jesús Jato and his unique refuge in Villafranca del Bierzo (supported by the International Association of Pilgrims, Ave Phoenix). One British cyclist wrote an article for the confraternity's bulletin entitled "The Jato Experience" and called her stay there "the ultimate refuge . . . experience."[5] The refuge is constructed of plastic sheeting and is variously described as "a makeshift circus tent," "a greenhouse," and "a miserable hovel." One's first impression of dirtiness and one's skepticism are overcome by the desire to know what the inside is like and to meet Jato, a man in his late fifties born the day a pilgrim passed through his grandmother's house in Villafranca. His fame comes from his refuge, his ability to heal, and his dedication to the Camino (he and his wife Carmen are full-time hospitaleros who offer all that they have to the pilgrims). Pilgrims often find at this refuge what they call the "true spirit" of the Camino—generosity, a sense of community, shabbiness associated with the nontechnological, a bit of magic, and always an open door. In the mid-1990s Jato began the construction of a new refuge in this same spirit. Pilgrims have brought stones from all over the world to be incorporated in the walls, which are built by Jato and the numerous pilgrims who stop to help. A Spaniard from Murcia wrote in the pilgrim's testimonial book: "To my friend [Jato] Jesús, with all my affection, in thanks for the excellent care given to me last year. I came without money and you gave me shelter and food. When I was broken and without hope you helped me go forward."[6] At night Jato often makes a *queimada*, a locally famous potent drink that has a base of the strong alcohol *aguardiente* (burning water), sugar, coffee beans, and lemon and orange peels which is set aflame. As the drink is passed around it makes a dramatic effect in the dark. Jato begins a humorous and ironic incantation (*conjuro*) adapted to the pilgrimage and the pilgrims. Despite his acclaim among pilgrims Jato is a controversial figure in the village. Sometimes he is associated with the esoteric element, and young men (usually) seek him out to be his disciples—which he firmly rejects. For some, it is an important part of the pilgrimage experience to share in these informal moments and rituals, to be able to compare later, and to joke about them with other pilgrims—"shared Camino moments," as one German put it. Some pilgrims even feel left out if they missed particular people or places.

The social element is vital for those on the Camino, not only for those people who live along the way but especially for those who are cycling and walking to Santiago. It is commonly said that many people start alone but always end accompanied by others. The formation of friendships and groups of walking and cycling companions that cut across normal divisions such as gender, age, class, nationality, and marital status is an important aspect of becoming a pilgrim and feeling part of a larger community. One Spanish pilgrim commented, "On my first day I've already met 3 Belgians, 2 Gallegos, 2 Germans and a Filipino. It's fantastic to know people in this way—traveling and walking."[7] This is a summer phenomenon, when the majority of pilgrims are on the road. Those who go from late October to May usually meet fewer people.

In the open social contexts of the pilgrimage participants come to trust themselves and others—even all of humanity—to a greater extent. Robbery is the exception in refuges and very rare among pilgrims. Values that participants believe have been lost in modern city life are found again through the simplicity and face-to-face relationships that the Camino makes possible and that pilgrims themselves nurture and strive to maintain. Jane, the Irish teacher, remarked, "On the Camino I had a friend, a Spanish bloke, very intelligent, professional, an achiever, multitalented, married to a woman who sounded wonderful, entertaining, funny . . . and one day while walking (we were both suffering terribly from our feet and both trying to keep our spirits up) we talked about 'life' and he told me that one of the reasons he did the Camino was, to put it briefly, to come to terms with the fact that people didn't like him! I found this very revealing." She was especially surprised because his statement contradicted their growing friendship. His declaration also illustrates his trust—he shared something deeply private with her—and his recognition of his own potential for achieving social ease.

As participants feel themselves more a part of a community and perhaps more fully "pilgrims" they often acquire nicknames or reputations among their companions relating to who they are on the road. An informal gossip network develops. William, an English physician who was described by one friend as a "joyous Catholic," wrote to me from the road as he finished a two-week portion of the Camino, from St. Jean Pied-de-Port to Burgos. I was an hospitalera in Rabanal del Camino, and he wanted to let me know who to anticipate. He wrote,

> A fine group of Pilgrims are on their way to you. First to arrive should be an Englishman on a bicycle, JP, who began at Burgos and I met when I finished there. . . . Behind him on foot will come Angel, a tall bearded Donostiarra [Basque for a person from San Sebastián] notorious for his snoring, and Luis from Pamplona and Juan from Teruel, who calls himself addicted to the Camino, and a large batch of North Americans, MH from Toronto, JM a teacher at Andover, Massachusetts, to whom I gave whiskey in the dark at Roncesvalles, and MK from Yale who's thinking about joining the Jesuits and started at Burgos. And at a slower pace Etienne, an elderly Belgian, who has come all the way from Belgium with Rosalie, his donkey.

A playful environment, almost like a summer camp for adults, pervades some moments. For some pilgrims, this does not detract from what can be a profound spiritual experience or a reflective time but is just another aspect of the journey. One Spaniard commented, "There are times when it is impossible to find the words to express what one feels when someone who you just met treats you like one of his best friends."[8] Through knowing one another in adverse circumstances and relying on others to help get through the fatigue of the day or the confusion of limited language, feelings of *communitas* (community) and a heightened sense of generosity emerge. A single Catalan woman who made the Camino in a group described her companions as being like a multipaned mirror.

Figure 19.   French pilgrims take a break under the eaves of a church.

While walking and getting to know them she could see different parts of herself in each. In this mirroring process she decided that she liked the reflections.

Many pilgrims also value the meaningful connections they make with people across cultural, national, class, and age lines. A working-class man from Burgos told me that he developed unforgettable relationships with two university students while walking. He was most impressed that he was able to get to know two people who in his daily life would be out of his social reach yet who treated him as an equal. Traveling alone for the first time and for two weeks on bicycle, an electrician from La Coruña met a French professor his first day who became a close friend and a "father figure." They were the best two weeks of his life. Learning not to judge by first impression led a walker from Madrid to forge a powerful friendship with a contemporary whom he originally rejected because of a superficial dislike. In addition, some pilgrims report feeling more European after making the Camino.

Frustrations on a social level also occur. It is not uncommon for pilgrims who go with one or two friends or in a group to come to blows at some time during the journey. On his way to Pamplona to begin the Camino, Jonás, a twenty-six-year-old cyclist from Madrid, met another

cyclist heading to Santiago. An avid photographer and interested in the
Camino's monuments, Jonás was soon at odds with his new friend,
whose interests focused on getting to the next destination quickly and
passing the rest of the day in a bar. Jonás was normally a shy person,
but he finally got angry, and the two parted ways after putting up with
a great deal of discomfort. This experience turned out to be the turning point of Jonás's pilgrimage—instead of a sport, it became an inner
search. Even among long-term friends the intense close living can cause
temporary ruptures and separations. Sometimes the friction is caused
by the different rhythms or a physical problem, which causes one of the
companions to make a choice: continue his or her own way or wait with
the friend. Existing friendships may suffer from the expanding sense of
self, different rhythms, renovation, and experimentation that are common in the way. Paths begin to diverge, leading to a temporary rupture
or misunderstanding.

The pilgrims' refuges play a fundamental role in adding to the human
dimension and the creation of communitas, in which intense personal
relationships are formed and enjoyed. In the early 1990s the refuge system barely existed; pilgrims slept in barns, abandoned schoolhouses, and
churches and, more frequently, under the stars. Since then the refuges
have developed into a vital pilgrimage institution. Religious institutions,
parishes, city and regional governments (especially in Galicia), and foreign (England, Italy, and Germany) and Spanish Friends of the Camino
associations all sponsor and fund the maintenance and construction of
refuges. The majority receive no public funds for their day-to-day maintenance. They are not hotels and do not take reservations as do some
mountain hostels. There is a great deal of variation among the roughly
seventy-five refuges, but most maintain a one-night limit and similar hours
and norms. Most share the same basic amenities: communal bathrooms
with showers and sleeping quarters, a place to wash and hang laundry,
often a common room for writing, resting, eating, or conversations, and
occasionally a cooking facility. Individual privacy is not often designed
into the refuge space: pilgrims sleep on bunkbeds or mattresses in one
large room or several small rooms. In some refuges there is segregation
of sexes for sleeping and bathing (one separates snorers as well).

Sleeping together can be trying, especially during the summer months,
when refuges are often overcrowded and pilgrims sleep in close quarters.
Spaniards have the reputation of sleeping with all the windows firmly shut
and the shades drawn—a cultural difference that drives many northern
Europeans and Americans crazy—effectively sealing the already stuffy,

Figure 20. Pilgrims prepare and eat the evening meal at the refuge in Santo Domingo de la Calzada (La Rioja). Note the woman reading the pilgrim's testimonial book.

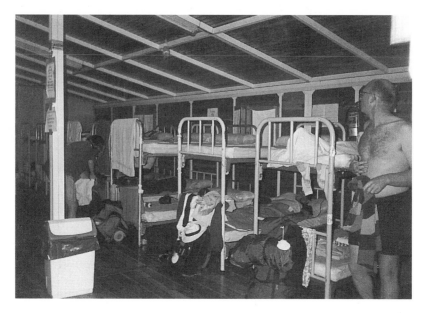

Figure 21.   Getting ready for bed at the Burgos refuge.

pungent sleeping hall. There are many jokes about snoring and the problems caused by the snorer. Nonetheless, through sharing a communal dinner and the day's stories, curing blisters, or giving massages, there is generally a high level of congeniality among pilgrims, even under difficult
circumstances.

Problems occasionally arise when someone has the attitude that pilgrims deserve special treatment and have the right to make demands of
refuges and local shopkeepers. In this case pilgrims nearly always have
the option of sleeping in a local hostel or hotel. Most, however, enjoy
the atmosphere fostered by refuges and are grateful for the refuges' hospitality and a simple place to unroll their sleeping bags.

Refuges are often maintained by *hospitaleros voluntarios* (voluntary
attendants), usually former pilgrims who spend at least two weeks attending to the needs of pilgrims. In the summer of 1994, 137 hospitaleros vol-
unteered in twenty refuges: 93 were Spanish and 44 were non-Spanish
(14 English, 6 Swiss, 10 Italians, 5 Germans, 4 Belgians, 2 Americans, 2
Dutch, and 1 French). By 1997 the number of hospitaleros had risen to
230, with roughly the same breakdown by nationality. The large number of English and Italian volunteers relates to the establishment of refuges
along the camino francés by their confraternities. German associations

Figure 22.   Pilgrims at the Santo Domingo de la Calzada refuge prepare for the next day. Note the sign for DONATIVO on the pillar.

helped in the construction of refuges in Azofra and Hospital de Orbigo, but the same spirit of volunteerism does not link them to those places as it does the English and Italians. Considering the large proportion of French pilgrims who make the way it is noteworthy that so few return to "give something back" to the Camino—as many hospitaleros claim to want to do. It is also described by some hospitaleros as an "extraordinary experience" and as "another way of making the pilgrimage."

The role of the hospitalero is multifaceted, ranging from bureaucratic functionary to nurturing attendant and housekeeper. Depending on the refuge the hospitalero is responsible for the financial and physical maintenance of the space and the well-being of pilgrims, including basic first aid, information on road and village conditions, emotional support, and in some cases spiritual or personal guidance. Non-Spanish hospitaleros tend to be seen as more rigid in terms of closing and opening times and keeping order. During an end-of-season meeting I attended with twenty Spanish volunteers many laughed about these differences and suggested sending all the German and Swiss volunteers to refuges famous for order.

Because there is a feeling of anonymity among pilgrims and hospitaleros a level of intimacy normally reserved for only the closest relationships

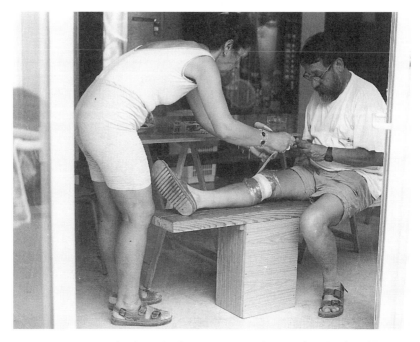

Figure 23. A Spanish pilgrim heals a companion's knee with a clay-based home remedy in the Estella refuge (Navarre).

can develop easily and effortlessly on the road. Some people are silent as they walk. Others talk incessantly as if it were the first time in years. Pilgrims tend to find in one another and in hospitaleros safe listeners— for confessing, testing new ideas, and processing past events. Hospitaleros are usually aware of this aspect of their role. A doctor from Barcelona commented that for her being an hospitalera was "a daily lesson in sociology."[9] For some pilgrims, the Camino is a catharsis for tremendous grief, personal shame, or despair, and a willing, nonjudgmental listener is a tremendous gift that some find difficult to repay.

Another level of solidarity fostered by the refuge system is a written one. In nearly all of the refuges there are books in which pilgrims write comments about the refuge (thanks, occasionally complaints), personal testimonials, and messages to other pilgrims. The testimonial books become an important form of communication as pilgrims track friends and leave messages. Pilgrims write of the pains of the way ("Today my right foot emerged from a blister"), personal revelations on nature, spirituality, and people, the course of the day, and poetry, or they sketch or simply leave

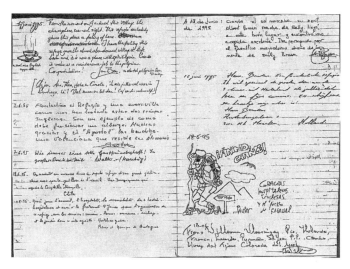

*Figure 24.   A sample page of a pilgrim's testimonial book from
Refugio Gaucelmo in Rabanal del Camino (León).*

their mark. Messages are usually signed with first name and country. Not
surprisingly, pilgrims write in their own languages, leaving a fascinating
network of transnational comments across the Camino.[10] Pilgrims frequently use these messages to cheer one another on, often writing "Ul-
treia!" (which roughly translates as "Onward ho!" and derives from a
twelfth-century pilgrims' song, "Dum Paterfamilias"). Curiously, many
pilgrims do not know what the word means but use it nonetheless as it
has become part of the folklore of the contemporary pilgrimage.

Refuges promote solidarity, but they are also points of tension. There
is a hierarchy among pilgrims in the refuges whereby bed space is distributed according to mode of travel. Walkers are given first preference,
then cyclists (there are so few horseback riders that it is usually irrelevant), and then support-car pilgrims. Before 1993, when fewer pilgrims
made the Camino, support-car pilgrims were accepted quite readily. With
the inundation of participants during the 1993 Holy Year, some pilgrims
protested the presence of those who used support cars. One Spanish hospitalero explained the distribution of bed space: "With the bike pilgrims,
except for a few exceptions, I had to put them in a place apart, their habits
and customs were totally different from the rest. They were always the
last to arrive (except for a few cases) and the last to leave from the refuge
in the morning."[11] In this discriminatory view cyclists are antisocial, ar-

rive late, are noisy, and dawdle in the morning. What many walkers and hospitaleros (who have not made the pilgrimage on bicycle) do not appreciate is how the refuge system favors the customs and habits of the foot pilgrim. Most walkers arrive between 1:00 and 5:00 P.M. and can shower, relax, enjoy the afternoon, eat, and tour the village. By the time evening wears on they are ready to sleep. In contrast, in the busy summer months, cyclists are usually told that refuge space is not distributed until after 6:00 P.M. The hospitalero quoted above complains that cyclists arrive at the last hour, but many have learned that if they arrive before this they will have to wait. It is a catch-22. In the morning many walkers leave at the crack of dawn to avoid the midday heat and maintain an average of 20 to 30 kilometers. Some "refuge pilgrims," as one hospitalera put it, leave early to get space in the next refuge, to save space for slower friends, to inspect the conditions and choose whether or not to stay. Cyclists never have this option. The road is dark between 6:00 and 8:00 A.M., the day's journey is longer (seven to ten hours), and more kilometers (60–80) are covered more quickly. The cyclists tend not to feel the need to rush, but not because they are lazy.

Cyclists are often considered antisocial because they do not mingle with the walkers. Since the cyclists and the walkers go at different rhythms they do not always develop the same kind of groups. When the cyclists arrive in the refuge they are like the last at the party; the walkers know one another, they have been there for several hours, and they have rapport with the hospitalero. Antisocial behavior can be read more accurately as social disadvantage. Hospitaleros comment that when they speak with cyclists on an individual basis what they hear often tempers their judgmental stance. One's rhythm also affects the formation of friendships. Walking more quickly, for example, the pilgrim constantly passes people, making it more difficult to establish friendships (and the opposite if one goes slowly). Some pilgrims want the solitude. This missing also occurs with cyclists who, unless they meet cyclists going the same speed, constantly pass the walkers. It is harder for cyclists to develop the same sense of community. Robert, a three-time German cyclist pilgrim to Santiago, suggests, "We bikers are individualist and a little bit like cats. There are of course exceptions, but for the most part bikers love contacts only for a certain time and prefer in reality the independence of traveling alone." Unless one goes in a group of cyclists or actively seeks riding companions, the journey can be much more of a solo, interior experience.

Contact between cyclists and walkers, consequently, is limited to one-night encounters in refuges and being passed during the day. The speed

Figure 25.   The day begins early at the Hospital de Orbigo refuge (León).

of their journeys is experienced by many walkers as quite distant from
their own. Despite their differences, both cyclists and walkers describe
feeling a social ease and openness unusual in most urban environments.
Pilgrims greet one another as well as those they encounter in villages with
smiles uncommon in the everyday, leading one to claim, "There are places
along this camino in which the people shine more brilliantly than the
stars."[12] For many, the Camino exists outside of normal time in neutral
and inspiring places, where stress is reduced to a minimum. In this environment pilgrims open up internally and externally to those around
them. One woman said she felt a strong sense of belonging and even
"home"—accepted and valued for herself—while making the Camino.
Walking with a group of generally like-minded individuals, heading toward the same goal, and sharing similar pains, joys, and trials provide
an opportunity for the development of friendships, love relationships,
and new visions of the self as socially adept and likable.

FINDING A SENSE OF DIRECTION

Despite all its varied routes the Camino has a fixed point of convergence,
Santiago and the coastal zone to the west. The goal is clear. The paths

are marked with distinct yellow arrows and often shells whose rays indicate the divergent routes that join at the center. Guidebooks also explain the nuances of the trail, the history of each Roman stone and the
legend of each place. Everything appears to be going the same way, including the stars and the setting sun. Unlike other long-distance journeys, the one-way quality of the Camino is unique.

The breakdown of the everyday and the new sense of rhythms are further enhanced by the clear sense of direction that the Camino provides.
Rarely is one so literally "shown the way" as with the Camino. Despite
exposure to cyclic ways of experiencing time and the rhythms of the day
the line plays an important role as a guiding principle via the *flechas ama-
rillas* (yellow arrows). Arrows have both temporal and spatial meaning.
On the one hand, the arrow signifies directional time toward a goal, which
is somewhere lodged in the future. On the other hand, the arrow signifies "movement in space towards a goal."[13] The arrows lead somewhere
specific. It is not simply a two-way route.

I am often asked how the contemporary Santiago pilgrimage compares
to other long-distance trail journeys, for instance, the Appalachian Trail
in the eastern United States, the John Muir Trail in California, or the
vast network of hiking trails in France and the Pyrenees. Others ask me
how journeys that appear to share a structural similarity, such as youth
tramping on well-traveled routes for long periods, compare to the Camino. Of course, in all these routes one can find similar types of personal
discoveries and triumphs and the use of the road as a metaphor for life.
The Camino is unique, however, for its religious and historical traditions, the presence of nonpilgrims who encourage the journey, the pilgrim's passport and the collection of stamps, its one-way nature, and its
network of refuges and hospitaleros. One is not just a walker but a pilgrim to Santiago: "You can't escape being called a pilgrim," as the Dutch
teachers said. The vast majority of pilgrims are making the pilgrimage
to Santiago. It is the rare individual who makes the return journey on
foot or bicycle. All the signs are marked for the westward-bound person
(the other routes are north-south). Return pilgrims are often told that
they are going the wrong way. The return journey is made alone, and
connections with other pilgrims are limited to brief encounters.[14]

Pilgrims experience a powerful feeling of being guided toward a goal,
of having a sense of direction, and of knowing where one is going that
is not so clear in daily life. Each day is an act of accomplishment toward
a stated goal in which everything seems to be going the pilgrim's way.
Andrew, a fifty-year-old Belgian businessman, wrote, "For two and a half

Figure 26. Three pilgrims pass the sign A Santiago —. *The cement marker (right) indicates the way over the Alto del Perdón (Navarre). Note the scallop shell on the backpack.*

months, I knew where I was going, what my objective was, what I had to do for the day. I had nothing to worry about. I had no possessions (save for my credit card that bothered me a lot), no agenda, no meetings, no important people to meet and convince, no television, no papers, no reminders of the modern life. It was 'Carpe Diem' to the maximum and every day was better than the preceding one." *Accomplishment, purpose, competence,* and *guided* are all words that pilgrims repeatedly invoke to describe the sense of direction felt while making the journey to Santiago.

GETTING LOST, OVERCOMING FEARS, AND PAIN

Pilgrims' stories also focus on experiences of doubt, despair, and pain. In getting lost the metaphor of directionality is equated with a loss of control, a waste of time and energy, and feeling inept. This state often provokes a sense of crisis until the way is regained through its resolution. While attending a Practical Pilgrim Day in 1995, sponsored by the English Confraternity of St. James, the theme of getting lost arose. One woman in her forties, Sara, entitled her presentation "Le Puy [France] for the Fainthearted," claiming that she felt a need "to speak for the pathetic and frightened" with so many "superheroes" on the road. Having attended a similar session the year before making her pilgrimage, she found that she did "everything wrong" yet still got to Santiago despite a great deal of solitude, doubt, and a constant sense of being lost. Sara began the pilgrimage with the preconceived notion that she must keep off the paved roads to make it in an authentic way. Somehow, she reasoned, the experience would be more real by following specific routes and types of roads. It was quite a shock, she said, when one day she encountered a tall German man in France and the issue of traditional roads arose. He told her that being a pilgrim does not mean that one has to follow just one trail.

In her presentation Sara emphasized the feeling of getting lost repeatedly, despite carrying guidebooks and following the way marks. Getting lost, rushing, pushing herself, all made her feel incompetent, and Sara believed that it diminished her ability to connect meaningfully with other pilgrims and the way in general. She would arrive later than others, and by the time she relaxed they would have left for dinner. Then she would go to dinner, and when she returned her companions would be asleep. Sara struggled with the Camino, maintaining her private urban rhythms rather than flowing with those of the Camino. Her preoccupation with trying so hard to find the "proper" way led her to lose her own. At one point she remarked, "I would have welcomed someone to come and tell me where to go." Despite this difficult experience of the "fainthearted pilgrim," the occasional sensation of being lost, while negative and difficult in the moment, may provoke a sense of crisis in which pilgrims garner new strength or insight through its resolution.

Others find lessons of humility in being lost. One man, an experienced hiker, described marching out of Cizur Menor assuming that he knew the way. Suddenly he realized he had lost the arrows. He would have to backtrack or wander in what he thought was the right direction. He chose the latter and passed through a small village with several vicious dogs that impeded his way and then made a long, rough crossing through a wheatfield, which, from above, had looked easy. Finally, on a distant road, he spotted another figure, a pilgrim. Once he regained the road and shook off the briars, he took his morning detour as a reminder not to "be cocky" and to keep his eyes wide open.

Some pilgrims who made the Camino in the 1970s or 1980s fear that the "positive" experience of getting lost is diminished by the development of the infrastructure and increased way marking. Getting lost, however, is frequently related to a distracted mental state rather than a lack of arrows. If pilgrims are "lost in their thoughts," which is normal while walking, it is easy to miss the arrow or shell. In general, getting lost is positively valued by pilgrims, even if disconcerting at the time. Lee quoted Thoreau after getting lost in the mountains outside Astorga: "Not till we are lost, in other words, not till we have lost the world, do we begin to find ourselves, and realize where we are and the infinite extent of our relations." For him, the doubt, fear, and uncertainty led him to feel more connected to a "common experience" from the past. Moreover, despite feeling lost he had the additional feeling he was going in the right direction ("My Guardian Angel?" he asks), which leads him to conclude, "I do not live in a world of chance, I do not depend upon luck."[15] This experience (like many others he had throughout the course of the journey) made Lee feel that his world has purpose: "I learn yet again: There are no accidents, no coincidences in creation; there are only gifts, whether of pain or of insight, the vision of place or the experience of prayer."[16] This conclusion corresponds to his religious beliefs and his faith in God's creation. Getting lost and other challenges compel some pilgrims to experience and overcome crises. As a result pilgrims often feel capable of dealing with the unexpected, acquire greater self-confidence, and have the sense of being more compassionate, generous, open-minded, and accepting of hardship. These experiences are part of how pilgrims explain how the Camino works on them to produce meaning and transformation.

THE HELPER AND MODERN MIRACLES

Lee is not alone in sensing unexplained help. Other pilgrims experience similar feelings of assistance, perfect timing, or synchronicity but find other explanations relevant to their own worldviews and beliefs or are simply left wondering, Does causality exist? The latter is the title of an article written by a pilgrim from Guipúzcoa in the Basque Country for his association's newsletter. He relates several extraordinary experiences: plays of light, being lost and someone appearing out of nowhere to guide the way, and the formation of his group by people who originally meant to go alone.[17] An American couple from Alaska who walked with their eight-year-old son (motivated by a desire for world peace, for spiritual and physical strength, and to learn Spanish and a bit about Spain) said, "We knew that it was the hand of God and the Apostle James at work . . .

when sickness, cold, failure, seemed to impede our progress and someone always helped us continue on." "[Through seeing the hand of God
in nature and the people of Spain,] it made us think about the goodness
in the world and it has renovated our faith in God's love."[18] Also, the
idea that Saint James comes in many, often unexpected, forms leads pilgrims to frequently attribute a seemingly miraculous or lucky encounter
to the saint even if they do not consider themselves religious. Faith in life
and others is thereby increased. Some actually see the saint himself in
these encounters; that is, he appears in the guise of a fellow pilgrim or a
local person.

Pilgrims do report a common experience with synchronicity relating
to help received along the way. One English pilgrim commented, "Luck
is 2 to 3 percent greater than it should be." Just in the moment when the
pilgrim senses failure the appearance of someone (another pilgrim or villager) or something (a sign, yellow arrow, rainbow, bridge, etc.) serves as
a bridge to show the way and resolve the crisis. It is also a common experience that an opportune meeting with a particular person serves as a
catalyst for change. A German pilgrim told me a story about another German pilgrim (as is often the case and is the stuff that legends are made of)
who entered the *parador* (four- or five-star hotel) in Santo Domingo de
la Calzada to have a look at the historic building and ordered a drink. As
he was waiting he felt a hand on his shoulder and looked around. It was
his brother, with whom he had not spoken for six years because of an argument. They embraced, the bitterness forgotten, and marveled at the co-
incidental meeting. The brother just happened to be staying at the parador
and the pilgrim had just happened to enter at that moment. "All these
'coincidences' helped me and made me feel that something (God, or whatever you want to call it) was with me," said Susan, the Protestant Swiss
woman who walked from Lake Constance on her way to Portugal.

DOGS

According to the old cliché, dog is man's best friend. But on the Camino
the dog seems to be more symbolic of the savage, untamed, and dangerous. The "nasty dog" anecdote is often an important part of the experience, either as an initiatory trial or as a personal encounter with fear.
I always scoffed at these reports of wild dogs on the outskirts of towns
or the necessity of carrying a walking stick as a weapon against the potential attack, but I learned that they do daunt many pilgrims with their
snarls and threatening postures. The dog, as an image, sometimes serves

as a link to the past or to the "primitive," a term used by some pilgrims to mean the human-powered, face-to-face, natural, or solo. In Spain dogs are often chained on long runners to guard homes and in the villages tend to be protectors more than pets.

The Camino of the late twentieth century is tame compared to the medieval journey. The latter was host to a variety of dangers: tainted water, unscrupulous innkeepers, highway robbers, dark forests, wild boars, and wolves. The dog, however, adds a dimension of adventure to the Camino. In a bulletin of the Alicante Friends of the Camino there is a description from a group pilgrimage made along the *camino del norte* in which the routes are rated in four categories: kilometers, number of pilgrims, temperature, and number of dogs. While this categorization is tongue in cheek, it points to the fact that dogs are on pilgrims' minds. Moreover, pilgrims' stories foment this fear, adding to the sense of accomplishment at journey's end once the trial is overcome. An English cyclist wrote for her confraternity's bulletin: "There were exciting adventures like sheltering in the porch of a church while thunder and lightning crashed all around us; or being chased by a pack of many dogs, who were, in turn, chased off by a lone hound who, taking pity on us (or so I like to believe), came from nowhere."[19]

The anxiety that dogs produce can even influence pilgrims before they set out. At the same Practical Pilgrim workshop in England a middle-aged woman asked me earnestly about the dogs outside of Santiago. Of all the questions to ask, she was concerned about whether she would be able to enter the city. What should she do about these beasts? Were they really such a threat? I reassured her that she would probably have no difficulty and thought to myself that this worry represented a general predeparture anxiety relating to the journey's uncontrollable elements as well as to a fear of the end. Anyone attending a Practical Pilgrim workshop is attempting on some level to gain mastery of the unknown and being "practical"—planning, organizing, informing oneself, attempting to take out the mystery, as one would for a vacation.

For one pilgrim, an experience with several dogs became an access point to his primitive self. The American writer Jack Hitt, in his popular account of his journey to Santiago, remarks, "Pilgrims don't like dogs. At the museum of Roncesvalles, the one icon I remember most vividly was a wooden bas-relief of a pilgrim being devoured by five or six dogs. . . . The pilgrim's expression of primal horror was finely carved and particularly memorable." He uses this memory as an opening to describe his own primal experience with wild dogs on the Castilian plain:

"A strange fear overtakes me, and it's one I have never felt. . . . I'm scared because I know that I am prepared to kill them. I have my knife in my left hand and my stick in my right. . . . On the plains of Castille [*sic*], I bark. I didn't know humans made the noises the way birds of prey caw, caters caterwaul, or coyotes bay. But we do. . . . My entire body convulses with explosions: 'Lalulalulaluaaaaaa.' More or less."[20] While this experience is clearly exaggerated for literary effect, Hitt's sense of being in touch with something more real in himself is probably not. In this moment he was pure instinct. Such a moment is important in reaffirming much of what the pilgrimage is intended to answer for some: I am alive. I am not merely a cog in the modern machine.

Dog anecdotes are also linked to place. Hitt's experience took place in the barren plains of Castile, as did other pilgrims'. An unusual clustering of stories also feature Foncebadón, a small, abandoned village below the Cruz de Ferro. The dog, in these latter stories, seems to be associated with a demon or something evil on the way.

In addition to the encounters with wild dogs that some pilgrims describe are the curious accounts of "dog pilgrims." Rather than being told with fear, these stories are often told with surprise, mystery, and affection. When I talked to pilgrims walking with dogs I was surprised to hear that their companions were often not pets brought from home but animals who had at some point joined them on the road and then never left them for the rest of the journey. Sometimes traveling hundreds of miles, these dogs would leave their local areas to follow a pilgrim; often their paws suffered from the uneven, stony roads, and some came into the refuges wearing bandages. The pilgrim "owners" remarked with awe that the dogs would continue despite the pain. These dogs, who had perhaps been abandoned, starving, or lonely before joining the way, were always docile, usually older, and extremely loyal to their new human companions.

A Portuguese man recounted that on his first journey to Santiago in 1995 he was joined one afternoon outside Logroño by a large, white, female dog whom he had given something to eat. He was convinced that the dog would not make it to Santiago, but each day she rose and set off with him and his companions. On the day they reached Santiago he said he sensed that she too knew the journey had ended; after having visited the cathedral they all went to a local park, and there she lay down and died.

This pilgrim, like several others whom I met, interpreted the unanticipated relationship with a canine companion as part of the mystery of the Camino and suggested that the dogs were pilgrims in their own right.

Some even suggested that they bore the souls of pilgrims who had never been able to reach Santiago.

PAIN AND FATIGUE

Nearly all pilgrims contend with pain and fatigue but they interpret these aspects of the journey differently. Some pilgrims claim that pain and fatigue are powerful vestiges of the medieval Camino. Practicing Catholics often interpret pain as suffering or penitence—"to cleanse your spirit by the sweat of your brow."[21] In many cases pilgrims who make the Camino to fulfill a vow arrive physically unprepared and suffer much more than the already athletically inclined. In general their pain is accepted as a sacrifice ("for the greater glory of God," as an American evangelical Catholic said) as a way of bringing one closer to God. A thirty-three-year-old man who is a government functionary from a small village in La Rioja described how, little by little, the pains of the journey were intimately linked to his spiritual transformation, to his return to religion. From the second day of the journey, with the help of the priest who led the group, he decided to "dive headfirst into the Camino with all of the consequences" and "to bear the trials necessary to achieve transformation." He continued, "Suffering heat, thirst, fatigue, and pain all helped me to change internally and to understand the longevity of the Camino." For him, the pain and suffering of the way is the access to a rediscovery of God, a link to the past, and a strengthening of his faith in everyday miracles and God's omnipresence. Pain may be interpreted as a gift that brings greater insight.

For some religious pilgrims, encounters with suffering also lead to other lessons of the journey that are given a religious interpretation. In a short article, "Pilgrim's Tears," an older Spanish man describes his journey from Roncesvalles to Santiago. He assumed that because he was an active person he would have no physical problems. A foot full of blisters the first day became, for him, a lesson in humility. As he continued the pains of the foot were transferred to his leg, and after crossing the meseta his pain was so great that, in despair, he sat down at the side of the road and began to cry, believing that his journey was over. At his wit's end, he prayed aloud to Saint James, begging him not to make him abandon the journey so that he could finish the Camino and give him a hug in Santiago. To his surprise a few minutes later two pilgrims arrived, one a woman who happened to be from the next village. On arrival at the village she gave him a massage, and he commented, "Chapeau, señor

Figure 27.   Exhausted, this pilgrim took advantage of the eaves of a village plaza to rest and escape the heat at midday. Note the wildflowers on the backpack, the staff, and the bandaged knee.

Santiago, esto sí es atender rápido una petición" (I take my hat off to you Saint James, this certainly is rapid attention to a petition). There also happened to be a French physical therapist among the pilgrims who gave him a massage then and in the following days. When he reached Monte del Gozo he broke into tears of joy and began to sing (a reference to Psalm 122:1–2): que alegría cuando me dijeron / vamos a la casa del Señor / ya están pisando nuestros pies / tus umbrales, Jerusalén (what joy when they said unto me / let us go into the house of the Lord / our feet shall stand / in thy gates, O Jerusalem). On reaching the cathedral, he cried with emotion, gave the saint a hug, and, unable to pray, wept in the crypt (or is this also praying? he asked). His tears of pain and joy were part of his process: "Making the way you take it in internally, you tire your body and you liberate your spirit."[22] Through the breaking down of the physical body, the inner ways of understanding, from this religious perspective, were also challenged, allowing the possibility of transformation or conversion to occur.

For nonreligious pilgrims, the pain and fatigue are part of the chal-

Figure 28.   Forced to stop by the pain of blisters, this Spanish woman cures her feet at the side of the road in Galicia.

lenge that must be overcome. Testing one's limits to feel one's body is sufficient for many pilgrims. The principal problems that pilgrims encounter are those associated with the feet and tendons and muscle pains in the legs, back, and shoulders. Many pilgrims elect to make the Camino for a period of a month, during which time they may or may not take rest days. For those unaccustomed to the rigors of exercise, the day-in-and-day-out effort necessary to go one or two or four months without stopping is demanding. Overcoming pain when it seems impossible to continue leads to a great feeling of accomplishment and satisfaction, a better knowledge of and respect for one's body, and a way of feeling alive.

Furthermore, the experience of pain plays a crucial role in the formation of solidarity among pilgrims and among pilgrims and hospitaleros. The pains that pilgrims suffer are an important topic of discussion as pilgrims give each other advice, help with cures, and lend each other band-aids, cotton swabs, and betadine. The sharing of pain also allows physical contact between people through end-of-the-day massages. The bathing of feet in cool water with salt and vinegar is a pleasure many look forward to at day's end. Most refuges have containers for the bathing of feet, an important symbolic Christian act of humility and equality. In

the Italian refuge hospitaleros bathe pilgrims' feet, reanimating this tradition. The elevation of the normally impure and low is possible in the
Camino as it is a space out of normal time and place.

Pilgrims often report feeling a greater bodily confidence, learning and
testing limits, and feeling empowered by the physical struggle. Losing
weight and feeling stronger boost the morale. Blisters themselves are used
as a metaphor for life, as Jose, a twenty-six-year-old pharmaceutical student from Madrid explained:

> If there's something I've learned in the Camino it's that life can be much
> easier than we make it. It doesn't matter if my girlfriend doesn't love me or
> is with another. Life has given me many other things to enjoy, and I can't stop
> when something doesn't work. It's like the Camino: if you get blisters, you
> cure them and go on. The Camino continues. You can leave it if you get blis-
> ters, but you will always regret it. Suffering makes us more human, if we fight
> to overcome it and don't accept it. Blisters of the Camino are the problems
> of life. To continue walking despite blisters produces both pain and joy. A life
> without problems is like a Camino without blisters: it's a dream and a tourist
> route, but not Life.

Pain is also seen as instructive by this pilgrim but not in a religious way;
rather it takes him closer to self-understanding and the development of
a personal metaphysics.

Seeing oneself as an athlete for the first time may also be empower-
ing both for the pilgrim and those left at home. A twenty-six-year-old
Spanish schoolteacher who was not athletic during his childhood decided
to make the pilgrimage with a friend. His father was convinced he would
never make it but began to have a new view of his son and enthusiasm
for his journey as he phoned from the Camino. The father developed pride
in the perceived athleticism of his son, bought a map of Spain, and began to chart his progress. The pilgrim benefited personally and also felt
that his relationship with his father was unexpectedly enriched.

Pilgrims note changes, and they often, simply, notice their bodies. Instead of selecting clothing and shoes, or worrying about norms of clean-
liness or appearance, as in daily life, these things become relatively unim-
portant on the road. Pilgrims may joke about the "pilgrims' smell" they
acquire from days of accumulated sweat and dust and inadequate washing of clothes, which may take their olfactory toll. Many older men who
have never had to care for themselves come to the Camino alone and
must do their own wash and attend to themselves in unaccustomed ways.
The body and the sensations it opens the pilgrim up to become a new
unexplored territory. An American professor commented as he finished

the journey, "Now my body seemed to walk itself, the road walking my body." Rather than walk on the road and dominate it (as one does in a car), one's body often responds to the road and its demands. In daily life most pilgrims do not depend on their bodies for their work. The same Englishman who did not bring his razor to the Camino because he did not imagine that pilgrims shaved also felt uncomfortable in his "pilgrim's clothing." He commented on arriving in Santiago that he always wore suits and that he liked them. On the Camino he was always fumbling for things in this "awkward" clothing. On the Camino the pilgrim depends completely on his or her body to get through the days. Some pilgrims express surprise at the body's ability to make the whole journey, to keep going when they are discouraged and realize what a foreign place the body can be.

The body also serves as an important conduit for knowledge as pilgrims learn to listen to or read their bodies through new sensations and pains and the development of muscles and endurance. It is commonly believed among pilgrims that the body somaticizes its psychic problems, compelling the pilgrim to slow down and possibly attend to conditions of both mind and body. A Dutch hospitalero commented, "We treat the whole pilgrim here—not just the body. We've now had four pilgrims stay an extra day because of spiritual, personal, internal needs, not just because of problems caused by their feet or tendonitis." According to a French hospitalero, "The pain of the feet is caused by poor mental preparation more than poor physical preparation." He made this comment after a woman said, "I have more pain here than here"—first pointing to her head, then her feet.[23] Others also suggest that many physical pains relate to personal problems—usually relationships—and some locate the problems in certain parts of the body. Shoulder and back pain is somaticized stress, leg pains are related to relationship problems, and lower back pain is related to an inability to bear responsibility or commitment.[24]

In the contemporary pilgrimage feet leave their normally cloistered space and become part of the public domain. They are touched, inspected, discussed, massaged, and pierced with needles to relieve blisters; they become signs of a journey well traveled, and symbols of power: "I did it all on foot!" In this way pilgrims elevate feet, removing them from the category of hidden objects. On the Camino pilgrims give feet a power and importance not recognized in daily life—as a causeway and direct channel to the road, the past, meaningful relations, nature, and the self. Feet are authentic.[25] This elevation of feet (and the democratizing effect it has) can be explained in part by the restructuring of values that takes

place on the Camino. It is not the $100 pair of shoes that count but the
feet inside the shoes. It is the feet that carry one through the journey and
connect one to what is perceived to be real—however that may be defined. The feet take one to the source, to the authentic, to the self, to the
origins of the pilgrimage. A Canadian woman found grace in her pain.
As she told me the following story she had her feet on the refuge's kitchen
table at which we were sitting—proud of them and their now worn, but
blisterless, condition. At the beginning of her journey she decided to give
thanks for each pain she felt, and as she did so, remarkably, the pains would
disappear. For her, the whole journey was one of thanks and joy.

The inability to overcome the trials and other frustrations of the road
also plays an important part in pilgrims' experiences. For example, at
times the pain becomes too difficult for pilgrims to bear, requiring them
to attempt to recover on the Camino by taking layover days, to return
home without completing the journey, or to pray to Saint James for the
arrival of a good Samaritan. Although it is difficult to calculate, an average of about 20 percent of the people who begin the Camino in Roncesvalles do not complete the Camino in Santiago for various reasons,
including time, failure to plan well, physical problems, and, rarely, disillusionment. The decision to leave the Camino is usually a difficult one
and is accompanied by a desire to return and overcome the pain or the
self-described failure of the first attempt. Even a limited time on the
Camino can have a great impact on the pilgrim, as this twenty-four-year-
old German woman expressed: "I absolutely want to finish the Camino.
Not so much because of the feeling 'I started something I also want to
finish it,' but because I discovered the power of walking for a longer time.
The Camino gave me a lot of power." She originally intended to walk
for a week and then go to the beach but, not wanting to stop, continued
for another week on the Camino.

Other surprising inversions of daily life on the physical level also occur through the surpassing of physical and mental barriers. Despite the
heavy physical activity during the day's journey, which can lead to pain
and fatigue, pilgrims express a surprising increased amount of energy,
optimism, and strength. Two women in their late thirties (one from
Barcelona and the other from La Rioja) shared with me similar stories
of bodily renewal, which they attributed to the reduced-stress environment of the Camino. Both chronically underweight, active profession-
ally, and with emotionally demanding home lives, they decided to make
the Camino alone but as part of a group. Both were concerned about
losing weight. One of the women also suffered from the demands of a

dominating mother and a severe case of psoriasis. The other woman's father had recently died. Much to their surprise, rather than lose weight while walking they both gained weight, slept more profoundly, and felt a general sense of well-being. The woman with psoriasis (which had been getting progressively worse) also noticed a remarkable improvement in her condition once she returned home; she attributed it directly to the decreased stress. Both have continued to be actively involved with the pilgrimage since their original journeys in the late 1980s.

An infrequently discussed, though important, bodily transformation that occurs in the pilgrimage's environment of reduced stress, free time, and openness is that which takes place on the sexual level. The topic first came to my attention in a public manner while discussing the personal renewal felt by Luis, a Valencian writer in his early sixties. When he arrived at the Camino in 1994, after his first pilgrimage in 1993, he felt *hecho polvo* (literally, "made dust," or wiped out). Tired of his work and the noise and pollution of the city, as well as mentally exhausted from a long, painful divorce, he arrived with few expectations for the Camino other than the desire to relax and walk without thinking. Luis found that, much to his surprise, he felt an immediate lifting of his spirits that increased throughout his journey and left him physically and emotionally recharged. At the very end of our conversation, as we were parting outside the door of the train in the Santiago rail station, he suddenly wanted to add one more detail. He told me that he only confided this in me because I was a researcher and he wanted to know if others experienced the same physical reaction to the Camino. Markedly embarrassed, he said that from the first to the last of more than twenty-five days walking the Camino, the lift he felt was not only emotional but literal: he awoke every morning with an erection. This was not normal for him. Luis did not experience an augmented level of sexual desire but a heightened physical potency that extended to all of his bodily functions. He felt a complete rejuvenation, like a teenager. On returning to Valencia this physical reaction ceased, but it continued the next year in the same way when he returned to the Camino.

The theme of sexual potency struck me forcefully a second time when I was talking with Robyn, a Frenchwoman in her forties, and a priest during a pilgrims' excursion. In the midst of a discussion of a medieval studies conference, my ears perked up when Robyn suddenly asked the priest if he knew about transformations that pilgrims experienced on a sexual level. She then commented that in preparation for the pilgrimage most participants discuss the physical, spiritual, and mental aspects yet neglect to mention the potential sexual aspects of the journey. During her first Camino, motivated by a strong need to have personal time to reflect on her life and spirituality, she was stunned and frankly quite disturbed by her body's reaction to the experience of being on the Camino, surrounded by its "energy," "power," and natural landscapes. One day while alone on the Spanish meseta Robyn had the following experience: "I was near the end and dead tired when the village suddenly appeared. The sun was on the horizon and the bells of the church were ringing, as if they were saluting my arrival. An explosion of emotion, tiredness, joy, all provoked an orgasm—so intense that in that moment I felt like all the women of the world were inside my body. I don't have words to describe this incredibly, fantastic experience!"

As Luis had found, this experience was repeated in the pilgrimage that year and in her second pilgrimage the next summer. This time Robyn accepted it as part of the experience. Similar to Luis, the increased level of sexual energy was not equated with an increased level of sexual desire but with revealing a potentiality that she was unaware of possessing. Unlike Luis, who felt like a teenager, Robyn felt more feminine and powerful as a woman.

Not surprisingly, other pilgrims found that with the easy sociability and the diminution of stress while walking, sexual barriers are brought down. Whereas in the two examples above the experience of sexual potency was a personalized one of renovation and potentiality, a heightened feeling of sexuality may also be projected outward. In the anonymous, open environment of the pilgrimage relationships of a temporary nature as well as romances that continue after the Camino are not uncommon. Experimentation with first relationships as well as affairs between pilgrims who have left spouses behind can be tempting and, at times, consummated.

Relationships between pilgrims and hospitaleros and between pilgrims and villagers also occur. While working as an hospitalera in Logroño I met a pharmaceutical salesman (who also happened to be a former hospitalero) who was making the pilgrimage with eight gynecologists. From his own experience he attributed the increased level of sexual energy among people to the lack of stress, even mentioning that a doctor in Pamplona recommended making the Camino to people who needed to relax. Increased sexual tension (*erótico light,* or light eroticism, as one refuge owner put it) can exist through the close-living, sharing, and relaxed atmosphere but is usually "kept under wraps." A man from Barcelona told me that while walking to Santiago over a period of thirty days he made love to three women (pilgrims) on three separate occasions during the day, which he attributed to being inspired by the natural beauty. He maintains a sexual relationship with one of these women; they get together for the occasional weekend. Some couples maintain their relationships only while making the Camino and are able to bracket the Camino and home as two separate realities. For couples making the way together, even those celebrating a fiftieth wedding anniversary, this increased physical and sexual energy can lead to a positive renewal of the relationship.

This type of physical renewal may shock some pilgrims. I asked a number of them about how their bodies were affected, and many felt none of the above. Many pilgrims felt a general sense of physical renewal, but not specifically sexual. Once again, the Camino affects each person differently.

BEING ALONE IN SOLITUDE

The pilgrimage provides numerous opportunities to experience solitude or solidarity. In both encounters pilgrims find and test different parts of themselves. For those pilgrims accustomed to being constantly surrounded by others (family, workmates, or friends), venturing off alone to make the Camino may be the first time in their lives that they are entering a new context completely dependent on themselves.

While profound experiences of solitude are often attributed to the open spaces of the meseta, they can occur at any time and any place depending on the personal worlds of the pilgrims. Overcoming a fear of being alone can lead one to personal understanding and change the Camino from an uncertain adventure to a more broadly conceived journey of self-exploration. Ramón, a cosmopolitan Spaniard in his early forties, went on the Camino after hearing a radio broadcast in which a popular Spanish bullfighter recounted how he found solutions to his personal problems. Feeling troubled and at a loss in his own life, Ramón impulsively left a week later for Roncesvalles, alone. More than a year later, dressed in suit and tie in a Madrid bar, he told me about being lost and alone: "My first night in the Camino outside of Roncesvalles in May 1993 was terrible. I had arrived in Roncesvalles with snow and the next day I began. Somehow I got lost. I didn't have a flashlight." Night came, and he found himself cold and alone in the dark—all terrifying to him. He slept outside that night in fear, huddled in his sleeping bag crying. He described crying for himself, for feeling utterly alone, and for himself as a little boy afraid in the dark with no one to comfort him. As he described this painful, cathartic moment he imitated the action of pulling covers over his head, as he did as a boy to comfort himself. He said that he felt idiotic, but there he was, on the Camino doing the same thing. Ramón did not think he would get through the night, but he did.

In this case Ramón's fears were immediately tested in the way as he found himself reliving a moment that was part of a painful childhood memory. On the Camino he was alone with no one to succor him. He needed to find the strength within himself to realize that he could survive and be okay. The next day, instead of leaving the Camino, he decided to continue, having passed an important personal barrier. While his fear of being alone did not vanish after this day, he felt greater confidence and was prepared to meet life alone or with others. Ramón suggested that he no longer needs to make the pilgrimage by himself because he knows that he can after passing this personal test. The next summer (1994, when we met) he went with his nephew. He had learned the value of solitude.

During the long stretches of continuous movement, which may be painful, boring, or exhilarating, the pilgrim also fills the time in novel or infrequently practiced ways—thinking, praying, meditating, singing. Many pilgrims describe singing every song they know two and three times and recalling tunes buried in childhood memories. On the ludic, Andrew, the Belgian businessman and father of three, who needed time to reflect on the course of his life as well as "make a journey of initiation to compensate for the one [he] could not take as an adolescent," described his journey: "I let myself loose, played like a child, sometimes with excess, let the emotions out, wrote silly poems, fell romantically in love for three days with a girl of my daughter's age and learned enough Spanish to communicate and say things I do not dare say in French." The long hours walking or biking day after day on lonely, open roads lend themselves to reflection. They provide the ideal space and structural break from normal time and life. A twenty-six-year-old German man described his first pilgrimage: "There was so much time for thinking. . . . The consequence was a confrontation with myself. . . . Past, present, future became a large mire. I noticed my fear of being frustrated for my whole working life. I said good-bye to engineering." Making decisions in solitude, where each step is a thought from which one cannot escape, is facilitated through the journey. Others simply find themselves lost in the rhythm of walking, trudging along like an "automaton that walks only to walk, unaware, with general indifference." Yet despite this feeling of being an unthinking, walking creature, one pilgrim, a Frenchman, found himself assaulted

Figure 29.   Pedaling through waist-high wheat in Navarre.

with existential questions: "Why am I here? Why do I inflict this sacrifice upon myself? To what end does this apparently useless pain serve? In the end, will Our Lord attend my prayer?"[26] This is another expression of the idea that the pace of the journey provides opportunities for the pilgrim to begin to find meaning in the questions and thoughts that inevitably arise on the way.

For pilgrims making a specifically religious journey, times of solitude and silence are crucial parts of the experience.[27] According to a Spanish priest from Madrid, "after walking many kilometers [solitude] helps open one's eyes" as well as practice spiritual exercises such as prayer, meditation, finding oneself, and feeling gratitude. In these moments, in contemplation of nature, union of the self with the religious inchoate can occur. Through silence "the Camino is converted into a sacrament of life" in which the many hours of walking serve to help internalize all that one lives and feels.[28] Meditating and thinking more deeply on passages of the Bible, feeling the Rosary with each step, repeating litany and prayers learned as a child—these may come to have new meaning when put to the rhythm of walking. Rather than rote exercises, they are described as helping one to experience the Camino more fully.[29] Lee described praying with his feet (a metaphor also used by other pilgrims). Walking gave him a new way to understand the Rosary—unhurried, with the rhythm of his motion, connected to the world around him. If pilgrims pray while walking, at Mass, or at any time during the day, it may consist in any (or more) of the following recognized by the Pilgrims' Office in Santiago: personal prayer to God, admiration of God's presence in nature, petitions, giving thanks, offering of sacrifice for pain felt in the journey, or for solidarity among pilgrims.

In the religious journey specific biblical passages are frequently used by organized Spanish catechism groups or individuals to help understand the process and interpret the pilgrims' experience—the feelings of community, the pains, the sense of union with nature. Perhaps the most common metaphor is that which a sixty-year-old retired Spaniard described as having helped him through a crisis of faith several years earlier: "Thanks to my first Camino in 1990, I rediscovered the Truth. The Way and the Life." For him, the Camino is meant in the religious sense as the way of Christ (from John 14:4–6 in the New Testament). His annual summer pilgrimages serve now as a thanks and a form of spiritual and personal renewal toward Christ that is both truth and life for him. Both religious pilgrims and the Spanish Church use the idea that communion with Jesus via the way (i.e., identifying oneself with His pain, suffering,

Figure 30.   The long road ahead in Castile.

and love) will lead one to God and salvation. Closely tied to this message is that of the Road to Emmaus (Luke 24:13), which underlines the
importance of the Eucharist celebration to the Church and provides the
model for seeing the hand of God in every action of grace associated with
the pilgrimage and three of its important values: fraternity, austerity, and
interior peace. From these two readings the Church sees the Camino "as
a parable of God as the goal, of Jesus Christ as access [to the goal/God],
of the Church as the caravan and shelter [to the goal/God], [and] of the
Lord's table as the bread of heaven, which is the true bread of the pilgrim."[30] In this model transformation or conversion is a process. The
vagueness in motives of many pilgrims on arrival is usually understood
by the Church as a latent spirituality that the Camino experience will release. Grace lies within each person, but for some there is an "obstacle"
that impedes communication with God. The action of the Camino helps
to remove this obstacle, in the least expected moments, allowing pilgrims
to realize and understand the religious root of their journey.[31]

Other pilgrims, making a personal spiritual or religious journey, may
have or find their own particularly meaningful liturgy. Some pilgrims
carry small psalm books, or they may read something for the morning
and then ponder it during the day. Among Spanish Catholics the Bible

is not as important a spiritual tool as it seems to be for Euro-Americans. A Basque pilgrim said simply, "Jesus said, Love one another. This phrase encapsulates everything that one ought to do with the people one meets and it is what one most often sees among people on the way—helping, understanding, encouragement and smiles."[32]

Feeling oneself at peace in nature and with others, living a healthy and simple life, breaking bread and drinking wine in communion with fellow pilgrims on a daily basis, and finding goodness in everyday acts on the Camino as a manifestation of "God's presence" can lead one to a greater sense of spirituality (which need not be interpreted in a religious way). A young German man explained, "My understanding of God is complicated and not clear. But in meeting people, in discussions and mental exchange, in confrontation with myself in looking at or living in nature, I meet God. We were allowed to see how easy life can be and how beautiful the human community could work. We were pilgrims to Santiago but also to life, to ourselves, and in a special way to God." The multiple ways in which he understood what it meant to be a pilgrim are important. To be a pilgrim is a life mission, a self-exploration, and a path to God. Also, his experience underlines how transformation is a process that takes place over time, discussing and then integrating the pieces of the way—step by step. It also appears that depending on one's orientation toward a Catholic tradition, the importance of the path as led by Jesus or God is fundamental. Often in French and German reflections the connection to God is made more directly, whereas in Spanish instances or evangelical orientations Jesus often mediates the spiritual connection.

Some pilgrims develop new ways to express their religious feelings. The idea of finding the light or illumination transfers to the language used by both religiously motivated pilgrims and those who define themselves more generally as being on a spiritual journey. The Camino is La Luz and La Vida (The Light and The Life), providing both inner illumination and the chance to renew one's spiritual life—as the "inward activity of growth and maturity." An Italian woman in her thirties, born Catholic, found the Catholic church "too dogmatic" and "guilt" oriented. Yet an inexplicable void existed within her, compelling her to make the Camino. The Camino gave her "the basis for [her] spirituality" and a way to express this internal welling. Her movement is toward an individualized religion yet based on experiences of the Camino—the power of silence, being open to everyone—where each person can "find herself or himself." Like the young German man above, many disaffected Catholics find comfort in the "truths" of the way; an idealized vision of the "human community" in its basic form, free of the politics and hypocrisy many claim to find in organized religious practice. Others find themselves drawn to Saint James but not to God or religion.

Others find in the Camino the desire to begin to pray or an opening to a religion rejected as a child. Often these desires come as a shock, the pilgrim being completely unaware of their presence. Feeling the receipt of gifts that have no price creates for some the opening to question their own lack of religious sentiment or to feel a greater openness to their spiritual life. A Canadian college graduate commented, "While I have no religious affiliation—my background was more Eastern than Christian influenced—my sense of grace (the gift that is bestowed on humanity, despite its weaknesses, failings, frailties) is inextricably linked with my feelings about the Camino." Pilgrims often enter churches or may attend Mass with greater frequency than they do in daily life. I sat in one Mass in Villafranca del Bierzo with an Anglican priest who walked to Santiago, and he expressed his disappointment in the Spanish services. For him, the people (mostly older women) and the priest seemed to be saying the Mass by rote without feeling its meaning. He found little inspiration. Often Euro-American churches have centers of welcome, brochures, and printed histories. Friends groups organize activities and raise money to improve the structure, repair stained glass, and so on. This atmosphere does not exist in Spain, and some non-Spanish pilgrims, like this Anglican priest, feel quite distant from Spanish Catholicism and forms of worship. Others are disappointed to find churches closed or to find that priests are unavailable to attend to their spiritual needs. Many non-Catholics attend the Masses out of curiosity, the spirit of communion, to enjoy the sound of the ritual in a foreign language, or to understand the experience of religious life in the local villages. A curiosity about, not necessarily a desire for, religion may be piqued for non-Catholics and non-Spaniards: Why do people light candles? Who are the saints? What does it mean if someone asks me to take their petition to the apostle? Why do only older Spanish women attend Mass in Spain? Why in some villages do women sit at the front and men at the back? Some non-Catholics begin to light candles or look for particular saints, simply because they like the gesture or what the saint represents, not necessarily tying it to a religious act. This is part of what pilgrims call the spiritual journey, for example, giving thanks for those of the way who helped them. They use the religious symbols to create their own private meanings and rituals.

EXPERIMENTATION AND ITS DANGERS

In this environment, in which new doors to the self are opened on personal, spiritual, physical, and social levels and the pilgrims experiment with emerging parts of their identities, a sense of danger or guilt may also surface. These reactions frequently occur when one's image of what a pilgrim's behavior "ought to be" while making the Camino conflicts with the reality of the experience. Robyn, for example, never imagined that on the pilgrimage she would experience a heightened sense of sexual potency and womanhood. This experience of pilgrimage did not correspond with her pre-Camino image, causing her to reevaluate and question the experience, not only with female friends but also with others, such as the priest.

Through the many days of travel the pilgrim develops a repertoire of stories and experiences created independent of the home environment. For those pilgrims who have left a spouse at home, a sense of guilt may emerge in the contrasting image of pilgrimage as a serious, spiritual venture and an often rollicking, personal adventure. Home is often very far away mentally and physically. An affair on the Camino may form part of the liminality of the whole experience but on reflection can be a danger for what was left behind.

This sense of danger through experimentation was profoundly illustrated by a chance encounter with a pilgrim I had met two weeks earlier. Visiting a refuge in which I would later be an hospitalera, I was very happy to meet Martin again. He saw me, his eyes widened, and as he said my name, his tears began to fall. "I have been a very bad pilgrim," he almost moaned. "I think I've ruined the whole Camino." It turned out that temptation had visited the sixty-year-old German, who had left his wife at home for the first time in thirty-five years to fulfill a lifelong dream of making the Camino after he retired. Temptation came in the form of a woman, a pilgrim with whom he shared an afternoon eating and drinking in a Spanish bar. A bit tipsy, they began to walk in the hot Spanish sun and realized it was impossible to continue. They laid down on the side of the road (nothing happened, he emphasized) and fell asleep. Later they continued to the refuge (where he and I met), and he remained behind to sleep off his hangover. His increasing guilt was augmented by her departure with no food or water for a difficult mountain pass.

On reflection his actions were foreign and disturbing to him. On the Camino he got drunk with a woman, crossing lines he felt were questionable, and even though "nothing happened" his behavior disturbed him and seemed quite unpilgrimlike. Sleeping on the side of the road added to his sense of vagrancy and shame. His lament became, How am I going to return to my wife? or continue the pilgrimage? Putting it into perspective through discussing it with me, he came to see this experience as a trial of pilgrimage. After the sense of guilt washed over him Martin began to see a reaffirmation of his values, the importance of his family and a greater acceptance of the fallibility of human character. His idea of being a "bad" pilgrim later became reframed as being a pilgrim who suffered a crisis yet overcame it to learn from the experience. The next summer he returned with his wife by car to share the road with her.

RESOLUTIONS AND DECISIONS

Through the course of the journey pilgrims often make decisions and resolutions regarding life "off the Camino." One woman wanted to maintain her physical conditioning after feeling the power of her body through living a healthy, active lifestyle. Martin felt a sense of renewal and commitment to his family and home life. Robyn and Luis wanted to return to the Camino to once again experience the powerful sense of rejuvenation and vitality that struck them on various sensual and emotional levels. The Camino also provides opportunities for making decisions that will be incorporated into home life regarding a job change, a personal relationship, or business relationships.

AUTHENTICITY

When Martin said to me with tears in his eyes, "I've been a bad pilgrim," he was also describing what a good pilgrim should be. He imagined his journey to be serious, focused on the road and certainly not bound up in personal compromise. For many, like Martin, ideas about the good and authentic pilgrim can come to be reconsidered during the journey. The authentic pilgrim is implicitly understood to be the one who most closely represents the iconographic image of the medieval pilgrim who walked to Santiago with staff, cloak, scallop shells, felt hat, and small pouch. The set of values attributed to this image include self-sufficiency, humility, decency, solidarity, generosity, and respect for nature, oneself, and others. One can be an authentic pilgrim in the present by emulating the image through behavior, mode of travel, and attitude. On doing so, the hope is that the pilgrim will better understand himself or herself, God, the way, and the past. Despite general agreement on these points notions of the authentic and proper guide, influence, and shape modern experience. As the anthropologists John Eade and Michael Sallnow suggest, it is "necessary to develop a view of pilgrimage not merely as a field of social relations but also as a *realm of competing discourses.*"[33] One aspect of pilgrimage is social—a place of heightened feelings of solidarity and goodwill between pilgrims and villagers—which may be more or less agreed on. Another reality is how people and institutions understand and use pilgrimage or being a pilgrim. Broner suggests that "authenticity" is used in at least four ways: as credibility, genuineness, originality, and certification. In the case of Santiago the emphasis is on genuineness of experience, which is produced through the process of becoming a pilgrim and personal knowledge: "I did it." Genuineness is attributed by people along the way, other pilgrims, hospitaleros, and the self. Credibility is marked by how one travels and comportment. The journey is certified through the credential and the *Compostela.* At each of these points one can see attempts to control the meaning of the pilgrimage, either consciously or unconsciously, by a variety of different institutions and people.

At the root of conflicts over what is and is not "pilgrimlike" one frequently finds a power struggle, personal debates with the pilgrimage's meaning, and claims to authority. Who has the right to tell the story of the site? Who decides what is and what is not authentic, when the pilgrimage is ultimately so personal? As Bruner suggests in his discussion of the term "authentic reproduction," the "more fundamental question to ask here is not if an object or site is authentic, but rather who has the authority to authenticate, which is a matter of power."[34] The story of the modern pilgrimage has been written by many hands. Obvious influences include the Church and government, but pilgrims themselves are crucial in attempting to "tell the story."

On the institutional level the Catholic church defines authenticity according to "tradition" and motive yet also recognizes the boom in popularity of walking and cycling to Santiago. The Spanish Diocesan Commission met in 1993 and developed this statement about the pilgrimage: "*The traditional pilgrimage to Santiago is made on foot,* for this, special merit is in order. However, the essential part of the pilgrimage is to make it *with a spirit of faith* and this is not linked to any mode of transport."[35] Of course, faith, belief, and devotion are the bottom line for the Church. Stating that modern pilgrims deserve special merit for making the pilgrimage by foot assumes that the pilgrim's motives relate to a devotion to the apostle Saint James—representing a sacrifice of pain for sin, gratitude, and identification with Christ's pain. The pilgrimage was "traditionally" made on foot before the twentieth century because the vast majority of pilgrims who went to Santiago then had no other way of getting there. The majority of modern pilgrims, however, are not walking or cycling from a worldview in which sacrifice and religious devotion predominate.

The Church does intervene in the pilgrimage through the pilgrim's credential and the receipt of the *Compostela*. The bearer of the credential claims to make the journey in a spirit of faith (according to the fine print on the document). When pilgrims arrive in Santiago they usually get the *Compostela,* the certificate of completion. The Church bestows the *Compostela* after asking the pilgrim to express a religious motive. In the 1990s the religious motive was amplified to allow "spiritual" as a separate category, after pilgrims repeatedly declared this motive instead of a religious one. The distances that are mandatory for receiving the *Compostela* were established arbitrarily. Through the distribution of the *Compostela* and the interpretation of motives, the Pilgrim's Office boasts a high percentage of the religiously motivated. And pilgrims often greatly value the *Compostela,* which is in Latin, as a special memento and sign of the journey. It is when alternative beliefs appear to compete with the Church's perspective that attacks begin to mount against "false" pilgrims. The Church is clear that "esoterics" and "gnostics" are not pilgrims and it discourages strongly this influence in the pilgrimage. A pamphlet on this theme is available in the Pilgrim's Office, and articles occasionally appear in *Compostela,* the magazine of the head confraternity of Saint James, which is closely tied to the Pilgrim's Office.[36]

The Church, though, hesitates to impose strict limits on the pilgrimage because it is precisely the Camino's openness that can bring more into the fold. A specific goal of the Church is to use the current popularity of the Camino to evangelize and convert European youth in the name of a future united Europe. The Church also recognizes that pilgrimage is a process and that sometimes people experience conversions while walking.

The Spanish Federation of the Associations of Friends of the Camino de Santiago, with support from the Council of Europe and the Spanish Ministry of Culture, produced a series of pamphlets for public distribution on how to be a pilgrim. One of these pamphlets describes the modern pilgrimage: "To go on pilgrimage to Santiago in the traditional mode, is more than a tourist or sport trip made on foot over an artistic route in contact with nature. It's all of this, but also much more. It is to find yourself in the religious and historical routes of Europe, to renovate a way of interior transformation, to walk at the rhythm of other centuries, it is to . . . wander." Not surprisingly this definition is broad— allowing for pilgrimage to be linked to art, nature, personal transformation, Europe, history, and travel. Anyone who goes to Santiago "traditionally," that is, on foot, is a pilgrim. Moreover, the federation is generally concerned with pilgrims' satisfaction of experience (like a tour holiday), and their questionnaire asks pilgrims to rank the regions according to services.[37]

It is no surprise that the Church would have one interpretation designed to support a religious view of the reanimation, or that the federation, supported in part by government money, would want to show a high level of pilgrim satisfaction among "traditional" pilgrims. What is more surprising are the divisions among pilgrims, who, in general, highly value solidarity. For example, a member of the Navarrese Friends of the Camino association published an article entitled "What Should the 'Authentic' Pilgrim Be?"[38] In tongue-in-cheek fashion the author outlines the ideal characteristics of the "true" pilgrim and pilgrimage using commonly heard comments and criticisms made by pilgrims, which often contradict one another. On the scale of the authentic the most important elements are movement (on foot), attitude (serious and austere), time (slow paced and long term), motivation (religious), performance (use of the Camino infrastructure, solo) and space (following the marked old way). Though presented as a satire it points to the power of the "cult of authenticity" that exists in the Camino, which often works as an exclusionary rather than an inclusionary force.

Pilgrims relate to and react to the authentic at many points along the way. During preparation for the pilgrimage participants may be aware of the "proper pilgrim," as in the case of David, the Englishman who structured his journey according, at least in part, to ideas associated with the authentic—where to begin, amount of time, how to behave, and so on. Alison, the English winter pilgrim, suggested that the idea of a "right" or best time dissuaded some people from going in the winter. Others, like the Englishman who saw the sailor cross himself as he got off the boat, feel like pilgrims when others recognize them as such, for example, when they are asked to be a spiritual messenger or are given the shell. The Englishman felt like a "fraud" much of the time, precisely because he felt like he was playing a role. If one behaves well, walks, goes by oneself, then one will be treated like a pilgrim and will receive the benefits therein. Some very few, creative people have latched on to this idea and live off of the Camino, playing at the authentic pilgrim by telling a story of false poverty. The listeners usually give such pilgrims money or food. They are part of the "pilgrimage underground," as one man called it.

Concepts of authenticity among pilgrims may focus on motive. An older Spaniard wrote in a pilgrim's magazine, "The pilgrim is a person who expresses his Christian faith in the pilgrimage and walks to the tomb of the Apostle as penitence or in search and encounter with apostolic roots."[39] His perspective echoes that of the Church yet is more severe. He suggests further that participation in the Camino should somehow be limited to only authentic, that is, religiously motivated pilgrims. For those who journey in faith, the pilgrimage of the nonreligious person often seems senseless. Others find the essence of the pilgrimage to be in its history and art and enrich their journeys by stopping in every church and analyzing the architecture. They may disparage those pilgrims who take little interest in the patrimony of the Camino, claiming that they fail to understand the road and what it means to be a pilgrim.

Rather than a lack of religious or historical motives, inauthenticity usually centers on being a tourist and how one makes the pilgrimage. As pilgrims travel the Camino these differences may become more pronounced and influence how they see themselves or others as pilgrims. It becomes clear that divisions that at first appeared to exist only between motor- and human-powered pilgrims exist *within* the latter group as well. Cyclists, as a category, often are seen to tarnish the sacredness, the "purity" of the Camino, just as bus and car pilgrims contribute to the desecration of the way. Even though there is communitas, rifts exist. Some Spanish walkers call cyclists *peregrinos descafeinados* (decaffeinated pilgrims), meaning they are a watered-down version of the real thing. Without realizing it pilgrims make sweeping judgments about others and at the same time put themselves into a category that claims to hold a "truth" about the Camino. The authentic says "We are all pilgrims," but at the same time it is clear that "some are better pilgrims than others." For some, being an authentic pilgrim raises one's status instead of serving as an equalizer.

I read the following entry in the Frómista pilgrims' refuge signature book, which highlights these conflicts clearly. The first pilgrim, a walker, wrote in Spanish: "Así no vale. El peregrino va a pie, el que va en bici es un turista. (That doesn't count. The pilgrim goes on foot. The pilgrim who goes by bike is a tourist.) What particularly intrigued me about this entry was the rather violent response written in parentheses below by another Spanish pilgrim: "Eres idiota porque mis huevos me ha costado subir las cuestas sin bajarme." (You're an idiot because I had to bust my balls to climb the hills without getting off my bike.) Both are pilgrims, yet they are worlds apart. The walker rigidly claims that the essence of meaningful pilgrimage is walking. The cyclist argues that pilgrimage is suffering or pain, not solely movement choice. Neither mentions motive.

Robert, a twenty-nine-year-old German graduate student, made his first journey on bicycle to Santiago in 1985 out of "curiosity" as well as for cultural and historical reasons. He repeated the journey in 1988 after finishing college, and we met in Santiago after his third pilgrimage in 1994 (after he had submitted the first draft of his Ph.D. dissertation). Noting a tremendous difference in attitude between 1985 and 1994, he reflected,

> There is now a very annoying discussion about the question of whether bikers are pilgrims or whether only pedestrians are "authentic" pilgrims. Those who plead for the latter indicate implicitly or explicitly that the pilgrim has to suffer; that you are more a pilgrim the more you suffer on the way. . . . Walking is always the most direct way a person can move in a landscape. You can't escape as easily as a biker from painful and unpleasant situations. . . . But who says a pilgrim must suffer? That's deepest medieval Catholic ideology which considered the sense of the terrestrial life of sinful human beings only in pain and in suffering. . . . So more tolerance for us cyclists!

Unlike the other cyclist, Robert rejects the idea that pilgrimage and suffering go hand in hand. He also traces this emphasis on pain to "medieval Catholic ideology," questioning the idea that being a pilgrim means trying to replicate the past. He follows the same routes, participates in the same rituals, and enjoys the same spiritual journey as walkers, yet he does not share the idea that authenticity is defined by suffering, speed, or an intent to replicate the past. A Spanish Basque man who made the pilgrimage first by bicycle and then on foot commented in an article on this theme, "People can think that anyone can do it on bike, that there's more merit in walking, but in all sincerity, I have to say that for me it was much harder to go by bike than by foot."[40] Again, this man emphasizes difficulty but makes no mention of motive. He concludes by remarking that he prefers walking, which allows him to enjoy the experience in a relaxed and open way. Among cyclists there are further divisions between those (usually mountain-bikers) who ride on the Camino and those who ride on the highway. Similar criteria based on speed, roads used, and perceived suffering may surface in cyclists' conversations in the same way it does with walkers.

Hitchhiking a bit or taking a bus for part of the way also scores very low points on the authenticity checklist. It hints at a lack of will and stamina and an unwillingness to put up with the pain; at a willingness to give in to the easy society, to forfeit the project of re-creating the hardship and recuperating the values of the past. It also is an abuse of the pilgrimage infrastructure, which is designed for those who are walking and in need of shelter, not to provide free lodging for those who want a comfortable walking tour of northern Spain's highlights. Some pilgrims are embarrassed to admit they hitchhiked or took a bus. Others have no idea that their actions appear disrespectful to those who have walked or cycled the whole way. Values of authenticity may be assimilated by cyclists, who frequently express a desire to repeat the Camino the next year—"to do it the authentic way." Or, alternatively, a young, unemployed Segovian learned about the pilgrimage when he met two pilgrims from Galicia outside the Burgos Cathedral and asked them what they were doing. They explained, and he and his friend decided it would be a good, cheap way to travel. They went home, got the pilgrim's credential, and came back to the Camino—walking some segments, hitchhiking others. The Segovian stayed in touch with one of the pilgrims he met in Burgos. He told the Galician that he felt guilty about how he made the Camino and wanted to repeat, to do it "right," and to become an hospitalero. He did all three, demonstrating how the existence of an authentic model can influence a participant's behavior.

Distance from modern technology plays a crucial role in determining authenticity. Pilgrims who make the Camino with a support car fall at the bottom of the group because they maintain a dubious connection to the trappings of modern society. Although cyclists use their own power, they are placed just above support-car pilgrims because their link to the Camino is mediated by the metal frame between their legs, rubber wheels, broken chains, oil, and, in this world, high speeds. Walkers reign supreme for their independence, physical effort, and slow pace. Those few who go by horse or use a pack animal fall somewhere between walkers and cyclists. Even though their physical effort is minimal, the horse is natural and linked to past ways of going and, consequently, is thought to be more authentic. Horses usually require a support car, and the romanticized pack animal is frequently problematic—it gets sick, there is no place to sleep or feed—and is much more time-consuming than the owner imagines before beginning the journey. What happens to the animal once in Santiago? Neither trains nor planes are amenable to such cargo. Pilgrims sell them, unless they have well-organized equine transport.[41]

Walking as a form of transport in modern middle-class Euro-American life is essentially obsolete. It is the rare individual who commutes to work

Figure 31.   A German woman and a Spanish man on horseback in Astorga (León).

on foot. Walking is usually linked with leisure. What pilgrims often do not realize is that their venturing out to discover something true about themselves and the world has a long history in Christian and Western philosophy centered on the debate over whether the locus of change is found in stasis or mobility.[42] Marshall McLuhan wrote in 1964,

> When machine production was new, it gradually created an environment whose content was the old environment of agrarian life and the arts and crafts. This older environment was elevated to an art form by the new mechanical environment. The machine turned Nature into an art form. For the first time men began to regard Nature as a source of aesthetic and spiritual values. They began to marvel that earlier ages had been so unaware of the world of Nature as Art. Each new technology creates an environment that is itself regarded as corrupt and degrading. Yet the new one turns its predecessor into an art form.[43]

One Irishwoman made a similar observation: "Just think, the two most important forms of transport early this century are now highly specialized hobbies!" In a sense walking the Camino has become an art: one's feet are the brush; the Camino, the canvas. The crucial measure of authenticity is not what is painted but the technique. Those who walk are purists, and others disrupt the purity of the form. From the walkers' point of view, their technique leads to more profound results.

One of the perceived threats to this art of making the Camino is the tourist pilgrim. A Swiss hospitalero wrote at the end of his volunteer stay in 1994, "Fifty percent of the pilgrims were essentially tourists. Keeping in mind that I am interested in interior, spiritual journeys, I didn't converse with this type of visitor."[44] Or: "There were some true pilgrims and others who took advantage of the infrastructure of the refuges to have a good walk with good company in the cheapest way possible." From a Spanish hospitalero: "Those pilgrims who began in León or Astorga, the majority, left a lot to be desired in their comportment—they didn't identify with the spirit of the Camino."[45] In this scheme the pilgrims who make an interior search, respect the infrastructure, and have the "spirit" of the Camino are the authentic ones. The superficial, the disagreeable, the complainers, those who demand, are tourists. Many are the "new" pilgrims who have not yet been inculcated into the "culture of the Camino" and therefore make behavioral gaffes.

The notion of the authentic is fostered through these kinds of sentiments in discussions among pilgrims and in the testimonial books. The position of hospitalero is a powerful one, setting the tone of the refuge and sending messages about what is and is not authentic through his or her behavior. Sometimes hospitaleros, trying to "educate" pilgrims about what is authentic behavior, make narrow judgments and privilege or impose their own knowledge and experience. Haab commented on her ambivalence regarding the care of pilgrims: "It seems to me that much care needs to be taken that one doesn't project his or her own idea of the best way to make the Camino onto others. If one does this, it isn't love, but a hidden way to impose power, nothing else. And it is even worse to impose power claiming that it is love—the pilgrim, as a pilgrim, is very sensitive to these ambiguities. Love is to give without conditions, to satisfy the basic needs of the pilgrim without judging who does and doesn't merit it."[46]

In 1997 I cycled the pilgrimage with a companion, and we found ourselves repeatedly engaging in discussions about authenticity with pilgrims, hospitaleros, and villagers who frequently told us it was better and more difficult on foot and often treated us, as another cyclist put it, as "second-class pilgrims." At least six of the ten hospitaleros we met expounded on the virtues of walking and assumed that we had never gone by foot. It turned out that none of them had made the Camino by bicycle, yet each felt that their experience and authority were adequate to judge others' journeys. We were also often encouraged to go on the main road rather than the Camino, which was deemed too difficult or more appropriate for walkers than cyclists.

Pilgrims who walk or cycle in a group are also marginalized from the cult of authenticity. A Spanish priest who has done both commented, "Making the Camino in a group and alone are two experiences so different that it's impossible to compare them. In some places I have met *hospitaleros,* usually priests, who roundly criticized the group experience, reducing the Camino to an experience which can only be personal."[47] Walking or cycling alone allows the pilgrim, according to the priest, to experience solitude and interior silence, to challenge and open oneself to new circumstances not possible when in a group. Going alone is understood to be the ideal way to experience oneself in nature and obtain spiritual and personal insight. Cyclists in groups are especially marginalized and understood to be tourists or athletes rather than pilgrims.

The nuances of authenticity do not end with the differences among groups, cyclists, and walkers. Distance and time traveled are two other important variables. Pilgrims who make the longest journeys, in terms of both time and distance, are considered the most authentic; the implicit assumption is that longer journeys have the potential to produce a more profound transformation. Long-distance cyclists and walkers are those who go for at least one month and as many as four months and begin at least at the French-Spanish border (Roncesvalles, Spain, and even better, St. Jean Pied-de-Port, France). Yet these distances and amounts of time are arbitrary, part of the contemporary trend. Part-time pilgrims— an option possible only in the late twentieth century—fall between the cracks of authenticity and foul the "length of journey–power of experience" continuum. For months I ignored this modern way of making the pilgrimage because I believed it was irrelevant to my research, reflecting my own struggle with the authenticity trap. After speaking to a number of part-time pilgrims during and after their journeys I realized I needed to revise my own narrow categories.

On the level of lived reality pilgrims choose (consciously or unconsciously) from these categories in constructing their experience. For some pilgrims, feeling authentic and having an authentic experience play a crucial role; for others, it has relatively little importance. A Swiss pilgrim commented, "I felt like a walker most of the time for the simple reason that I did it for the physical and mental challenge. When I stayed in the big towns like Burgos and León and did sightseeing, I of course felt like a tourist and I was one. I never felt like a pilgrim even though I thought about it." Some pilgrims find that their motives change as they walk and they unexpectedly feel like pilgrims when they reach Santiago, or even when they return home and reflect on the experience. In the case of the Swiss man, his long-distance journey, his foreignness, and his comportment gave him an aura of authenticity, yet on the inside he felt like a tourist. The cult of authenticity establishes the expectation that one should feel like a pilgrim or become one—reinforcing for some the common sense of personal dissatisfaction and incoherence. When the Camino is over and they do not feel any different, even though they did it authentically, they wonder what they missed.

There are other pilgrims who wear authenticity like a badge of honor and expect or feel entitled to special treatment instead of moving toward a position of greater humility. This is not necessarily done on a conscious level. Being a pilgrim "has a lot of benefits," as the Dutch couple observed, and some pilgrims get accustomed to these benefits and expect them—often insulting villagers, hospitaleros, and other pilgrims. For example, a Spanish priest who began making the pilgrimage in the 1970s alone and in groups, reported that during one of his numerous pilgrimages he and his companion arrived late in a small village of the meseta. Commenting at first that pilgrims should not expect villagers "to be able to fund the necessities of all the pilgrims that pass," he proceeded to tell how they asked the woman at the bar where they stopped to prepare them dinner. She said that she had nothing. The priest continued, "We insisted on explaining our need and the day that we'd had. We got another negative response." They commented that it was obvious they would be going to bed without dinner and that their beds, the terrace of the school, would be less than desirable. The priest's friend, not being resigned to this fate, decided to call home and complain loudly about the bad treatment they received. He also said that they would write in a pilgrim's book about how badly the people of this village treat pilgrims. The woman heard, prepared two tortillas with chorizo (an egg, potato, and meat pancake), and asked her husband to drive them to the next village where they rented beds.[48] In narrating the story the priest expressed no remorse, nor did it cross his mind that the woman may have given him the only food she had because of their threat of slander. They used being pilgrims to get what they wanted. They are not alone.

For some pilgrims who do not attach great importance to the concept of authenticity, it is the travel that is important. Traveling forms part of their identity. They either work to travel or are experienced long-distance walkers. In other journeys they have experienced the pains and disorientation of solitude, the joys of stunning natural beauty, and the experience of living with little. The Camino is just one more such path. "I have always been a walker, my life one long itinerary. . . . The Camino de Santiago didn't bring me anything special, except the pleasure of walking and meeting a series of interesting people. . . . At its root, it's a bourgeois way full of bourgeois people." Like this fifty-year-old man from Granada, pilgrims who feel unaffected by the Camino usually have a storehouse of similar experiences. A German carpenter, who stumbled on the Camino while hiking through the Pyrenees and decided to continue, said to me in Santiago, "I'm a traveler. I've never been a Santiago pilgrim. I'm always a pilgrim on my own private camino."

Although authenticity is believed to reside in the past, pilgrims find their own meanings through identification, questioning, and reflecting on the image of the authentic pilgrim. The Camino has become a space in which meanings emerge for the individual who can play with identity, search the soul, find the past, create friendships, engage in serious religious or personal reflection, or simply have a good time. Pilgrims often find something essential (authentic) within themselves or others. The point is not that there is no authentic pilgrim but that there are many authenticities. Each person creates his or her personally meaningful experience. The Navarrese pilgrim who originally posed the question, "How should the authentic pilgrim be?" concludes with the idea that authenticities are ultimately "personally negotiated."[49] "With almost complete certainty, one can say that there is no 'best' or 'most authentic' way. These ways change with time and the social, geographic and religious circumstances that revolve around the Camino."[50]

CHAPTER 5

ARRIVALS AND ENDINGS

How should I your true-love know
From another one?
By his cockle, hat and staff
And his sandal shoon.
         —*Shakespeare*, Hamlet

An Italian physical therapist sent me a postcard two weeks after she began the pilgrimage in Roncesvalles which announced, "The pilgrimage
has just begun in Burgos!" This declaration surprised me, for it implied
that her pilgrimage either had never really begun or had ended at some
point after leaving Roncesvalles and begun again with new spirit. On
learning that she had intended the latter meaning, I began to see how
endings and arrivals may or may not be place- or space-specific. Depending on the pilgrim's goal and motivation different internal endings or resolutions can come at any moment and may not be linked to the physical arrival in Santiago.

    While the vast majority of pilgrims reach the geographical goal in San-
tiago, there are pilgrims who find resolutions at other points along the
Camino, which may make the arrival in Santiago irrelevant for them,
even though they may continue the physical journey. A well-known example is Paulo Coelho's (1996) journey of esoteric initiation. He recounted that the Camino ended for him in Cebreiro when he found his
sought-after spiritual enlightenment and the sword that would convert
him into a *mago*, or magician. At that point his primary goal was reached,
he found himself at peace with his mission, and he continued to Santiago
by bus.

    On a less esoteric level a young Brazilian lawyer explained that friends
who had made the Camino shared their stories and positive experiences
with him and finally persuaded him to go. He began the Camino alone

in October and encountered cold, lonely days interrupted by torrential rain. One of the first stories he recounted to me on arrival in Santiago was of the priest's kindness at San Juan de Ortega. The priest helped him to thaw and dry out with a hot fire and a bowl of garlic soup when he finally managed to drag himself to the doors of the twelfth-century monastery and pilgrims' shelter. Despite these unexpected hardships (to which he was not accustomed in daily life), he continued to Burgos and entered the meseta. In the process he realized that the Camino he was making was not his own. He found himself trying to conform to a standard of authenticity (walking alone) set by his friends. At one point while walking in the meseta he realized that it was not important to make the Camino in a prescribed way and experienced an immense sense of relief: "It finally became my Camino." Once he made this decision, he took the bus from the meseta to Santiago. He felt his journey, on an internal level, was complete, and he was pleased with its outcome: his sense of self was strengthened and his priorities reoriented in a positive way. The physical arrival became irrelevant.

Lee, after walking eleven days, began to understand more fully his motive for being on the Camino: "to become a man of faith." After reflecting on this gift of faith he commented, "So, as I end my life, I begin it. As I approach the end of the *camino,* I arrive at its and my source, faith."[1] In the view of the Church the apostle's tomb is the goal that should be constantly before the pilgrim and that makes the pain and the fatigue understandable. The pilgrim's religious journey is not merely a personal one but is placed in a larger, holy context: in walking to Santiago the pilgrim walks to the roots of Christian faith. In the Catholic view the pilgrim's journey becomes a testimony to the longevity of faith and the pilgrim becomes a new apostle. As Lee's testimony demonstrates, beginnings and endings and arrivals emerge and occur within the same spaces.

These stories reveal how the idea of the journey's goal is often flexible and variously situated. While Santiago is an obvious geographic goal, it is not necessarily the end of the interior journey. Journey's end and the pilgrim's goal should not be conflated.[2] The multitextured quality of endings is visible in the closure of the physical journey and the turn toward home. The pilgrimage does not simply end with the pilgrim's arrival in Santiago but is a process that often begins well before the pilgrim reaches the city's gates and is prolonged indefinitely as the pilgrim continues to interpret in daily life the experiences he or she lived while making the way.

ENDING'S ARRIVAL

The geographic ending in Santiago is often preceded by a sense of arrival felt long before the pilgrim actually sets foot in or cycles into the city and starts up the granite path to the cathedral. Approaching the geographic goal is felt most strongly in the last week for walkers and in the last several days for cyclists. Clearly, time begins to play a role if the pilgrimage has been made within specific limits and the days, rather than seem more than numerous, begin to pass as in a countdown.

Changing geography and weather also influences the sense of transition in the last two weeks of walking. As pilgrims reach Astorga they leave behind the flat, sweltering, brown meseta and pass through the large fields of Castile-León and the large cities of Burgos and León. They then enter yet another zone of climatic, geographic, and cultural differentiation, La Maragatería and then El Bierzo. La Maragatería is frequently mentioned as a step into the past: few modern structures exist, most of the inhabitants in the villages are elderly, and the main highway bypasses the area, leaving it largely undisturbed by rapid transit. In addition, the music, food, and dance all have a distinct flavor.

Nicknamed the fifth province of Galicia, El Bierzo stands at its doorstep, rising to greet its neighbor near the highest point of the camino francés—Cebreiro, the first major hamlet of Galicia. Though the area is small (walked in three days or biked in one) it is important as a hilly transition between the long stretch of the meseta and the verdant, rolling footpaths of Galicia.

Depending on the season in which the pilgrim makes the Camino, the changing composition of the pilgrimage group also signals arrival at Santiago. In summer it is common for participants to make the Camino for a period of one or two weeks, usually departing from León, Astorga, Ponferrada, or even Cebreiro. The increase in pilgrims is felt profoundly by those who have come from longer distances. The latter may have the feeling of simply being one more among many but at the same time experience a sense of awe at the long journey from both pilgrims and villagers.

ENTERING GALICIA

As they approach Santiago pilgrims often react to the journey's physical ending through changes in the rhythm of their movement and myriad emotions ranging from elation to profound sadness. There are two places in Galicia that pilgrims repeatedly associate with the process and real-

ization of the journey's end. The first is El Cebrero (O Cebreiro in Gallego), the last major physical hurdle that separates pilgrims from Santiago. The second is cresting the Monte del Gozo (Mount of Joy), the last
rise before and first view of the long-awaited goal. While Cebreiro and
Monte del Gozo are commonly referred to by pilgrims I do not mean to
imply that the sense of ending is in any way limited to these two locations. But at these two there is a strong linking of place and recognition
of ending, achievement, or perhaps even fear of failure.

One enters Galicia going up—up 1,300 meters to arrive at Cebreiro's
doorstep. It is a difficult, long, and steep climb that is often made more
difficult by the fog, rain, and wind typical of the area. The final approach
is made along a *corredoira,* a path of earth and stone used by rural Galicians to move from village to field. One guidebook writer describes the
ascent dramatically: "In the ascent to Cebreiro, the heart beats faster,
not because of the physical effort, but for the emotion provoked by reaching Galician soil. Now there is no mountain in the world that can stop
the pilgrim."[3] Haab describes the arrival here as a positive threshold,
"where one is filled with new strength,"[4] and pilgrims may even shout
with joy.

The pilgrim's goal suddenly looms large, and reactions of triumph and
achievement are common. Inner ups and downs mirror the physical ones.[5]
For some, after weeks of walking the body is accustomed to the physical exertion, but the summit presents one last challenge and even place
of doubt. On cresting the top 150 kilometers separate pilgrims from Santiago, meaning less than a week walking or a few days cycling.

For pilgrims who have traveled the Camino since the border of France
and Spain and passed through distinct geographic zones, reaching Cebreiro marks another abrupt change. Until the sixteenth century the pass
at Cebriero was one of the only access points for travelers entering Galicia. Not only a vital communication link to the rest of Spain, the village
has had a long-standing important relationship to the pilgrimage dating
back to the founding of an eleventh-century pilgrim's *hospital* (which
existed until 1854), the twelfth-century church of Santa María, and a
fifteenth-century Eucharist miracle in which the host and wine were trans-
figured into the flesh and blood of Christ.[6] The sacred chalice remains
there. For some modern Catholics, this miracle motivates the climb up
and reaffirms God's omnipresence. An important watershed lies here,
leaving it to fate to send the waters from the frequent storms down to
the Atlantic Ocean or Cantabrian Sea.

In this dramatic border crossing a sharp architectural contrast is also

noted, adding to the mystique. From the red adobe typical of Castile-
León, suddenly the pilgrim encounters the use of stone and, most no-
tably, the *palloza,* a type of dwelling of pre-Roman, possibly Celtic, origin. Nine of these low-walled circular dwellings topped by high thatched
roofs still stand in the hamlet (one has been converted into an ethnographic museum) but are no longer inhabited. Galicia, in general, is famous archaeologically for the large number of what are believed to be
Celtic remains and *castros* (fortified circular villages), attracting pilgrims
who are partly motivated by a search for their Celtic roots. Until the 1993
construction by the Xunta of the ninety-bed refuge in Cebreiro, pilgrims
slept in one of the pallozas. In short, pilgrims report the experience of
arrival in Cebreiro as a shift to another time and stage of the Camino.
Within this environment pilgrims experience many of these changes on
the internal level as well.

Cebreiro is often a point where stories of vision and insight surface after the physical trial is overcome. Reaching the top of Cebreiro gave Anton his first vision of the end and what he described as a near-mystical
experience. After a cold, wet ascent the clouds cleared for a moment just
as he crested the summit. In this pause he could see Galicia for the first
time, and "it was as if the clouds were opening up exposing the sea." He
could smell the salty spray carried in the atmosphere by the strong wind,
even though he knew it was impossible given the great distance separating him from the ocean. The end and the sea were linked as great and
powerful. He had already moved beyond Santiago in his mind.

The crossing into Galicia puts most European pilgrims at their farthest point from home, but for Galician pilgrims it has the double significance of reaching the goal and of coming home. For those who come
from Santiago or other parts of Galicia, it is especially curious to take a
bus to the border of France and Spain and then walk home more than
750 kilometers. Other Spanish pilgrims may pass their village or city while
making the Camino, but in going forward they continue to leave it behind, unlike Gallegos who have it constantly before them. One Galician
sailor who had not lived in Galicia for fifteen years and made the Camino
to fulfill a vow called the arrival at Cebreiro unexpectedly "important
and traumatic." He was left with a profound sense of coming home. Thus
the arrival at the border of Galicia puts the Galician pilgrims both closer
to the goal and closer to home and adds the curious twist that they have
reached the center. The majority of Galician pilgrims begin at Cebreiro,
"from their front door," as one study put it. Instead of getting farther
away from home on reaching Santiago, Gallegos get closer to it.

Figure 32.   Palloza and stone house in Cebreiro (Galicia).

Once pilgrims leave Cebreiro behind the last portion of the pilgrimage takes place in Galician countryside and villages that have welcomed
pilgrims for centuries. The twelfth-century *Codex Calixtinus* says of this
moment: "Then, after crossing the territory of León and going over the
passes of Monte Irago and Cebrero, you come into Galicia, a well wooded
and well watered region with rivers and meadows and fine orchards, excellent fruit and clear springs, but with few towns and villages or cultivated fields. There is little wheaten bread or wine but ample supplies of
rye bread and cider, cattle and horses, milk, honey and sea fish both large
and small."[7]

Despite the passage of eight hundred years Galicia still retains its image as an area of high precipitation, abundant seafood, and a dispersed
population. Galicia has long been an extreme zone of Spain, the hinter-
land, the mystical, green place behind the mountains, the sanctuary of
Saint James's bones, and the home of the end of the earth (Finisterre).
In Galicia, oak, eucalyptus, pine, and chestnut trees become the constant
companions to pilgrims, who may also be struck by other differences,
such as the Galician language (Gallego), village structure, nonmechanized
farming techniques, house construction, and an emphasis on the rural.
Passing through the more rural areas one encounters *cruceiros* (stone

Figure 33.   Samos monastery and village (Galicia).

crosses marking crossroads) and *hórreos* (elevated stone granaries) characteristic of and unique to the Galician landscape.[8]

Once the entry into Galicia is made the changes wrought by the Xunta
de Galicia (Government of the Autonomous Community of Galicia) for
the 1993 Holy Year to improve (depending on one's perspective) the
Camino for pilgrims also clearly mark the approaching end. Cement way
markers now dot the Camino every five hundred meters and begin the
countdown with Santiago as the zero point. In addition, the creation of
refuges from abandoned schoolhouses and other buildings nearly every
10 kilometers as well as changes in the Camino—it generally avoids the
highways and is tree-lined—signal an intensification of the journey. The
combination of these changes in the last week influences the sense of proximity to the goal. Space, time, and population converge, creating an hourglass effect with Santiago representing the narrow waist and point of greatest pressure. Pilgrims experience this effect both emotionally and physically.

THE AMBIVALENCE OF ARRIVAL

A common sensation that pilgrims experience in the last portion of the
journey is ambivalence.[9] The end of the long physical, personal, and

often spiritual journey is tangible. Each pilgrim's journey has a different rhythm. One may arrive strong and powerful on a physical level—feeling new muscles, trust in knowing one's limits, wearing the pack like a second skin—yet feel totally unprepared on a spiritual or personal level to reach Santiago. Awareness of this process often presents itself only in the return home. Haab suggests that on the approach to Santiago pilgrims demonstrate "two quite different tendencies. . . . [S]ome try to put it off, walking more and more slowly, and are troubled by the thought that their long journey is nearly over, their return to their everyday lives so close. Others can scarcely wait to arrive, walking faster and faster."[10] In part there is a physiopsychological explanation for changes in rhythm. Some people increase their speed because it is easier to walk in Galicia, with its cooler temperatures and hilly, verdant geography. David, the English pilgrim who found the meseta frustrating, commented on how different the horizon was in Galicia: "Our travels were dominated by mountains the height of Ben Nevis, by forests of tall eucalyptus trees, winding paths round the hills, some beautiful wild flowers and delightful little villages surrounded by green fields."[11] Except for the eucalyptus, this could be a description of an English country walk. Thus it is that much more curious that some pilgrims would slow down when certain factors favor speed.

Changes in rhythm may have nothing to do with geography but with pilgrims' inner worlds. One young Austrian I met during the last week of his journey of more than three months expressed a desire to speed up in the last ten days, feeling that the time had come "to get there." I asked him if he was preparing for the arrival in any way. He replied that he would not feel a letdown, that he was ready to go home; three months had been long enough. The questions he had brought to the Camino were resolved while walking, and the journey felt complete. Now it was time to draw the experience to a close. Instead of simply leaving the Camino and going home, he wanted to reach the geographic goal in Santiago so that he could complete the journey on the physical level. Speed was a means to the literal end of a physical journey, having already closed on the internal level. Moreover, his uncle had arrived two days previously to walk with him to Santiago, and he said, "He brings me back home, too."

It is not uncommon for relatives to meet a pilgrim in the last week or two and walk or cycle the rest of the way to Santiago. There may be ambivalence associated with these meetings. Pilgrims develop a whole world throughout the journey and incorporating "home" into

Figure 34. Eucalyptus footpath in Galicia.

the adventure and perhaps new discoveries may be difficult. Others look with great joy on the arrival of a relative or friend so that they can share the experience.

In addition, a large group of pilgrims make the Camino as a search for spiritual or life answers, and there is a sense of feeling pressured to "find" along the way. Others come to the Camino with little or no expectations and find themselves unlocking doors and making a host of unhoped-for discoveries. Reaching Santiago often comes as an unpleasant surprise as the joy of discovery comes to a sudden halt. And, of course, there are those who do search and find and those who do not search and do not find anything particularly compelling.

For those who are seeking yet not discovering, a sense of crisis may darken the latter part of the journey because the Camino has not opened them to what they hoped to receive. At the same time these same pilgrims often feel frustrated about not simply enjoying themselves. It is the paradox of the moment. I met a German woman in her thirties while at the refuge in Rabanal ten days before her expected arrival in Santiago. We were talking about ending, and she said,

> Before I began I had fantasies about what the Way would be like. I needed to get away, to deal with personal problems, and I thought that I would walk and think and all would come clear. But it hasn't, and now I'm almost in Santiago and I don't want it to end. I'm planning to go to Finisterre, and I'd like to spend time in a monastery that I've heard about from another pilgrim. In my fantasies I didn't think about my body. But I've suffered from foot problems and they distract you from the surroundings and taking in what is beautiful. It's just like life though. You can have many little things which distract you from seeing and experiencing the world fully.

In this case, rather than the bodily pain and blisters helping her to resolve the internal pain, tending the physical pain distracted her from tending her inner world. Now the proximity of the pilgrimage's end left her feeling pressed. Already she looked beyond Santiago and extending the journey, hoping to find an inner resolution that she feared would not be reached with the geographic end in Santiago.

Unresolved issues or unfulfilled expectations can drive some to escape from the Camino before reaching Santiago. The arrival anxiety was so great for one Swedish woman that on getting to within one day of the city she decided to turn around. She flew home and then returned a week later, having decided it was essential to end the journey in Santiago. While more the exception than the rule, her (literal) flight strongly demonstrates the complexity involved in the end. The title of the Spanish journalist Gregorio Morán's book, *Nunca llegaré a Santiago* (I Will Never Get to Santiago), illustrates well his disillusionment with the journey. Walking the Camino until he reached León, he found only the same superficiality and commercialism that he hoped to leave behind in Madrid and decided one should go directly to "the end of the world"—Finisterre—without passing Santiago to leave behind the "lie" of the Camino. He bought a staff, boarded a bus, and left León, frustrated by the Camino and the miserable state of the world he saw while walking.[12]

The ambivalence about arrival can occur to a pilgrim even before embarking on the adventure. George, the part-time English pilgrim, told how before he began the pilgrimage he imagined "turning back at the gate of Santiago" based on a combination of "the Buddhist Arahat ideal and a desire not to be disappointed by something to which I'd built up for so long." That original thought disappeared as he came to see the arrival in Santiago as the halfway point "in a journey whose true destination was [his] own front door."

The passage through Galicia may also be characterized by anxiety, as expressed by thirty-year-old Marina from Madrid, whose heart leaped with joy when she began to walk in Roncesvalles: "Since I entered Galicia my anxiety for getting to Santiago was so great that I realize that it was the part of the trip I enjoyed the least, in part because I had the feeling that the Gallegos treated us more like tourists than pilgrims." Her statement indicates the continuing importance of the social element in the Camino. Her sense of identity as a pilgrim is destabilized as the external reassurance she may have received in other parts of the Camino is lacking for her in Galicia. Already there is a sense of loss, that of no longer feeling special or treated well, because the pilgrim's role cultivated during the Camino through personal and social negotiation of meaning is transformed once again in the new context of Galicia and the impending end. As a side note, it is interesting to observe that Marina uses the Spanish word *viaje* (trip) to describe her journey rather than *peregrinación* (pilgrimage), desacralizing the experience and her role as pilgrim.

Some villagers do in fact think of pilgrims as tourists. In speaking with the citizens of a village that lies 18 kilometers east of Santiago in Arca, several of them told me that the best thing about the way's reanimation is regular garbage disposal. Many villagers find the pilgrims incomprehensible and the majority are thought to be tourists, especially the young Spanish pilgrims—who seem to make it because they have nothing better to do or it is cheap tourism (*turismo barato*). It is hard for these villagers to relate to the idea that some pilgrims, tired of materialist values, want to do the pilgrimage austerely, with little money. Going without money is seen locally as having *mucho morro*—a lot of nerve—as a desire to abuse the road and the goodwill of the people. Also, pilgrims before the 1993 Holy Year were, according to them, more authentic. Now, it is just *de moda,* in style, to do the Camino. Older foreigners also appear more serious, usually come from longer distances, and therefore fit more closely their image of the authentic pilgrim, the religious traveler.

The villagers were also disturbed by the sense of "ownership" of the Camino that many pilgrims expressed while walking on the back roads. Villagers, passing from field to field with their tractors, noticed that pilgrims often looked indignantly at them for somehow having disturbed their peace without realizing that these roads have been in use by them their whole lives, and they, the pilgrims, are the visitors. There appears to be a clash of values with these encounters. The villagers, as a group, did not have much sympathy for the existential worries that draw many city folk to the Camino. The villagers' understanding of the Camino and being a pilgrim is that it is a religious endeavor, which seemed to be lacking among most participants. One man, living his whole life with the Camino at his door and watching thousands of pilgrims pass it, never felt attracted to the pilgrimage as a personal activity in any way. It was just always there.

Incomprehension may be mutual. While most hospitaleros try to develop a positive relationship among the refuge, the pilgrims, and the village, one French hospitalero commented about the people of the village, "The only thing you can talk to them about are harvests and tractors." His remark was preceded by an anecdote in which the mayor commented to him that if the hospitalero gave free soup this year, next year the pilgrims would want pork chops—expressing the concern that the refuge competes with the local village economy and that most pilgrims only want cheap tourism. This hospitalero, who felt great goodwill toward pilgrims and an elevation of their status, responded, "It seems that they also have a right to eat pork chops. And for me, it would be an honor to be able to give them to the pilgrims, if I had financial backing."[13] As with the villagers of Arca with whom I spoke (one of whom was a restaurant owner), the perspective of the mayor in this village was economic. Since the existential motives are hard to identify with, the only motive that does make sense is the financial one. Why should pilgrims receive special services, when they are just tourists? some wonder. And while most pilgrims and hospitaleros want to make connections with the people of the villages, this man saw himself with a mission—the pilgrims. The local people and their lives were uninteresting to him.

In the village of Arca the Galician government made changes to accommodate the pilgrims without consulting the villagers, with some negative consequences. Some of the fountains in the area were destroyed and never repaired by the government. The village's refuge has hot water, a privilege some villagers do not have. One man commented that the Camino is good because it brings life to the village, but at the same time he has to pay for hot water so pilgrims should as well (none of the refuges in Galicia charges a fee, so they rely on pilgrims' donations). Many pilgrims who take hot running water for granted do not pause to consider this is a luxury. For the villagers, the irony was the garbage pickup: before 1993 there was none; in an effort to clean up the Camino for foreign pilgrims and the press the Galician government began the service. This type of whitewashed facade is typical of the thinking of Santiago's mayor, Xunta officials, and others involved with exploiting the Camino for short-term benefit.

This sense of contrasting values is not unique to Galicia. It also struck me forcefully when I was an hospitalera in a small village at the west end of the meseta, Hospital de Orbigo. One day I found a sturdy branch broom in the refuge (a converted parish house) and put it in the corner, thinking it looked "quaint and rustic" and added a bit of charm. Much to my surprise a woman from the village who helped with the refuge entered and asked in horror, "What is this doing in the entrance? It goes behind the door!" I realized that what I had done was, in essence, put the vacuum cleaner or mop on display at the entrance rather than in the closet with the other cleaning implements. The broom was still part of her daily experience, and I was trying to elevate it to art, because it was so far from mine.

MONTE DEL GOZO

Monte del Gozo, located approximately 6 kilometers outside Santiago, is the first point from which the towers of the cathedral are visible to pilgrims. It has become a highly contested knoll whose transformation and urbanization (desecration, for many) for economic and political reasons has caused outrage and protest. The long-awaited first vista may be an-

ticlimactic as the pilgrim struggles to discern the steeples amid the out-
lying urban sprawl of Santiago. The English confraternity's guidebook
reads: "It was once a tranquil green hill. For 1993 the Xunta de Galicia
erected a number of unsightly buildings on this historic site, including . . .
800 free refuge places for pilgrims; also an amphitheatre, campsite, roads,
car-parking and restaurants. . . . The site is crowned by an inappropriate modern monument. It is hoped that the many trees planted will have
softened the whole area in 1994."[14] The dismay at the encroachment of
what appears to be thoughtless modernity imposing its crude development on the sacred medieval Camino is common. Traveling through many
rural environments, being constantly exposed to the history of the way,
almost builds the hope in pilgrims that they may find Santiago as it was
many years ago. Instead, the city looms large.

Nonetheless, the site is still one of key transition for many. Even after making the pilgrimage numerous times, a middle-aged priest from
Zaragoza described feeling "a knot form in his throat" and his eyes brim
with tears on seeing the cathedral's spires.[15] Some pilgrims pass through
the site wanting to arrive at Santiago as fast as possible, feeling attracted
to the city as if it were a magnet. Another expressed this urgency as a
need to get the "pain of arrival" over quickly. Others pause in Monte
del Gozo, perhaps to prepare mentally or to cleanse themselves before
the final push. Lavacolla, several kilometers before the Monte on the
River Sarela, is a long-standing site of ritual cleansing.[16] A pilgrim related to me the feeling of great surprise when a companion pulled out
clothes from his backpack that he had carried since Roncesvalles and
never worn, wanting to arrive in Santiago and greet the saint in the best
way possible.

Pilgrims often plan their entrance, desiring to enter at daybreak, with
friends, or perhaps alone. Despite the best-laid plans for the physical arrival, the experience of Karen, a young Canadian college graduate,
demonstrates how the desire for a climactic ending did not materialize
until after the actual arrival and visit to the cathedral.

> You know I didn't feel very welcomed to Santiago. . . . We stayed at Monte
> del Gozo. What a horrifying place! Like barracks. We looked all over and had
> no idea what lights were Santiago. The next morning we woke up early (5:30)
> so we would walk with the sunrise. The sun never came up that day, or even
> during our stay in Santiago. We had no idea we had arrived in Santiago. We
> went up to two churches before we found the cathedral. Even then I was un-
> sure if it was it. It was nice to hug Santiago, I think I loosened some of his
> jewels. But I didn't truly feel welcomed until we met Peter in Bar Suso. Peter

Figure 35.   Looking from the west at Monte del Gozo and its 800-bed refuge, or in the words of one guide, "a number of unsightly buildings."

was so enthusiastic to see us, he gave us a huge hug, he congratulated us. Then I realized it was over. I had wanted so much a hug on my arrival to Santiago. Peter gave that.

Karen hoped that a dramatic entry from Monte del Gozo, the site of joy for many pilgrims, would help end the journey. But this did not occur until it was made real through social recognition rather than a personal coming to terms she later longed for. The final push to arrive is not always easy, as this young woman painfully expressed by her sense of disorientation ("we looked all over") and disgust with Monte del Gozo ("that horrifying place"). Instead of being a place of joy, vision, and celebration before the final entry, it became the marker of a difficult finish. The way had become dark (the sun never came up) and without direction (she was not able to find the cathedral). The physical ending was disappointment in a dark and damp place. It was the same place in which Karen found herself emotionally, despite being proud of the physical achievement. She arrived with her feet but not with her heart.

The final descent can also be a crucial point of reckoning and reflection, as expressed by Edward, an American professor of Spanish: "I take a final look at Santiago. A waning moon hangs palely over her in the western sky: the identical phase I saw coming out of Roncevaux after my first night on the road. Is it possible that only thirty days have passed. . . ? How much have I changed . . . ? . . . The heat, sweat, dust, mud, rain, fog have weathered this body, broken it down, made it supple and uncomplaining. . . . I've seen so much land, met so many people, had so many thoughts . . . that I feel overwhelmed. . . . Too much has happened. . . . [P]erhaps I'll never fully grasp it."[17]

CHAPTER 6

SANTIAGO

As the days passed and we kept coming back and back to the
Cathedral, we ceased thinking of it as arch and vault or even
as sculptured saints and began to perceive the moving forms
that belonged to it.

    —*Ruth Anderson,* Pontevedra and La Coruña

After leaving my post as hospitalera in Roncesvalles in mid-October 1994
I returned to Santiago to spend the winter. On arrival I went to the cathedral and, as I had hoped, encountered Susan, the young Swiss woman
who had begun the Camino in Roncesvalles at the beginning of the month.
With tears of joy and fatigue she recounted her journey—the failures, the
aches, the triumphs. We spent the day together and the next, too, like
old friends. And then one day she left on the train for her home in Switzerland. And I wondered, What now? Not only did she feel the loss of ending the pilgrimage, I felt the personal loss of her departure as well.

  Thus I began a daily ritual of welcomes and good-byes, an informal
hospitalera. I attended the Pilgrim's Mass and went to the Pilgrim's Office so that I could see once again a large number of the walkers and cyclists who had passed through Roncesvalles. Some of these pilgrims I
never heard of again; they ended their journeys early, or we did not manage to reconnect in Santiago. For the most part I accompanied pilgrims
as they meandered about the city, restlessly anticipating the next step,
listening to their stories from the way and their thoughts about the future. The old section of the city retains its medieval layout, small-scale
construction, and covered granite arcades. This area is the hub from
which the newer parts of the city have expanded in all directions. Of the
seven original gates of the city only one remains, but the medieval urban
space is easily distinguished from the looming sprawl of the 1950–70s
expansion.

The focal point of arriving pilgrims is the cathedral. Pilgrims enter the city at the Puerta del Camino (Door of the Way; one of the original seven doors of the walled medieval city), passing several churches on both the right and left sides and ascending one last time to "paradise" at the Puerta Santa, the Holy Door, which is only open in Holy Years. Crossing the stone pavements the pilgrims make their way finally down to the granite cathedral, suddenly reaching the expansive Plaza del Obradoiro. One pilgrim commented, "Slowly, as in a dream, I walk across the enormous expanse of stone hearing no sound except the regular tap . . . tap . . . tap of my staff on the pavement."[1] Bordering the granite plaza, which is dedicated largely to pedestrians, are the Rajoy Palace, the University Rectory, the fifteenth-century pilgrims' hospital of Ferdinand and Isabella (now a five-star hotel), and finally the stunning façade of the cathedral, which dominates the east side. "In front of its [the cathedral's] great door two staircases rise so jauntily from the level of the square that they seem to be leading to a blithe belvedere. And in the centre of the composition the twin west towers of the Cathedral soar into the blue in a sensational flourish of Baroque, crowned everywhere with figures of Saint James in pilgrim guise, speckled with green lichen and snapdragons in the crevices, and exuding a delightful air of cheerful satisfaction."[2]

In the summer, when pilgrims arrive, the plaza is vibrant with action—visiting tours, other pilgrims resting on the ground or on the stone benches around the perimeter, nuns and priests, government officials in suits, and residents of the city. Santiago Matamoros, captured in stone, his sword raised, looms large from atop the Rajoy Palace, which now houses offices of the municipal government. The four sides of the plaza represent a commingling of power: religion, politics, knowledge, and tourism.

After spending a great deal of time with pilgrims in their transitory arrivals I began to see how a goal is both a point in time and a point in space.[3] As a place, a goal may be the proverbial promised land, or Santiago, located in the far reaches of the Iberian Peninsula, constantly ahead of the pilgrim. It may be abstract or literal. As a goal, Santiago is both a physical place and an abstract idea; an imagined vessel into which pilgrims may have poured hopes and dreams. As a place and an abstraction it can be attained by movement away from the starting point and mediated by pauses or rests. Reaching the physical goal does not necessarily entail a parallel arrival of other goals—spiritual enlightenment, a decision made—as is clear from pilgrims' stories of arrival in the city. For some, the end in Santiago marks the beginning of a new journey. For others, it is a great letdown or simply a stopover point. Several of the salient issues at play in the end of the pilgrimage are reassessment of the journey's meaning, search for closure, dialogue with the past, contemplation of the future, symbolic death of the self, and preparation for the return home. Just as pilgrims must draw the physical portion to a close at some point, the arrival in Santiago marks a geographic end, even if it is not the ultimate goal in an abstract way. The pilgrim still needs to get home.

When pilgrims arrive in Santiago they frequently describe both a sense of elation at having reached the goal and completed a physically and mentally challenging journey and despondency at seeing the experience come to an end.[4] For a large group of pilgrims, the pilgrimage reaches its climax and termination on arrival at the cathedral. A great feeling of joy, exhilaration, and accomplishment are often expressed, based on the feeling that a great challenge has been overcome. Pilgrims may cry as they see the towers of the cathedral, reach its steps, or enter the impressive sanctuary. Unlike the Canadian woman who found disappointment in her arrival, one Spanish man, a former pilgrim, walking with friends in a rainy Santiago at 2:00 A.M., found an unexpected sight on the Plaza del Obradoiro and a way to illustrate the profundity of the Camino: a young Frenchman, on his knees in prayer before the cathedral. After a moment they slowly approached him, and he lifted his head. They noticed "the tears falling down his face and landing on his old scallop shell that hung at his chest and read: Camino de Santiago–PARIS." Seventy-five days earlier he had struck out, and his desire to reach the goal was so great that he continued into the city, leaving his friends at Monte del Gozo. "His goal was Santiago, but he cried for something more. He realized that after this moment he was to begin the real Camino, knowing in this moment that his vision of life had changed. He knew that he was different and, like everyone before the unknown, he was scared . . . yet happy . . . for the first time in many years."[5] For those whose journey is religiously oriented, there is often a strong sense of joy and satisfaction in reaching Monte del Gozo and the tomb of the apostle. They are places that have meaning in their faith.

A group of three German graduate students who made the Camino together described the arrival as one of great exhilaration. Sophie wrote, "On the last day we had to run in the rain—it was a downpour, we wished to arrive to celebrate the Mass [and] therefore we were running, . . . but we arrived in time! We were very happy. In the Mass we met pilgrim friends from the Netherlands, France, Spain, and so on—beloved *peregrinas* and *peregrinos*. The Mass was (for us) very essential, it was good

to be together. We were also sad because we had to part; the tie that had
bound us together was to be undone." Running, the desire to reach and
participate in the Pilgrim's Mass, the unexpected reunion with new friends
made along the road, the sense of communion—all move and strengthen
the sense of arrival. Rain is a common companion for the pilgrim in Santiago, where it is said locally that Santiago is *donde la lluvia es arte* (where
the rain is art).

In the pilgrims' testimonial book in the cathedral's office of welcome
for pilgrims the most common reactions expressed are intense joy and
triumph. Usually there is an acknowledgment of the difficulty of the physical trial in getting to Santiago, but the arrival makes it all worth the pain
and effort. Not only is it deemed well worth the pain, but a majority express a desire to repeat the experience as well as give thanks to God, Santiago, or others along the way for helping them make the journey.

A sixty-year-old Spanish man from Toledo, who cycled from Roncesvalles, described what are fairly typical rites associated with the arrival at the cathedral: "The arrival in Santiago, after the long Camino,
consists of an obligatory visit to the Saint to give him thanks, attending
the Pilgrim's Mass, and perhaps proposing, if it's possible, that He give
you the strength to do it again."

Entering the cathedral from its east entrance, up the double staircase,
one encounters what is considered the masterwork of Romanesque sculpture, the *Pórtico de la Gloria* (the Doorway of Glory) by Maestro Ma-
teo, which has been greeting pilgrims for more than eight hundred years.
In remarkable detail the stunning three-arch doorway includes repre-
sentations of the four evangelists, the twenty-four horsemen of the Apoc-
alypse holding musical instruments, and figures from the Old and New
Testament. The central column, crowned by a seated Santiago, is known
as the Tree of Jesse and bears a magnificent testament to the longevity
of the pilgrimage—a handprint worn into the marble. Placing one's right
hand in the grooves created by millions of others making the same gesture brings many pilgrims to a powerful sense of union with the past.
For Haab, the column served as another link between heaven and earth:
"[It] was the axis along which my soul, led by St. James, arose."[6] Prayers
or wishes are commonly made as pilgrims press each finger into its re-
spective groove.

Greeting the apostle through a hug and paying respect or praying to
him in the crypt below the altar are also common acts. Behind the main
altar is a large seated James, who can be reached by climbing a small
staircase that rises behind the statue. Reaching around his broad, be-

Figure 36. A Spanish pilgrim hugs the apostle in the cathedral of Santiago.

jeweled shoulders the pilgrim can finally "hug the apostle" and at the same time (with light blazing in one's eyes) look down the main nave. Exiting left and entering the crypt below, an ornate silver chest contains the supposed relics of the saint. For the religiously motivated pilgrim, these acts often produce outpourings of emotion such as tears and falling to the knees in prayer.

Many pilgrims learn of these rituals from guidebooks, from other pilgrims, or from observation on arrival. Some told me they participate in the rituals as celebration and thanks, as a way to connect with those who came before, because "it felt like the pilgrim thing to do," as a form of devotion, or to gain closure through ritualized action. One's feeling of belonging can be enhanced by the sensation of being welcomed by the saint himself, who is now like "an old friend, a fellow pilgrim"[7] to whom you give a friendly hug—the Everyman saint. This sense of familiarity helped ease the transition for one twenty-five-year-old South African man: "Santiago was there to welcome me. It's good to feel that there's someone at the end to acknowledge your arrival. Perhaps that's one of the reasons why people make the pilgrimage—there's always someone at the journey's end, if not physically, imaginary." Although the young Canadian woman did not find acknowledgment in arrival through the hug she gave to Santiago (which nearly "loosened some of his jewels"), such familiarity with the saint suggests that for many he has become a companion along the way as well as a goal. One pilgrim sent me a Christmas card that featured a photo of himself hugging the apostle, representing his gratitude, joy, and personal connection to Santiago.

Though individualized, these rites rarely occur in solitude. The cathedral is an important attraction for nonpilgrims, who also attend the Pilgrim's Mass and engage in the same ritual actions as the pilgrims themselves. A major source of curiosity is the 160-pound incense burner, the *botafumeiro,* which is raised by eight men and swung across the altar through both the north and the south transepts, spewing incense smoke at the crowds of impressed below. The botafumeiro is used at irregular intervals, but during Holy Years it is swung every day (other than on special occasions, it must be sponsored to be used). The hubbub of the crowds does not pause during Mass. And as one sits in the main nave during Mass the hands reaching from behind the saint's back in the gesture of a hug rarely cease.

Pilgrims at times describe feeling like objects of attraction and resent the pushing crowds of "tourists." For some, the noise and crowds detract from the initial entry. Betsy, the American psychologist who carved her staff, described going up the stairs of the cathedral, tears streaming down her face, when she suddenly realized that people were taking photographs of her. Her discomfort continued, as if this special moment were being invaded, on reaching the Pórtico. To her chagrin she found a long line of "tourists" and bus pilgrims waiting to touch the column, and impulsively she went to the front of the line, feeling that she deserved to be there and thinking to herself, Why do I have to deal with tourists now? During our interview, which was the day after she arrived in Santiago, she asked me if at one time the rites of the cathedral (the hand on the column and the hugging of the apostle) had been limited to people who had suffered physically to get there. "What is a pilgrim?" I asked her. Many pilgrims' sense of authenticity is often at its height in Santiago and sometimes, as one pilgrim said, "we feel better than the rest."

The power of the Pilgrim's Mass lies more in its ritual form than in its content. Offering the daily noontime Mass is one of the most important services the Church provides to contemporary foot and bicycle pilgrims, though the Mass is usually said only in Spanish. Occasionally an arriving pilgrim who is a priest will request or be invited to celebrate the Mass, and often does so in his own language. The countries of origin and mode of transportation of the newly arrived pilgrims are read aloud by the delegate of the cathedral in charge of pilgrimages to Santiago. In the mid-1990s this delegate, Don Jaime García Rodríguez, began to ask pilgrims to read the lesson or to write a prayer for the Mass, most frequently non-Spanish pilgrims, who describe this as a positive experience of closure. Pilgrims may also confess. Most frequently, according to the priest, they ask for forgiveness for things that have surfaced during the journey and have been lurking in their conscience. In an unusual but noteworthy case, a thirty-year-old American disc jockey from Houston, Texas, was baptized on arrival from Roncesvalles after fulfilling the requisite spiritual training in the United States. To confirm the pilgrim's story, the Pilgrim's Office faxed Houston. In the delay the baptism occurred, not at the Pilgrim's Mass, but later in another chapel of the cathedral.[8]

For many religious and nonreligious alike the Pilgrim's Mass serves as an essential rite of closure, a moment to contemplate what has come before and what lies ahead, to celebrate the Eucharist at the feet of the apostle, to rest at the long-awaited goal, and to languish in the joy of arrival. The Mass also serves a crucial social function: it is a common point of reunion and departure for groups of pilgrims that may have formed along the way. The Mass is personal yet communal. It is one more time to share together, an often cathartic experience and moment of closure.

Another key rite of closure common to the majority of pilgrims is the acquisition of the *Compostela* from the Pilgrim's Reception Office located in a building adjacent to the south side of the cathedral. In the later Middle Ages the *Compostela* served as a credential for the return pilgrim to acknowledge his completion of a religious or civil sanction. At the close of the Middle Ages it "served the additional purpose of separating false from genuine pilgrims."[9] Currently, the *Compostela* serves as a personal marker of completion for pilgrims and as an important mechanism of the Church to control the religious meaning of the pilgrimage through its distribution.

To receive the *Compostela* one must go to the Pilgrim's Office and demonstrate to an attendee that one is an authentic pilgrim by presenting the pilgrim's credential. The attendee in the office may ask the pilgrim if he or she is Christian, and then the pilgrim is asked to give basic information about the journey (where it was begun, the date, name, address, motive, age, and gender). The pilgrim must have traveled a minimum of 100 kilometers (62 miles) walking or 200 kilometers (120 miles) on bicycle or horse. Some pilgrims report feeling pressured into stating a spiritual motive by attendees who explain that if the motive is only tourism, sporting, or cultural, then they will have to receive a different, smaller certificate reserved for pilgrim-tourists.

The Church's attempt to control the pilgrimage's meaning becomes apparent when pilgrims are asked to give the motive for the journey. Without a religious motive, the *Compostela* is not given. This occurs in approximately 4 percent of the cases. Most pilgrims who want the *Compostela* are prepared when they arrive in the office to answer the motivation question. Many pilgrims feel trapped: they want the document, their name written in Latin, and the proof and souvenir symbolizing the pilgrimage's end, but they may not feel that the journey was motivated primarily from a religious fount. The office, though, is quite generous in how religious motivation is defined: (a) spiritual, (b) religious, (c) religious-cultural. In this way the Church claims that the motivation of 96 percent of pilgrims is religious or religious-cultural, conflating religious and spiritual without explanation. Under "spiritual" a range of motives are accepted, including personal search and education or learning.

Two anecdotes illustrate particularly well the conflicts that can arise over the competing definitions of who and what is a modern pilgrim. On one occasion in 1994 a Japanese pilgrim wrote a letter to the editor of the national daily *El País* in protest of his treatment at being denied the *Compostela*, the most disappointing moment of the pilgrimage. He explained how he, like his companions (many were nonreligious and received *Compostelas*), had walked from Roncesvalles, experienced joy in nature, suffered through inclement weather, felt spiritually moved, cried on seeing the towers of the cathedral, yet because he was not Christian, he was denied it. He wrote, "My sincerity wasn't acknowledged and my efforts didn't merit the small acknowledgment of the certificate. . . . The Church discriminates against belief, or better said, discriminates against sincerity."[10] For him, being "sincere" in his spiritual search was sufficient. Curiously, he made a public appeal about a private religious institution. For him and many other pilgrims, this experience contains all the elements of an authentic pilgrimage—temporal, spatial, and physical. He clearly developed a different sense of the authentic pilgrim during the journey, which did not correspond with the Church's.

In the second case an English pilgrim who first heard about the Camino "in 1983 during one of [his] annual visits to the fiestas of San Fermín" in Pamplona decided to make the pilgrimage from his home in England in 1992 after the tragic loss of his thirty-year-old son to cancer. Acknowledging from the outset that he went without any kind of religious

Figure 37. A Frenchman and an American woman, united by the Camino, display their laminated Compostelas.

belief (rather from a desire to get to know French and Spanish people in their daily lives), he decided to walk in winter to raise money to fight against cancer. On arrival in Santiago he went to the Pilgrim's Office with some anxiety about his reception, not having any religious motives or belief in God. The Englishman continued: "Without hesitating, he [the canon in charge] declared me an authentic pilgrim with the right to receive a compostela. I hadn't foreseen the strength and emotion of this deed and, in this moment, I cried. Then, I explained that in every step of the way I had felt the presence of my son Guy, in whose name I had made the pilgrimage. . . . I asked him to write the name of Guy on the compostela in front of me. When Don Jaime agreed to this petition, I began to cry again."[11] In this instance, despite the pilgrim openly acknowledging his lack of religious sentiment, his journey, made from a religious viewpoint as a sacrifice or in the name of another, merited the stamp of authenticity.

Despite these noteworthy examples, for many pilgrims the receipt of the *Compostela* is often anticlimactic, especially in summer when hundreds of pilgrims wait to be processed by the overburdened office staff, who are described as bureaucratic. "We were attended by a very bored student who gave us our *Compostelas* like a druggist sells aspirin," lamented Robert after completing his third pilgrimage to Santiago since 1985. Outside of the heavy summer months the pilgrim has the chance to enter in a relaxed way and converse with the less-harassed attendees. On request the cathedral's delegate, Don Jaime, whose office is in an adjacent room, is also available to pilgrims. Next door pilgrims can get the *Compostela* laminated for 100 pesetas (85 cents). Some carefully do so; others fold it up and put it in their back pockets.

TRANSITIONS WITHIN SANTIAGO

Unlike on the Camino, there are no more yellow arrows to guide the way in Santiago. Unless one is with other pilgrims one is suddenly alone at the goal, with no idea where to go. After the initial surge of arrival and participation in the customary rites, pilgrims begin to make the transition away from the Camino. Ellen Feinberg commented on this moment in 1982: "Unlike the bus excursion pilgrims, [the foot and cycle pilgrims] may feel alienated and isolated, a single pilgrim (or several), lost in the crowd of fervent worshippers. . . . [T]here will be no specific rites of reaggregation when they return home. . . . This lack of closure is what we and other 'foot' pilgrims found so dissatisfying when we reached Santiago: it didn't feel as if this could be the 'end.'"[12] This time can be a moment of truth and a point of reckoning. After sitting down for the first time in Santiago after arriving, sixty-five-year-old Lee movingly wrote, "I feel a slight tinge of fear. I begin to perceive internal motions that I don't recognize. . . . I can't figure out what's happening. . . . [I]t seems that a weighty sadness descends and muffles my spirit. . . . Today, I will go no farther. . . . The pain is past, the thrills are over, the magic is finished."[13] The French pilgrim who cried on his knees before the cathedral in the early hours of the morning also expressed fear of the road home.

Some pilgrims have little time to adjust and must immediately get their train or bus ticket home. The questions What next? and Why am I here? often loom large after the initial semistructured rites of arrival are over. Pilgrims generally spend between an hour and four days, usually one day, in Santiago before turning around and beginning the voyage home. During this time the transition to daily life begins through losing the constant rhythm of daily movement, the feeling of becoming a tourist in the city, the anticipation of the return to a home and a life whose future is uncertain, and saying good-byes. A Spanish priest described the brusque turnaround as "like being kicked out of Eden."

My sister met me in Santiago, and we spent the next week in a rented car traveling the Galician coast. I was there, but I wasn't. It was good to be with her, but I also wanted to be alone to reflect on what had happened. She was too close to what I was returning to, and I could not talk to her about what was most personal—as I might be able to do with someone from the pilgrimage, someone anonymous. Things about my life that were stable and secure before I left seemed to have lost a bit of their foundation. I had called my mom from one point on the journey (more than halfway), and she asked how I was. I felt bad, in a way, that instead of being homesick I was having the time of my life: I had discovered a circular room within myself that had many unopened, opened, and slightly ajar doors, each with its own beckoning call of sensations and possibilities. When I entered the cathedral after finishing the pilgrimage, I was startled by how my eyes, now trained in medieval art and architecture, could perceive differently since my first visit to the city in 1992. I felt this new perception internally as well. There was a deep hurt in my stomach and a gloom about some parts of my future that I could not share with my sister. I was restless, and I was concerned about going back for fear of what might happen, for fear of what I might do with my new way of feeling and seeing the world.

Those pilgrims who spend one to three days in Santiago experience a range of emotions. Describing the arrival in Santiago as *la gran depresión del Camino* (the great depression of the Camino), a woman in her thirties told me that it was the combination of feeling sad at finishing, not feeling welcome in the Pilgrim's Office, and finding Santiago surprisingly cold. Rather than feel special when they arrive, pilgrims describe feeling like "one of many." They are surprised that the pilgrim's refuge is barely operating and disappointed with the cathedral's commercialization of the pilgrimage. A few people even imagined that there would be greeters at the city's gate to welcome them with cheers. The people of Santiago are quite accustomed to pilgrims. As one local-turned-pilgrim told me, "As a girl growing up I thought they were all crazy, but then when I made it myself I began to see pilgrims with new eyes and to realize how cold the reception is here in Santiago." Perhaps the cold reception by those who live in Santiago relates to disinterest in the everyday. Pilgrims are just another common feature of the landscape.

New sets of emotion arise as pilgrims begin to reflect on what they have seen, felt, and experienced on arrival in Santiago. Wim said, "I arrived in Santiago and I spent the morning in the Cathedral. It was the end of my journey and I had problems realizing and accepting that. I sat there and let all kinds of memories pass by, the good and bad things, my walking problems in the first weeks after I left home, the places and the people I met, and I finally I sat there crying as a way to try and cope with it." Wim had been walking for four months from his Dutch homeland. Memories seemed to play across his mind as if they were pictures on a movie screen. He relived the movements bodily, spatially, and temporally. The flood of memories turned into a flood of tears as the final pause in movement allows the release of all the pent-up emotions and feelings long directed toward a goal, a place (physical and inner). This spilling over of emotion is common. It is as if the experiences have been accumulating without release and finally the floodgate is opened. Pilgrims may not find themselves mentally ready for this release and may have trouble finding an outlet for the stored sentiments or letting go of the experience. Extremes in behavior are common, such as drinking, eating, talking, and even continuing to move. While these are extreme reactions, the end in Santiago often has destabilizing effects that, at the same time, are healing. The physiological factor in the sense of letdown—fatigue, tears, and restlessness—must also be taken into account. After growing accustomed to walking or cycling for five to eight hours a day the sudden change produces a shock to the body now inhibited from maintaining its daily rhythm.

The structure of life enjoyed and lived on the Camino is also gone, leading to further destabilization. Even the Pilgrim's Mass, which is generally positive as a rite of closure, can be bittersweet. A twenty-five-year-old Dutch woman who had walked from the Netherlands with her boyfriend put it like this: "At first it was good to see everyone in the cathedral but now it's too much, too overwhelming, with all the people around. It was a strange moment in the cathedral. Those pilgrims who were ahead on the Camino knew that those behind were coming and today would be the big day of the reunion. All were sitting in the Mass and there were big hugs of welcome but awkwardness—What now? Also, the knowledge we share of each other and the experiences you've had or known about. It's all awkward."

The young woman shared these thoughts with me after several days in the city. She realized that many of the elements enjoyed on the Camino as liminal are lost in the return to structure represented by the Mass and the cessation of movement. She added later, "On the Camino we were all the same, but now we are all different. When you went to refuges it was easy—you all had something in common but now it's changed—the need to make appointments to see one another. Everyone's oriented toward going home." Roles that are clear on the Camino no longer fit the new circumstances encountered in Santiago. She mentioned several times how it was all "different" and "awkward." What before was organic and natural is somehow changed by the reorientation toward a new goal—making appointments brings people back to their daily planners and work life. The common goal that united the group, the new community, feels broken as each seeks a new end. Again the metaphor of the hourglass seems appropriate. In Santiago pilgrims are at the point of intensification found before the grains fly out into the undirected open space on the other side of the perpetual goal.[14]

This reorientation contrasts with the disorientation that may provoke the fear that what occurs in the Camino only lives within that space. Guy, the French psychologist who found the Camino to be a different time and space, remarked on arrival, "Disappointment is what I felt upon our reaching Santiago. Everyone had to return home to the intimate and the familiar, to work again. One went by train, another by bus. . . . We were like adolescents in separation. . . . [T]he speed, the hurry in our common departure and the sudden break as if now, in Santiago, the pre-Camino links were more important. It was as if our common walking story wasn't very real anymore." Guy expressed a profound sense of rupture, dissolution, and loss as the intimacy of the Camino suddenly gives way to the preoccupations of the end and return to the mundane. In the departures pilgrims often express the desire to maintain connections with one another, but with the abrupt change to the "real world" this may not seem possible. Feinberg also described the feeling of losing one's "new community": "There was no reformulation, no working through, no 'reaggregation' after the separation of the prolonged rite of passage, our physical passage through a foreign landscape, our social passage into the identity of pilgrim."[15] The common walking story begins to cross the threshold into memory.

One of the factors contributing to the sense of change is that during the transition in Santiago pilgrims generally begin to drop their role as pilgrims and become tourists. By taking off the backpack and putting down the staff, walking into the streets of Santiago one is no longer a pilgrim as on the road. Although pilgrims may remove the signs of their pilgrim's status and buy new clothes, now well-tanned, fit, and in moments radiant with accomplishment or appearing confused and disoriented, it is fairly easy to identify those in transition. Andrew, who had the "time of his life" while walking, describes his three-day stay in Santiago:

> I cried when I arrived to Santiago at the Pilgrim's Mass, watched in awe the botafumeiro, prayed at the grave of the saint, visited this marvelous city, got my diploma in Latin [the *Compostela*] and drank to excess with other pilgrims in the bodegas. I walked for three days in the city, visited every corner, bought a seventeenth-century painting of Santiago Matamoros, as well as tons of books and souvenirs (with my credit card). I was a perfect, dumb, obnoxious tourist who could brag about his "exploit." I was very sad to leave as I was closing a page of my life and would have paid a fortune for the privilege to walk back home instead of flying a silly, smelly, and noisy plane full of "perfect, dumb, obnoxious tourists." I was conscious of starting a new pilgrimage, the "Camino of Life," but this one is a lot more difficult for me. To start with, the "where I go" question is not so easy and knowing that it is the "Eternal Jerusalem" is not a great help for the moment.

In becoming tourists in Santiago pilgrims refer to engaging in activities involving consumption: purchasing souvenirs, visiting monuments, staying in hostels, drinking, and eating. On the purchase of souvenirs, a Brazilian pilgrim explained that he bought a small statue of Santiago to represent and remember all of the effort he had made in the Camino. He added that he needed an object, an amulet "to remember the thirty days I suffered."

Interactions among pilgrims to process the events, to debate the significance of the journey, to share fears, and to discuss the future are an important part of the transition in Santiago. Pilgrims congregate in the many bars and cafés in Santiago to converse in a way that is familiar— seated, facing one another, open. Pilgrims talk and listen. Those having just arrived and possibly feeling disoriented or elated mingle with those who have already spent some time in the city. There is a constant flow and exchange of figures coming and going. Others write. Jean-François wrote eighty-seven postcards. Some of his cards simply read, I DID IT! Occasionally he interjects his comments into the conversations of companions from the road. The French doctor and the German teacher embrace, separated in the last week. Smiles of reunion often seem to thinly cover preoccupations with uncertain futures. A restlessness with immobility and the loss of the daily structure and the direction of the yellow arrows are present in conversations. It is time to move on to the next stage. But to what? What next? How do you say good-bye to a man whose presence made your ovaries pitch and turn one night simply by being in the next bed?[16] It is a city oversaturated with experience; and the end must be negotiated through these informal acts.

One exception to the distant reception in Santiago is found at the Bar Suso, a common congregation point for arriving pilgrims. Suso, the seventy-six-year-old proprietor and native Santiagan whose spritely manner belies his age, has created a special niche for himself through his relationship to pilgrims and the pilgrimage. Each time pilgrims arrive at the bar he joyfully greets them, asks them from what country they hail, and then runs off to his back room. He then produces a different book of pilgrims for each country, complete with letters, photos, postcards, and drawings from pilgrims. Full of stories and energy, he helps pilgrims feel that they have a place in Santiago and renews the sense that their journeys are special.

Andrew, the Belgian, commented that he enjoyed bragging about his "exploit," revealing a hubris that pilgrims acquire and often recognize themselves. After making the pilgrimage three times on bicycle since 1985, Robert remarked, "Many pilgrims (like me the first time) reach Santiago in the quite arrogant conviction that they are now, after having crossed Spain as a pilgrim, something special and—at least a little bit—better than the others." Others believe that because of the pilgrims' physical efforts and "sacrifices" they deserve to be treated better than other travelers.

In fact, it is quite a common reaction to reject the push of the crowds who fill the cathedral. This rejection stems not only from the abrupt change from the solitude of the Camino to the bustle of the city but also from the feeling of superiority fostered by notions of the authentic pilgrim. An irony of the contemporary pilgrimage is how the ideal of the authentic pilgrim—humble, patient, grateful, accepting, sharing, uncomplaining, simple—is inverted and used to demand more and better. A Spanish Catholic woman arrogantly asked on arrival, "Why are we pilgrims great? . . . For the simple reason that one needs a great deal of humility to walk thirty days and arrive a new person in Santiago and to be able to get down on your knees before the apostle and . . . in the crypt." This kind of self-importance is extreme but reflects the pride that some acquire through walking and cycling a long distance over a long time.

The sense of difference is fostered in Santiago. In addition to continuing its original (fifteenth-century) purpose of sheltering pilgrims on their arrival, the Hostal de los Reyes Católicos has maintained a curious tradition for at least fifteen years. The five-star hotel gives the first ten pilgrims at each serving (there are three a day) who present a copy of their *Compostela* a free meal in a small staff dining room accessed through the hotel's underground parking lot. A pilgrim can in theory receive three free meals a day for three days. Even if pilgrims do not need the free meals for financial reasons, they often take advantage of the offer for its novelty, the experience, or out of a sense of privilege. The doorman of the hotel told me that guests—who pay up to $250 a night—often join the others for their free pilgrim's meal. Travel guides and some pilgrims' stories falsely build up the hopes of pilgrims by leading them to believe that the hotel will serve them free meals in the main dining room.

Instead of being grateful to the hotel for maintaining this novel custom and generously offering a simple, free meal to many people who can afford to eat elsewhere, some pilgrims complain—about the quality of the food, the meagerness of the portion, and the location of the dining room. In Santiago I met a well-to-do, retired Dutch pilgrim and his wife who walked to Santiago in 1996. The husband had cancer and did not believe he would make it. Both were radiant with joy and accomplishment, grateful for having made the long journey, eager to go home and share the Camino with friends and family, proud of their achievements, and pleased to meet again a fellow pilgrim, my companion. It was a remarkable journey. At one point the conversation suddenly turned to the hotel and the free meals. To my surprise, the Dutch pilgrim unexpectedly declared, "I'm a pilgrim, not a dog. In the hole, is where they wanted to put us." He was referring to the hotel's dining room for pilgrims, which was apparently dirty and the free meal unsatisfactory. Instead of accepting the humble meal or offering to donate money to the hotel to improve the dining room, they walked out, indignant, arguing that medieval pilgrims were not given such shabby service.

Unlike this Dutch pilgrim, another pilgrim, a cyclist from England, found her own healing and closure in the disappointing dining room. She rejected most of the meal except for the bread and wine, in symbolic recognition of the basics of communion. She wrote

> It seemed the loneliest, most derelict moment of the entire journey. I tried the bean stew and it tasted repulsive, the chicken was exactly as it looked; even the apple was flaccid and flavourless. It was strange that in a country where the food was so good and inexpensive, the first uneatable meal I was offered was the one that should have been a celebration. It left just the bread and the wine, and it was as I broke the roll in half that I suddenly knew that this was the moment that had brought the completion of the pilgrimage. Like the unnamed disciples on the road to Emmaus, I too had needed to encounter the reality of the Risen Christ. He had been there in every meeting I had along the way, and perhaps I had known this in a remote corner of my

mind. But to realise it fully had required this ordinary, everyday action in which the symbol could suddenly break free and be recognised for what it was. "They recognised Him in the breaking of the bread." Of course.[17]

A religious interpretation of the moment, the New Testament passage Luke 24:35, helps this woman to put into context not only the meal but also the whole journey.

Despite the sorrow that I felt for the Dutchman with advanced cancer, I saw in his attitude a rejection of the values held by many pilgrims whether religious or not. The Camino gave him an opportunity to apply his accumulated knowledge and new sensibility, yet his interpretation of the moment was to reject the gift as inadequate rather than recognize it as such. The cyclist's interpretation was religious: she saw in the bread and wine a holy communion. For another with a nonreligious perspective, that a private institution voluntarily gives away hundreds of meals without asking for thanks is a small miracle in itself and worthy of appreciation. Reaching the end is often bittersweet.

The city is a point of supersaturation. Pilgrims begin to shed their months of experience, leaving a wake of uncertainty, joy, pain, and discovery. Eventually the break is made and the pilgrim puts away the scallop shell, packs the bag and staff, and makes the turn that ends the physical journey and returns home. The linear journey becomes a circuit.

CHAPTER 7

TO THE END OF THE EARTH

The waves echo behind me. Patience—Faith—Openess,
is what the sea has to teach. Simplicity—Solitude—
Intermittency . . . But there are other beaches to explore.
There are more shells to find. This is only a beginning.
    —*Ann Morrow Lindbergh,* Gift From the Sea

The Camino officially ends in Santiago.[1] But Santiago is not the only physical or mental goal for many pilgrims. While the majority finish in Santiago and spend a day seeing the city before going home, others feel a need to continue beyond Santiago. Edward, an American scholar, wrote, "I left that city of stone to follow the path toward the sea and the setting sun at the end of the world. . . . Now my body seemed to walk itself, the road walking my body. . . . My old body has died; in many ways I have also died to my old self. . . . My life, my work, my family will never be quite the same."[2] The continuation of the pilgrimage beyond Santiago today is focused on the coastal zone to the west, on Finisterre, the medieval end of the earth. Once in Santiago there are very few pilgrims who want to visit other sacred sites connected with the presence of Saint James in Galicia. Those few who are fascinated by the legends associated with the translation of Saint James's body usually will continue to three or four locations other than Finisterre: Noya, Padrón, Pico Sacro, and Muxía. Some claim that the word *Noya* comes from Noah and that the town could be the site of the ark's mythical landing. The boat that carried Saint James and his two disciples from Jerusalem, according to legend, moored in Padrón. Today the mooring stone—the *pedrón,* or big rock, as it is called locally, gives the town its name—is kept below the altar of the Santiago Apostle parish church and shown on request. According to legend, on the way to present-day Compostela Saint

James's disciples passed what came to be known as Pico Sacro (Sacred Peak), named for the miraculous conversion of the pagan queen Lupa who tried to kill the disciples with wild bulls, which were tamed by Saint James's holy presence. These bulls are later seen in iconography hitched with a yoke carrying the body of Saint James in a cart the rest of the way to Compostela.

Another site that has an equally rich link to the historical pilgrimages, but is not a common destination for contemporary pilgrims, is the sanctuary of La Virgen de la Barca (the Virgin of the Boat) in Muxía, north of Finisterre. Not only was a pilgrim's hospital established there in the fifteenth century, but a well-known miracle relates the appearance of the Virgin Mary to Saint James during his original evangelization of the peninsula: carrying the infant Jesus in the stone boat, manned by two angels, her presence instantly calmed the raging sea.[3]

FINISTERRE AS END

Finisterre, a small fishing village located about 100 kilometers west of Santiago, is the dramatic geographic end that Santiago is not. It is another contested space on the Camino that is open to wide interpretation from various fronts. The Church (in this case, the Pilgrim's Office) states that Finisterre is not the end of the Camino and discourages pilgrims from continuing there, claiming it to be a site of esoteric practices detrimental to the pilgrimage. The Galician government encourages the movement west, declaring Finisterre one of the various tourist destinations on the Galician coast. The city seal of Finisterre reads "Fin da Ruta Xacobea" (End of the Jacobean Route).[4] In 1997 the Ruta Xacobea de Fisterra was officially institutionalized with a well-publicized three-day group pilgrimage/walk from Santiago to Finisterre and then Muxía. On finishing, the participants were awarded a certificate, the *Fisterrana,* by the mayor's office in conjunction with Neria, an association of municipalities of the northwest coast of Galicia whose aim is to develop and promote the region. The certificate is awarded to pilgrims who present their *Compostela* in the town hall; it accredits one's arrival at "the end of the Camino."

Pilgrims often learn about Finisterre from other pilgrims during the journey or from oral or written accounts before leaving home. Those who know about Finisterre frequently plan to continue there as a second physical goal either walking or going by bus. It is difficult to gauge the num-

ber of pilgrims who continue west, but of those who arrive in Santiago
approximately 10 percent continue. Most (in proportion to the total number of pilgrims) are foreigners. The majority go by bus, often claiming a
desire to walk or cycle but feeling rushed by time and the need to return.
Most make a one-day trip, but some spend the night in a hostal or ask
in the town hall for shelter. Pilgrims are directed to the village's gymna-
sium as there is no refuge (a plan in constant debate) in Finisterre. The
way marking does continue for those who wish to make the overland
route, and the route is described as being much more rugged than other
parts of the Camino. Maps are necessary. Even in the summer it is unlikely that pilgrims will encounter many others on the overland trek,
though they may hear that one or two have passed from villagers, whose
first language is Gallego. From Santiago to Finisterre the rural dominates
and pilgrimage infrastructure is scarce. Curiously, the way marks on this
route are often two-way, indicating that once the end is reached the journey back home or back to Santiago is inevitable.

As a way of understanding the meanings that Finisterre has for pilgrims, I quote the comments of a German student in his twenties at length
as they incorporate a number of the elements that draw pilgrims to this
alternative end point. The student alternately refers to the village as Finisterre (Spanish) and Fisterra (Gallego).

> Together [with his German companion and two Belgians] we reached Finis-
> terre, but . . . by bus. There was no possibility for us to find the "Camino"
> [in Santiago] and we didn't get good maps so we took the bus. Crazy. After
> 26 days [walking]: in a machine, in a bus. When we reached the village we
> first ordered beer. It is interesting that we drank and ate very much in the last
> two weeks. Seeing the Atlantic was great. We climbed down to the shore,
> smelled the air, felt refreshed by the water. We sensed: Yes! Now we are near
> the end of the pilgrimage. Santiago was, as I had feared, a disappointment,
> as a big city. Many tourists . . . or bus pilgrims. It was a horror. The Belgians
> felt as upset as we did in Santiago, and it was a great relief to them that we
> "invited" them to Fisterra. Both were interested in the old European history,
> so we filled them with enthusiasm while we described the Celtic roots of the
> Camino and Fisterra.
>
> We had our own Celtic rites. We waited for the sunset, made a fire, burned
> our clothes and at last ran into the ocean at midnight. At first Peter and I be-
> gan to sing German medieval music with a flute and tambourine and then,
> suddenly, the Belgians took the tambourine and sang old folk songs, too. Our
> faces were filled with joy the whole night. After a dinner of meat, cheese, bread
> and wine we fell asleep very satisfied with dawn's light breaking. That was
> the real end of our journey, our pilgrimage. . . . We spent another starlit night
> accompanied by a noisy and wild sea. The last morning the sky was gray and
> we felt that it was time to return.

Figure 38.   Finisterre, "where all drops off until there is nothing more."

Themes of the disillusionment with Santiago, the significance of Finisterre's geographic placement, the contact with a physical end, the personalized rites of ending and purification, the relationship to the past, and the sense of closure are all elements commonly found to motivate and inspire pilgrims' journeys to Finisterre.

GEOGRAPHIC END
AND SYMBOLIC DEATH AND RESURRECTION

As do other dramatic geographic points, usually located on extreme west coasts, Finisterre attracts Europeans. It is the end of the end. One can go no farther. This part of the coast, the site of many sunken vessels and deadly storms, is also called Costa da Morte (Coast of the Dead). The pilgrim arrives at Finisterre, walks the final kilometers up to the lighthouse, and is finally confronted with "miles and miles of water," "where all drops off until there is nothing more." "It's a wonderful feeling to stand out on the edge," "with no one around," "where the air is full of life and energy."[5] As one Belgian pilgrim wrote, "I was filled with a great sense of Le morte no existe—Death does not exist. Everything is alive."[6] The combination of wind, endless water, a limitless horizon, sea spray, pounding waves, and another vital element, the setting sun, all lead many pilgrims to see Finisterre as a point of symbolic death and rebirth or destruction and resurrection. Edward, an American professor, states, "I walked across the final stretch of land where the coast juts into the Atlantic: Finisterre, end of the earth, known for centuries as the dark waters, mansion of the dead who await the resurrection of the body."[7]

In the Camino the pilgrim follows his long shadow in the morning, crosses over it at midday, and then loses it in the afternoon, replacing it with the blazing setting sun as the goal's marker. Finally, confrontation with the ultimate goal is felt where the sun both rises and sets over water, sinking and burning into the sea. Pilgrims claim that one must experience and feel the end through the geography by coming to this extreme point before one can be reborn in one's everyday life (spiritually or personally). This interpretation is offered by both religious and nonreligious pilgrims. Or, alternatively, on contemplating the immensity of the sea another concludes that the "true Ways" never end, they simply continue into the infinity of the ocean. According to this view the celestial dimension is also central to the union of sea and sky as represented by the Milky Way (Camino de las Estrellas), which is believed to run parallel to the Camino and leads to the end of the earth.

PURIFICATION

Consistent with the idea that people must symbolically die or cleanse themselves before passing from the Camino to daily life, pilgrims often engage in rites of purification. The German student quoted above speaks of "Celtic" rites, relating to a vague notion of the sun cult (*Ara Solis,* believed to have existed in Finisterre), the building of a fire, the burning of clothes, and the midnight bath in the ocean. The burning of objects—boots, socks, and walking sticks—is common. I asked one Catalan cyclist why he chose his socks, and he replied that he had two pairs and would not need the other. Besides the practical choice, the symbolic dirtiness of the past was burned away for him.

The same objects may also simply be thrown into the ocean. A Belgian man in his late forties described taking his staff to a pier in the village and flinging it as far as he could. Much to his surprise, when he returned two hours later he saw it floating back in. He reflected with me later in Santiago, "I can't explain exactly what the symbolic meaning was that it carried. It was really just a piece of wood, but I decided not to retrieve it, despite the meaning it and its return had." He had launched it out to sea to mark the end and to let go of the experience, yet it came back.

Another common form of purification or rebirth is stripping, bathing, and washing one's clothes in the frigid Atlantic waters, drying in the sun, and thereby cleansing the body. Edward recounts, "Peeling off my wet clothes, I ran into the surf. After the shock of the first cold, the sea felt warmer than the air. I dove under a wave, . . . the water slipping along my arms, sides and legs, stinging my pores, soothing my limbs. I rolled over on my back, floating, the drizzle caressing my face, the swells rocking me back and forth as I looked up at the sky. . . . And I walked out of the water hearing the wind and crashing waves, the mighty rhythm of the world."[8]

RELATIONSHIP TO THE PAST

One of the motives for continuing to Finisterre is its believed links to the Celtic past. I have noticed, especially among northern Europeans, the common goal of connecting to one's pre-Christian roots. There is evidence of Celtic occupation throughout Galicia, including Finisterre. Pilgrims oriented toward this search for Celtic influences imagine what would have appealed to Celts in the past and drawn them to this jut of rock: the position of the sun, the proximity to water. Imagining early pilgrims or Celts inspired one pilgrim to remark in the 1995 pilgrim's testimonial book in the town hall of Finisterre, "I arrived yesterday in time to watch the sun falling into the sea and to marvel at the whole system of things as the ancient Celts must have when they too undertook this road along the Milky Way (which actually does go over this place)." Linking of heaven and earth via the ocean leads this pilgrim to envision a Celtic past living in harmony with nature and being part of a holistic system. This nostalgic view of the past as harmonious parallels a vision of the medieval pilgrimage as less complicated and more authentic which is found commonly among pilgrims seeking to re-create the footsteps of their medieval predecessors.

The internal journey that did not find its end in Santiago may be resolved at Finisterre. Haab suggests that the experience of going to Finisterre is "a consolidation of what has gone before."[9] It may give pilgrims additional time to reflect on the pilgrimage's conclusion and the return home. It may also be a way to keep walking, a way to keep searching and possibly avoid resolution, a way to smooth a potentially difficult transition, a way to end a pilgrimage of initiation through confrontation with the natural elements. Going to Finisterre has many meanings produced socially and individually, based on oral traditions passed on among pilgrims. In the case of the German friends and their Belgian companions, the culmination of experiences and turn in the weather helped them to turn around and continue their journeys home. At this point those who have ventured from Santiago usually return there to begin the journey home.

CHAPTER 8

GOING HOME

The road goes ever on and on, Down from the door where it began, Now far ahead the road has gone And I must follow If I can.
Pursuing it with weary feet, Until it meets Some larger way, where many paths and errands meet, And wither then? I cannot say.

—*Tolkien,* Lord of the Rings, Part 1

I am frequently asked, What made you focus on the return, or the post-pilgrimage? The answer is simple: friendship, curiosity, and loneliness. When I was living in Santiago I met pilgrims on a daily basis. I associated with them and their friends in bars and cafés and heard both their innermost secrets and their favorite public stories, stories of triumph in the meseta, anguish on the Cebreiro mountain, curious synchronous encounters, and ambivalence about the future. From listening to the laughter and the tears it was clear that for most the Camino reached a geographic end in Santiago, but there were too many other things—emotion, pain, growth, hope, doubt—that would not come to a halt once the pilgrim took off the scallop shell. After sharing the arrival with countless pilgrims, watching them go through various stages of transition, and then, often painfully, saying good-bye to many who became my friends, it became crucial to understand what was next. From my own return I knew that the next months could be tumultuous. How did other people sort out the experiences after they turned around and went home?

Oddly, most narratives, both academic and personal, end when the goal is reached: the apostle is hugged, the *Compostela* is duly granted, and the pilgrim bids the Camino farewell and goes home. Although most first-person pilgrimage accounts are written after the journey is completed, the authors generally reveal only a glimpse into how the Camino continues to exist within their own lives. The experience is treated like a photo, a frozen memory; as if there were no flow between the pil-

grimage itself and daily life. As pilgrims enter more deeply into the
Camino it appears to leave an indelible mark, yet it is hard to discern
the nature of this mark. George's postreturn poem eloquently points the
direction:

> For all that they follow the Milky Way,
> Pilgrims aren't homeless—
> For it's the leaving home
> And the coming back
> Which give shape and meaning to the journey.

Through reflection, the journey is given shape and meaning in the return home.

THE RETURN IN ANTHROPOLOGICAL PERSPECTIVE

Despite the fact that pilgrimage is almost always a round-trip, as Ann
Gold writes in her pathbreaking anthropological study of pilgrims' daily
lives in a Rajasthani Hindu village, the focus of most studies of the phenomenon is the "journey's destination—the riverbank, the temple town,
the lake, or mountain shrine with little attention to its closure or return
lap. The student of pilgrimage, then, interviews and observes pilgrims as
pilgrims in the context of their journey's goal, but not of its end."[1]

   In the introduction to a collection of articles on modern pilgrimage
E. Alan Morinis states, "The return to the everyday is a component of
almost every pilgrimage. While the sacred place is the source of power
and salvation, it is at home once again that the effects of power are incorporated into life and what salvation is gained is confirmed. The return journey and the reincorporation of the pilgrim into social life are
the test of the pilgrimage. Has there been change? Will it last?"[2] Morinis implies that an inherent outcome of the religious journey is change,
which reaches its greatest point of confirmation in the home context.
Change and transformation are assumed, yet how these occur or how
home serves to cement what has transpired is not clear. He asks about
the endurance of the effects of pilgrimage. Many pilgrimages (and other
rituals, for that matter) are made and repeated precisely to renew the
teachings or faith of practitioners, not to produce change in oneself or
society. In the case of the Camino, the "source of power" is not the sacred place (Santiago) per se but how the pilgrim relates to the landscapes
of the Camino and the meanings that emerge as a result of this process.
Radical change is not as vital as is understanding the various experiences

and meanings of common participation in an event that often leads one ultimately back to home and to the self with a "difference."[3]

The questions need to be reformulated. They should not focus on the presence or absence of change (a vague concept that fixes meaning to time and place and assumes that this should be a goal) but on how the pilgrimage endures, if it does, and how the experiences are interwoven into daily life, influencing future actions and ways of being. Furthermore, the question, On what level (personal, spiritual, creative, physical, etc.) does change occur (if at all)? needs to be addressed. One does not simply return a "new person," as if the old were somehow erased. What has been acquired through the pilgrimage needs to be renegotiated into daily life. Sometimes the experience of the pilgrimage results in changes in occupational or marital status, the pursuit of creative personal projects, the discovery of prayer, an emphasis on maintaining friendships or an identity developed in the way, or an enduring memory such as a lovely walk taken in Spain.[4]

Again, the end of the journey and the goal of the pilgrim should not be confused. They may coincide, but often they do not, at least in the case of Santiago. Within a linear worldview journey's end is usually equated with the goal, effectively negating the return. What happens when the goal is the way and not the shrine and the end comes while making the journey or after the goal is reached or once the pilgrim returns home?

THE RETURN

Despite the stated interest in experiencing the medieval pilgrimage, it rarely occurs to contemporary pilgrims to consider returning home in the same manner, as did their historical compatriots. When I asked pilgrims, Why not return the same way you came? most claimed that time constraints would impede such a journey or that the Camino is only one-way. Very few pilgrims return home this way, and most of those who do are non-Spanish. One Englishwoman was writing a guidebook when our paths crossed going in opposite directions. Another pilgrim had planted the possibility of the round-trip before setting off from his home in Lyon, France. When he reached Santiago he did not feel ready to return home, so he turned around and walked back. Several pilgrims reported seeing an Italian man who went in reverse, praying the Rosary, without food or money. He was labeled "strange" and "crazy" by those who passed by him.

The vast majority of pilgrims elect to return home by train, car, or bus and very often regret the speed with which they are carried back to their

normal daily lives. Some pilgrims extend the journey a few days, to ease
the transition, but in general pilgrims are back home within twenty-four
hours of deciding to leave Santiago. One of the common experiences that
walkers report is a sense of shock and even vertigo at the speed of motorized transit. Moreover, as the pilgrim passes over the same lands
through which travel has taken place day by day, mile after mile, and re-
alizes that the same distance can be covered in twelve hours by car, for
example, a sense of letdown may permeate the moment. The achievement is somehow slighted and put in perspective: was this just a dream?

In the return home pilgrims may also experience a finality to the journey's end not felt in Santiago. A flood of memories can wash over the
pilgrim, whose relationship to the landscape is no longer characterized
by active participation but instead passive observation. Esteban, a thirty-
three-year-old writer from Madrid, explains,

> The Camino's sentimental ending came with a Castilian sunset, riding in the
> car that took me back to Madrid, when the N-VI [where the national high-
> way turns south] definitively left behind an Astorga growing smaller in the
> rearview mirror. Once again I felt how fast distance is covered in a car. No
> longer did I comment to the driver "Here this happened" or "Around this
> curve I stopped to do some other thing." . . . This was where I no longer had
> the chance to run into a pilgrim, shout from the window . . . and wave my
> hand in a sign of encouragement. The only thing I did was to gaze at the set-
> ting sun, daydreaming, comfortably planted in my seat and listening to the
> song "I Will not Go Tomorrow" by Antonio Vega.

When Esteban leaves the space of the Camino, which he knew with all
his senses, the end of the journey comes into focus. Places are no longer
marked by experiences; hardship is replaced by comfort; and the sunset,
now just a vision in the rearview mirror, no longer marks the daily goal.
Moreover, Astorga grows smaller, in the same way that the experience
recedes. It is clear that with the setting sun, the speed of the car, the change
in direction, and the music's theme, part of Esteban's identity as pilgrim
slips away as if he were shedding a cloak.

The return by transit reintroduces the pilgrim immediately to many
of the qualities of life left behind with the decision to make the Camino—
speed, noise, the separation of the individual from the natural world—
and the sudden reacquaintance with them puts the pilgrim immediately
back into the quotidian. An English couple wrote for the confraternity's
bulletin, "We knew we were going to have problems before we arrived
in Santiago, but it found expression on the plane home. Our eyes met,
and simultaneously we exclaimed, 'I don't want to go home!' While re-

building our bikes in the terminal at Heathrow we took the next step. 'Let's get on the bikes and ride home.'"[5] Which is just what they did, extending the journey five more days. The return forms an important part of finalizing and adding some closure to the experience, but for many others the return is over and home is reached more quickly than anticipated.

THE HOMECOMER

In their study of pilgrimage in world religions Simon Coleman and John Elsner claim that "the extent to which pilgrimage involves so strong a sense of transformation or indeed an explicit confrontation with the new, either for the traveller or for those to whom he or she returns, is obviously subject to particular circumstances. Pilgrims who travel in a group of like-minded companions may not need to deal directly with the challenge of the exotic."[6] The comment was made in reference to the fifteenth-century religious traveler Felix Fabri, who on his return from the Holy Land to his native Ulm, Germany, expresses a sense of being transformed. His detailed account of the return is rare not only for accounts of today but also for those of his period. Writing six years hence, he calls Ulm "the place from which my wandering began, and at which it came to an end." Entering Ulm, he wrote, "I would hardly have recognised the look of the city . . . if the surroundings, which could not be changed, had not proved that it was the old Ulm." Not only does Fabri view the journey as a process of going and returning (home to goal to home), he remarks on how Ulm appears to have changed during his period away.[7]

Pilgrims often speak of learning to see with new eyes during their journeys, which suggests that vision is transformed through travel. Fabri's reencounter with home is also a reflection on how he has changed. Home is different yet the same: his eyes see with a new filter of accumulated experience, and he himself is marked by the long journey away.

The homecomer is both familiar and strange. On leaving, argues the sociologist Alfred Schutz, one becomes the stranger who "is about to join a group which is not and never has been his own. He knows that he will find himself in an unfamiliar world, differently organized than that from which he comes, full of pitfalls and hard to master."[8] Consequently the stranger, or, in this case, the pilgrim, anticipates an encounter with difference and adventure on leaving home. Pilgrims often express nervousness and fear before departing.

In contrast, the homecomer, writes Schutz, "expects to return to an

environment of which he always had and—so he thinks—still has intimate knowledge and which he has just to take for granted in order to
find his bearings within it." The stranger anticipates and the homecomer
recalls. In this recollection, as in the case of Fabri, "home shows—at least
at the beginning—an unaccustomed face."[9] Home appears different in
large part because of the new ways in which the returnee has learned to
see. Furthermore, not only does home seem unfamiliar, but both homecomer and those left behind in the home context are also different. Schutz
adds, "Even if he does not find that substantial changes have occurred
in the life of the home group or in its relations to him . . . the home to
which he returns is by no means the home he left or the home which he
recalled and longed for during his absence. And, for the same reason,
the homecomer is not the same man who left. He is neither the same for
himself nor for those who await his return."[10] Stephanie, the American
who at fifty-eight decided to walk for two weeks by herself, recounted
at journey's end, "When my husband, son, and Spanish friends greeted
me with a bouquet of wild flowers at the Alicante Airport where I flew
from Santiago, they met a different person housed in the same body!"
There is mutual dissonance: the homecomer often feels disoriented as the
experiences away from home, as stranger or pilgrim, are reincorporated
into a home life that may or may not seem particularly relevant to the
recent past. This feeling of disorientation after long-term immersion in
another cultural context is similar to reverse culture shock—not the shock
of entry into foreign circumstances, but of confrontation between one's
society and one's personal transformation.

When imagining the return home while in Santiago some contemporary pilgrims express nervousness, not knowing how they are going to
reincorporate the pilgrimage into daily life, or feel uncertain about seeing a spouse after the period of separation, fearing that an unbridgeable
experiential gap now exists between them. Others, however, are eager
to share the experiences with a loved one or friends and to return to the
Camino with them. Others are enthusiastic about making decisions or
changing parts of their lives due to a new sense of energy and motivation garnered along the way. Most others are not yet aware of how the
experiences influence them, and home is still far away. For some, the
Camino becomes "home," leaving a question mark as to where to go next.

Anton expressed well the paradox of the "familiar stranger" when he
said, "Change will not come from me but from the outside. What concerns me is how the others are going to respond to this." The others he
referred to were his family, friends, business associates, and priest. His

decision to make the journey produced a small shock wave within his social network. Being a very private man, his desire to make the pilgrimage came as a surprise to those closest to him, as it does for many. He became a stranger to those around him even before he left home. Pilgrims must also face the possibility that "home" has changed. Will they accept me now as before?

The pilgrim is a stranger by definition, not only beyond the city limits but within them as well. Becoming a pilgrim may reveal to intimates or associates a stranger behind what was thought to be a known face. Often an individual has been thinking of making the pilgrimage for a long time but does not announce the decision to colleagues or family until shortly before departure. A Basque man described the moment when, with great anticipation, he told the people at work he was going: "Some of them laughed. Others said, 'You're crazy, what kind of vacation is that.' Not wanting to give these comments any importance, I shut up."[11] He also became a stranger. Their beliefs concerning what might be a meaningful break from the quotidian diverged. This, it seems, is part of the pilgrim's power—the ability to arouse fear or surprise in others, to risk, to challenge, to become and do only what others dream. In the return the stories of the road, the loneliness, perhaps a bit of the mystery are shared, but the pilgrim harbors within the knowledge of the stranger and the power of having done what most would not do.

ARRIVALS

Pilgrims infrequently discuss the arrival home.[12] Instead they describe an extended vacation, the familiar rush of home life, and the difficulties they had adjusting. Some pilgrims have family celebrations or an acknowledgment of their arrival in their religious community, but most arrivals are quiet. Again, the pilgrim's goal is generally personalized and the act individual. It is not a community event unless the pilgrimage has been intentionally made in this way. A Swedish journalist sent articles to his local paper every week, and his return seven months after starting was nearly a national event.

The homecomer's return can attract attention among those close to him or her, as did the decision to leave. Relief and doubts about the pilgrim's return can be experienced in what Susan described as the "hero's welcome" when she returned to her home in Switzerland: "I surprised my parents by just ringing the doorbell on Sunday evening. There I was. Back safe and sound. My mother took me in her arms and didn't let me go for a long time, repeating my name over and over again, tears rolling down her face." For the parents and especially the grandparents of young Spanish pilgrims, whose Catholic reality was very different from that of the secularized 1980s and 1990s, the return of the pilgrim can create a great feeling of familial pride. The grandmother of one pilgrim from Santiago felt great pride about his journey (even though he is an atheist and his motive was nonreligious) and repeated the fact to her friends over and over. It was as if his act were at the same time her act; he became the representative of the family. The pilgrim (a lawyer) gave her the *Compostela* and credential, which she now keeps as if it were her own.

The welcome can be more meaningful to the friends and families of those with a Catholic background or familiarity with the Camino. Other pilgrims without the cultural markers, especially Americans and non-Spanish in general, to help explain the journey may experience greater incomprehension at home. Not only is the pilgrim faced with the monumental task of putting an array of senses and experiences into a coherent set of stories, but the basics of the pilgrimage need to be explained: who and where Santiago is, what the Camino is, and so on. Spanish pilgrims usually do not contend with these issues as Santiago, as a cultural reference, is immediately identifiable.

In the return the surprise evoked by the pilgrim's original departure announcement may still remain, but now awe, relief, and a great deal of curiosity may accompany this reaction. Anton, reflecting on his family's response, wrote,

> When I met my son I saw his joy and could feel his relief at my being back home from a journey he couldn't quite understand. . . . Until the last days before I started he was always thinking that I would not make the Camino. . . . This relief I felt by all members of my family. . . . [I]t is obvious also that it must have been a very strange situation for all of them. The husband and father is on a pilgrimage and nobody knows exactly where he is and how he is feeling on his lonely way. . . . The joy was very deep . . . and was shown in a rare quietness which lasted a very long time. I felt observed in a good way—how I was feeling, my behavior, my change in doing my work, my being different than before.

Both Susan's and Anton's accounts of return reflect a positive sense of being welcomed by those who were left behind when the decision was made to make the pilgrimage. To feel oneself missed and to miss those left behind during an absence can help reaffirm relationships and values associated with them. Reflecting six months after cycling to Santiago in October 1994 and returning to his job, a thirty-year-old American wrote to me,

> Doing the trip meant a lot . . . but most of all, I think that I am just glad to be home. In the end, all trips, sojourns and pilgrimages have as much or more to do with coming home than they do with leaving. Don Quixote had to go home three times before his trip was over. If he had never gone home, he would not be the charming character that he is. He would have been merely a pathetic slayer of windmills. Because of my trip I feel different about home and my life here as I start the "New York lawyer" phase. . . . I feel very, well, centered. And I thank god for my friends and family: I would not want to be an eternal wanderer.

In addition, pilgrims report the sense of "knowing who and what is important to you" as positive feelings of arrival. One pilgrim, a Spanish parish priest, unexpectedly found the pilgrim (another priest) who had originally urged him to make the Camino waiting for him in the Burgos train station at 4:00 A.M. He described feeling a rush of emotion, and in their embrace he felt himself hugging the apostle for a second time. It is the affirmation of belonging.

In contrast, Anton's sense of being watched by his intimates reflects precisely how Schutz describes the homecomer's additional quality as a stranger. He is the same father and husband yet different. There is readjustment and negotiation on both sides. In a society in which rites of reincorporation for the homecoming pilgrim are virtually nonexistent, pilgrims frequently describe a period of adjustment and disorientation consistent with that described by Schutz. In a lovely bit of understatement, Roy, the Dutch pilgrim who had the close call with bulls in Sahagún, wrote six months after returning home to his wife and retired life, "After seven weeks of being alone in the beautiful Spanish landscape and desolate dry meseta, you have to get used to normal life again. Some things don't seem to be as important as they were before." Not only is one's vision changed, but one's perception is changed also. Getting used to life at home entails putting into context the discoveries made during the pilgrimage as well as becoming accustomed again to the rhythms of society. It is very common for pilgrims to express, for example, "how hard it was to get back into life," meaning that life at home is much more complicated than it is on the way. But it is clear that the return home is an essential part of pilgrimage: one needs the Camino to put daily life in perspective, and one needs to be back in the daily routine to appreciate the Camino.

The homecomer's "difference" may be noticed by those close to him or her, reaffirming the personal sense of transformation. Susan's father, who had always been critical of her posture, remarked on her return that she seemed to be walking differently. She, too, had noticed her more upright bearing, attributing it to the necessity to walk with the weight of the backpack and also to the greater sense of confidence she acquired during the course of the journey.

Pilgrims usually arrive home with a difference, not only the ineffable and subjective but also the physical trappings of the journey: the backpack, now dirtied and broken in; the scallop shell and staff; souvenirs of the way; perhaps a diary; addresses of new friends, both pilgrims and villagers; the pilgrim's passport, stamped, perhaps warped by water; the *Compostela,* folded, rolled, or laminated; and photographs or film to be developed. Each object is marked by a wealth of experiences and stories known to its carrier: triumphs, difficult days, friendships, fears, anecdotes of village life, odd encounters, crises. There is no way that a pilgrim could recount all of the stories and experiences contained within each object or the meanings these objects have for the pilgrim's journey.

What pilgrims share on return is selective and interpretive. In the retellings meanings of the journey continue to emerge and the adventure grows as the pilgrim edits and elaborates on the journey's stories.[13] The returnee may realize only in the retelling that she is or was a pilgrim and the secular journey a pilgrimage. Retelling plays an important part in the return, whereby one is able to reinterpret, process the experiences, and create oneself as pilgrim at the same time. In this way the reactions of family and friends often help the pilgrim put the Camino into context through the acts of narration and fielding questions. At first Susan's return did reaffirm the experience through her ability to share it. She wrote, "So you see, I sort of flew on this cloud of 'Welcome back home, tell us all about it' and celebrated my hero position." Through the narration of the experiences the pilgrim relives the drama of the Camino and the audience responds with varied reactions, among them, admiration, interest, and questions usually oriented toward the superficial (food, weather, lodgings). Perhaps the why questions (motivation? alone? now? at your age?) surface, but only rarely does the pilgrim have the opportunity to process what has occurred on a more deeply personal level. In going home pilgrims have the opportunity to remember, re-view, and analyze the pilgrimage from the perspective of daily life, though they still may be lacking a vocabulary, voice, or an audience to express what has happened on a more profound level.

The homecomer's return opens the Camino to a wider audience, drawing curiosity and perhaps inspiring others to make the journey with the tales lived and shared. The material objects enliven the stories, making real the friendships, the extraordinary landscapes, the adventures, the distance, the wild dogs. The pilgrim's enthusiasm for the uniqueness of the way, or the power it seems to have had on his or her life, may plant the seed of curiosity for another. The adventures of a sibling, friend, or spouse make the journey seem less distant and more accessible. Stephanie, the fifty-eight-year-old American woman commented, "My family and close friends respect me for my venture; I think it has motivated some people to go and 'DO IT' even in other areas [of their lives]." Some few may be critical. Robert, the German cyclist, found that "militant Catholics" criticized his motives, which were not specifically religious, and others criticized him for going to the same place three times in nine years.

Despite the positive aspects of retelling, pilgrims repeatedly comment on their inability to transmit the experiences of the Camino on a deep level because "no one really understands." This perceived lack of comprehension often leads to feelings of isolation, or what pilgrims describe as long periods of reflection, and possibly the seeking out of others who have made the Camino. One Spanish priest from La Rioja said more than a year later that after returning he only told people about the superficial aspects because "it's useless to talk with people who haven't made it. They think that you're telling jokes." Others comment on how the eyes of friends and family begin to "glaze over" when they speak about the pilgrimage, alienating the homecomer from those around him or her.

The priest made the above comment to me during a weekend spiritual retreat conducted by two other priests who, themselves former pilgrims, in 1994 recognized the need for participants to process the experiences of the Camino. The retreat, held in the monastery of Silos (from which came the Gregorian chants on the compact disc *Chant*) was designed to help pilgrims put into a religious frame the experiences of the way through the sharing of experiences, reflecting on biblical passages, celebrating Mass, and walking. Some of the twenty attendees (two Brazilian women, one German man, me, and Spanish men and women from age twenty to sixty) had never spoken to anyone about their experiences and found the context of comprehension cathartic. Others had processed the experiences on a superficial level but went on the retreat with the desire to hear others' stories as well as to attend to their own often confused feelings in the return. Most described not having an adequate outlet to channel their new or unexpected feelings in their social and religious communities.

Pilgrims with a religious orientation frequently repeat the same idea about the arrival in Santiago and the return home: *el regreso es la salida* (the return is the departure), or the real Camino begins in Santiago. As one pilgrim put it, "You are not the same when you return as when you started out. Your very soul is on the move."[14] Continuing the metaphor of Jesus as the Way, for many Catholics the physical journey concludes in Santiago where the real spiritual journey begins. Ideally the pilgrim experiences a symbolic death and resurrection: the old self is transformed and in the return one has a new life focus. Part of this new focus is the pilgrim's evangelical mission, to spread the word to one's family, friends, and community that the Camino (Jesus) is the metaphor for life.

Many return home inspired with a new sense of having (re)discovered God through the road but do not find in their own religious or personal communities an adequate way to assimilate what has transpired during the journey. Often the messages of the journey remain, but it is difficult to apply them to daily life. Several testimonials from young Spanish pilgrims made in a group with a religious orientation illustrate this. "I went to think and to think about my faith. Now I don't think: I see. But I still lack security. The Camino is a reinforcement that gives you life. And, later, Jesus, the strength to continue walking." Or: "My faith is stronger: in the day to day and above all in the Eucharist. The daily prayer helped me a lot. . . . In the Camino you live closer to utopia. Perhaps this is naive, but I saw what I have given and what I should give and I saw an abysmal difference. I saw that everything in the Camino is a gift, my life should be a gift for others. I want this to grow."[15]

In her article "Strangers, Homecomers and Ordinary Men," Deirdre A. Meintel suggests, "The most important 'shocks' to be encountered by those who enter another culture or subculture are those of self-discovery. Revelations about oneself may become clear only upon return home; moreover they may also be engendered by everyday social experiences in one's own cultural setting."[16] Applying this to the Camino, discoveries that emerge on the journey may be truly felt only when the pilgrim returns home and shape and meaning are given to the experiences. As with the arrival in Santiago the initial weeks and months of the pilgrim's return to daily life are often characterized by strong poles of both positive translation of experiences and a negative sense of loss and depression, especially when the pilgrim cannot adequately express what has happened.

WHAT HAPPENED TO THE YELLOW ARROWS?

The sense of direction and purpose felt so strongly during the journey may be lost at home when the yellow arrows of the Camino no longer indicate the way. Instead the path seems to be signposted by question marks. In the words of one, "I don't get to Santiago anymore." Wim quit his white-collar job on returning home and described his immediate postreturn in this way:

> I had my photos developed and made extra copies for those I met on the road, anxious to send them around and hear from them. It was remarkable to see how I started hesitating. What to write, what to say. How do you continue a contact that was so exclusive and bound to a special situation? . . . Are we interested in telling and hearing what is bothering us in daily life? So I spent a few weeks [vacillating] and then started writing. I discovered that the others had the same kind of hesitation. It took until the end of December before I received my first answers [he wrote the letters in early October 1994]. Two of them had been depressed for weeks after returning, others didn't do much more than chopping wood for their fireplaces and ordering their diary, one found me some conchas [pilgrim's shells] at Finisterre in September and does not seem to find a way of sending them to me.

The contrast between the space of home and the space of the Camino is felt in Wim's hesitation. It seems as if the foundations of his "Camino reality" are shaken. He feels uncertain about relationships that before were welded strongly through trial, experience, and action. He asks the question, Is the Camino real? He found similar reactions in his companions. Rather than be reincorporated into the quotidian, these pilgrims were still betwixt and between—neither on the Camino nor fully at peace at home. The words *morose, depressed, lost,* and *difficult* are used by pilgrims to describe the first period of return. I add *stagnant,* because it is also seems to characterize the feelings inspired by immobility. Homecomers may initially flow easily back into social life but then many find themselves mired in the old vicious circles and problematic society, believing that what they felt they had acquired in the Camino is now lost, for naught, or was even a dream.

There tends to be a pattern of direction lost and gained that continues over time in the short- and long-term postexperience. Susan, who experienced an extremely positive return by riding the wave of the hero's welcome, wondered how it was possible one and a half years later to feel lost again and to believe that *la luz* (she used the Spanish) she discovered ("my personal little [interior] home") in the Camino might be gone forever. She wrote, "I feel as if at the moment I'm climbing a hill with a heavy backpack, though I also know that there will be easier bits of the Camino in front of me." Using the Camino as a metaphor for the current experience of doubt and despair, she takes solace in what she learned about life and herself on the Camino in her present-day circumstances, knowing that pains are inevitable but eventually will pass. And three months later she wrote to me again: "This time was nothing but a rainy, soggy, cold and windy pilgrim's day. . . . I'm trying to find an end to that part of my life which I find difficult but as this little home within myself has space again to grow and air to breathe, I feel that I'm getting stronger within myself again."

For Susan, the Camino as a sensory experience provided useful metaphors to help find the way in daily life. The confidence that the road or the weather is bound to improve if she continues to persist as she did in the Camino allows her to find her light and home within herself. The Camino still exists within her, and she translates the lessons to the problems she encounters.

These feelings of stagnation or disorientation after the Camino is completed may also be influenced by the inability to translate the Camino's experiences into daily life. After the initial rush, when the energy of the experience is quite present, immediate changes may occur, such as making a pending decision or returning to friends, former lovers, or a therapist to share the "new me." But other aspects of the inchoate are harder to bring to life in the home setting. Values garnered or clarified while in the Camino may not be compatible with a work or personal environment. Anton, reflecting on his return to work, wrote that "business life is diametrically opposed to a life which concentrates on the real existence of human beings." He refers, of course, to the Camino's positive social environment, now at odds with his work environment. Being unable to leave his work, he found that his greatest struggle was how "to compromise without giving up essential points," having lived another reality in which compromise was unnecessary. Wim commented, "I'm still trying to find a job that will please me more. In the meantime, I volunteer as a windmiller in a cornmill and work for an art-house cinema. I maintain the house—paint and renew parts I should have done last year."

The challenge of compromise is also expressed through vision metaphors. Having had one's eyes opened while on the Camino commonly appears in pilgrims' accounts. Guy, the French psychologist, shared with me part of a letter he wrote to a German companion on the Camino after they both had been home for six months: "From this experience it is no longer possible to look at reality with the same eyes. It is not the reality which is different, indeed: but how I look at it and which I now realize, I can't endure anymore."

The decision to ignore what was strongly felt to be true on the Camino or to accept the reality of home life is felt to be strongly in opposition to a desire to change. An Italian man, in his late thirties and at a difficult point of transition in his home and work life, commented, "When I went home, to Milan, my old habits were very hard to break and took me away from the hearty contact of the Camino. . . . The fear to change pushed me to protect my old ways. . . . To continue in the direction I felt during the Camino meant big changes and [caused me] big fear. . . . So, it has been 'impossible' to write you and even to other dear friends I met during the Camino." How to join the desire for change and the reality of a familiar but perhaps no longer comfortable home life is a struggle that pilgrims continue to negotiate in a variety of ways in the months and years after the pilgrimage is completed. As he struggled to express his sentiments in English, the effect is illustrative: making "big changes" produces "big fear" in him. His silence was indicative not of disinterest but of the struggle to reconcile his fear to change the quotidian with what he discovered in the Camino. In both of these instances the importance of the groups that formed on the Camino play a central role during the period of transition. Pilgrims reach out or remain silent to cope with the return.

Some pilgrims do not respond at all, as I learned while trying to follow up. I made a particular effort to track down these pilgrims to see if there was a connection between the impact of the Camino and their silence. While in Barcelona I contacted a thirty-year-old man whom I had met in Hospital de Orbigo and who works for a multinational insurance brokerage. For him, a self-described loner, the Camino had been worthwhile and meaningful in the moment, but it was over. He showed me photographs of his pilgrimage that were mixed with another trip he took to Cuba, like it was just another vacation. He did not feel any need to join an association to keep the spirit of the pilgrimage alive. He did maintain contact with a few people he met (especially women) but that was it. A Dutch graduate student in his thirties finally responded, to my third letter, by e-mail a year and a half later, explaining that the return had been too painful to rehash in the moment. Breaking up with his longtime girlfriend after making the Camino together sent him into a downward spiral. An Englishman in his fifties responded to a letter of mine a year late, saying, "I feel terrible for not replying. . . . So much for a pilgrim who purports to travel light." And a Spanish man admitted that he did not wish to tarnish his images of the Camino through maintaining a correspondence with companions and thus kept silent. I was never able to contact some pilgrims despite repeated attempts.

The sharp contrast between the easy flow, purposefulness, healthy lifestyle, and directionality found and often lived on the Camino can in the long-term postexperience give way to feelings of failure when it seems that it is difficult to maintain these "lessons" or ways of living in one's own life. Like Susan, Andrew, who had the "best time of his life" making the Camino, began to miss the "simplicity and peacefulness of the Camino" one and a half years later. Finding his life ruled by the same chaos as before (overeating, overworking, poor spiritual life), Andrew says, "Something is still missing. . . . I still carry with me the inner strength of the Camino, talk a lot about it, but, deep inside, I do not live it." As a memory and source of strength the Camino's presence cannot be taken away, but the day-to-day realization of it for him is harder and harder to achieve. In fact, the Frenchwoman, Robyn, who experienced the powerful orgasm on the meseta, commented five years after it first occurred, "Now I'm very reserved about some aspects of the Camino. It's not from shame, but because every time I speak about the Camino in this way, I feel like I'm losing the fabulous internal power that I earned while walking. I don't know if you know what I'm talking about. It may seem crazy, but that's how it is." Sharing experiences may become a drain, or it may simply be difficult to keep the Camino experiences burning in daily life, where the same stress and pressure from before the Camino work against the special feelings strongly felt while walking or cycling.

However, another outcome of the pilgrims' interactions with the Camino that continues to work in their daily lives is a sense of personal empowerment acquired through the way. A German engineering student wrote to say that he finally decided to switch to the study of psychology as his heart was urging him to do. In addition, he was returning the next summer with his father, hoping to strengthen their relationship by walking. Pilgrims claim in the postexperience that perhaps they were not changed by the Camino but it "reaffirmed" values or directions in which their lives were already moving. Stephanie, the American, wrote, "My faith has deepened; what I thought was very foundational to my being— IS! . . . I am delighted in my physical capability and continue to work on it. . . . [T]he relationship between my husband and me has deepened; we have a far greater sense of appreciation for each other and our capabilities." These affirmations give an extra impetus to continue in life with additional confidence. A thirty-five-year-old German priest said, "My confidence in God and people is greater now. I learned to save water; when you feel thirst you recognize the value of water." Placing value on the simple is reinforced by remembered experiences that are applied to one's personal and spiritual life. At home I had always talked about wanting to participate in adult literacy—some day when I had time. On the Camino I realized that my "imagined future" (an oasis where time is plentiful) exists in the present and that if I remained apathetic on this issue I would be saying the same thing until I was eighty. When I returned home I called the local library, and after eighteen hours of training I began this rewarding work specifically because of the Camino's influence and the alternative sense of time I felt while walking. As each person brings his or her social and personal world to the Camino, what is taken home is also unique.

Perhaps even more profound is the sense of the "potential me" the Camino reveals on the return home.[17] The Camino provides opportunities that compel the pilgrim to confront challenges. Through overcoming pain and fears and testing one's limits the pilgrim often reports a sense of "grounding" and strength in daily life. The result may be the mundane desire to keep physically fit after the return or, on a more interior level, a greater sense of self-confidence after surviving an overwhelming fear. An Englishwoman in her fifties reported, "The Camino has converted me into a Spanish teacher! I've still got my French class but also have first-, second-, and third-year Spanish." She is not alone in taking a greater interest in the Spanish language or Spanish society as a result of the pilgrimage. Others have become teachers or have learned to read and write in Spanish or English to communicate with new friends. Some pilgrims develop an artistic or poetic voice or decide to go back to guitar lessons given up years earlier.

Others develop a particular interest in Saint James, a personalized devotion toward him, or a greater religious faith in the apostle. Many pilgrims return to their hometowns and begin to look for signs of scallop shells or images of Saint James the Pilgrim in their local churches. Often pilgrims are surprised by the number of marks left by historical pilgrims. Others continue to see how Saint James works in their lives, attributing a positive coincidence to the power of the Camino. Just as pilgrims often attribute a chance encounter on the Camino to Saint James, they also often interpret luck and chance meetings off the road to being influenced by him. This association is not necessarily religious but is a sign of the power that the pilgrimage as a symbol can have in one's life. In Appendix A I mention that one pilgrim wrote in his memories of the journey that I spoke to Saint James "in extremis." It is true, despite being a nonbeliever, I somehow have faith and great affection for Saint James. It is a completely irrational sense of trust that I feel toward him as a symbolic figure—as if somehow he and the pilgrimage associated with him have influenced my life positively. I do go to the cathedral, smile at his gilded baroque figure, hug his back, and thank him.

Many pilgrims venture to the Camino at a breaking point in their lives or to make a decision. Returning forces the confrontation with what was left behind—quitting a job, resolving a relationship, or continuing the grieving process. Through confrontations with the self, God, and others on the Camino, postpilgrims describe an ability to confront quandaries with a new attitude or resolution. Jonás, the young man from Madrid who found his anger and strength while cycling, six months after returning home was able to apply his new self-confidence to a work situation and liberate himself once again from a stifling relationship. He linked this act directly to the strength he developed on the Camino. An American woman who cycled alone in 1990 opened a bicycle shop after returning and made the pilgrimage again in coming years. She hoped to find "new openings" to herself and to reinforce her self and sense of strength. A thirty-six-year-old Italian woman remarked three years after finishing the way, "I remember the physical problems and asking myself why I was suffering and not on the beach. Above all, I believe that it isn't just any trip (because it changes you radically) but because it gives you the capacity to make decisions with much more courage."

Her use of the phrase "change radically" is reminiscent of Victor Turner's claim that a pilgrimage's power is to "make one" a better person.[18] The idea of radical change generally refers to conversion or a dramatic resolution of a problem. On some level there is the belief that the pilgrimage will solve or provide the magic key necessary to understand life's problems. The locus of change is seen to be lodged in the Camino itself rather than in the individual interacting with what the Camino offers (which is how transformation is usually noted). A doctor from Barcelona first made the pilgrimage after she suffered a professional setback and was fed up with the politics and nepotism of her medical institution. Commenting that in Spanish society doctors usually see themselves, and are treated by their patients, as superior for their knowledge and power, she came to terms with her own arrogance while making the pilgrimage. There she felt an equalizing and a leveling of classes. Instead of distance based on social power, she felt connected meaningfully to a wide variety of people. Back in Barcelona she began to treat her clients with much more equality, wanting to ensure their comfort, and now she counts many of them among her friends. This kind of transformation occurred through opportunity, personal reflection, and then action. Some pilgrims are able to do this; others are not. The power does not reside solely in the Camino or in the person.

Sometimes unexpected outcomes are more dramatic—a divorce, a pregnancy, or a new intimate relationship. It surprises me how difficult it is to share my own homecoming four years after the events occurred. The pilgrimage brought me both intense joy and bitter anguish. Once I allowed the doors to open and began to walk through them on the Camino, I discovered when I returned home that I was no longer able to pass through the doors of my past. I left home and a stable long-term relationship. When I returned, despite intense personal struggle, I realized that what I had unleashed within myself while walking could no longer be contained by that relationship. Much to the shock of everyone close to me, I ended my marriage. Despite the deep pain it caused both of us, it was an outcome of the pilgrimage that I could not ignore and also the last place I thought my research would lead me.

An American evangelical Catholic couple wrote to me to announce the birth of their son James (named for Saint James), who was conceived during their honeymoon on pilgrimage in 1994. A twenty-one-year-old Spanish woman, an art history student, attributed her continuing tie to the Camino to a young man she met there: "I'm still living the Camino thanks to this guy, Juan. I would like to walk it with him." Others meet future husbands or lovers—other pilgrims or even villagers—while walking and cycling.

Just as the Camino draws some to the fold, it also takes some away from it. Conversion to Catholicism is not the norm, but it does occur from time to time. Conversion often takes the pilgrim by surprise. Often the conversion occurs among people whose opinions are strong to begin with, and the change is like a leap—a leap to faith rather than a leap of faith. Others find a budding spirituality in the Camino which may or may not be interpreted as a religious awakening. An athletic Basque man from San Sebastián first made the Camino in 1993 "por cojones," for pride, guts, stubbornness.[19] His friends at home had said that he would not be able to do it, and he was determined to prove them wrong. He cycled for two weeks. When he arrived in Santiago he was shocked to find himself crying at the apostle's feet. As a child he had hiked extensively in Spain and Europe, and as an adult he cycled through France and Spain. But on the Camino he found something different. While listening to the prayer in one village he felt an immediate sense of illumination. When he returned home his wife looked at his face and said,

"What happened? I want your expression too." "What expression?" he asked. "It looks like you've just spent all night making love," she replied. Whatever he found seemed to radiate from his whole body.

The next year he decided to repeat the experience on foot with his wife and two children, ages 9 and 13, and we happened to meet when they arrived at the refuge in Hospital de Orbigo where I was a hospitaler. Commenting on how the Camino is a symbol, he said, "During my first Camino. . . . I noted this mystery that hides in the way between the rocks and its people. When I returned to my daily life I didn't know how to keep this spark burning, and after several weeks nothing remained except the memories of the physical journey." Before 1993 he had a dim view of the Church—specifically, of priests—but in that first trip he began to feel a change in his spiritual life and a tempering of the negative sentiments. The next year, 1994, he repeated the pilgrimage again to find this spark, almost lost from the first journey. "I believe that I returned to find where it was, inside of me, but that I need the way to be able to find it." He added that although it is inside of him, every time he gets far away from the Camino he loses the spark and therefore needs to repeat and return via reunions. His spirituality and prayer is not focused on the Catholic church; it is part of a faith within him. Little by little, he explained, his spirituality has begun to grow, and now he prays every day. The next year he became an hospitalero with his daughter—"as another way to make the pilgrimage." He also attended the retreat in Silos and from this experience continued to learn about himself and apply lessons of the Camino to his daily life. On reflecting more than a year later on his work as an hospitalero, he said, "[I saw how] my pride was on top of my humility, that I acted like an hospitalero who knows everything, that I wanted to impose on others my supposed experience and knowledge of the way, giving advice without being asked, true or not, that I shouldn't have given."[20] For him, as for many others, the Camino is a continuing avenue to self-understanding. Curiously, I met his wife by chance in 1997 when she was making the Camino with her sister and I was an hospitalera in Rabanal. She painted a different picture. Only making the Camino because her sister had asked her, she found that her husband's involvement had become excessive, and she did not understand his deepening interest. She believed it was having a negative effect on their relationship. Instead of devoting his time to her and the children, every free moment was Camino, Camino, Camino. She felt impotent and frustrated by the situation. It seems that the original light that her husband had brought home from the pilgrimage has dulled for her four years later.

A dramatic spiritual transformation also led a French couple in their early forties toward a desire to give back to the Camino. Leonard, a medical doctor, and his wife, Elisabeth, were both born Catholic but were not strong in their faith. Their life was comfortable materially but unsatisfactory spiritually. One day in his medical clinic Leonard suffered severe pains that did not diminish despite medication. Much to Leonard's chagrin Elisabeth disappeared while he was in pain. Finally the pain receded, and it turned out that in that instant "Elisabeth was praying before the image of the Virgin Mary" in a nearby chapel. Their conversion began after this realization. Leonard decided to make the pilgrimage in 1991 to give thanks to Santiago, and "he discovered the new world of spiritual life in the Camino." During the journey he received a message from God that he should "live in a community of the Camino de Santiago to attend pilgrims." It became an obsessive thought in the return home, which he fought vigorously over the next months but to which in the end he succumbed. Leonard and Elisabeth established a lay community for the care of pilgrims in Estaing, France, and found their vocation in life.[21]

Participants can also come to identify themselves fully as pilgrims—a conversion not to religion but to being a pilgrim. The Camino becomes the savior and the salvation. One Spaniard carries business cards printed with his Camino name—"Paco, El Peregrino"—and address and spends all his spare time walking, essentially living for the Camino. In his daily life he works for the city government and claims to have found in the Camino the means to overcome an addiction to alcohol that was destroying his life. Some pilgrims carry deep despair to the road. On the Camino the discovery of new hope and purpose through friendship and a sense of common humanity can help ease the sense of loss and doom. An English pilgrim found his calling and raison d'être in the Camino. When asked his occupation by a customs officer he stated, "I am a pilgrim." For him, the pilgrimage became a return to life. Now he dedicates his life to the improvement of the pilgrimage routes, hoping to encourage young Europeans to follow this path of peace and hope and create a better Europe for the future.

These types of conversion are rare. Most people barely realize what has happened to them during the journey. It is only later, perhaps months or years later, that its meanings become clear. The realization at journey's end that illumination is not automatic sometimes hits pilgrims hard and in part explains Guy's disappointment on arrival. On some level, Guy, the Frenchman who walked to Santiago and back home, believed that after going through the motions of the way the reward would be resolution, conversion, and understanding. For most, the reality is that the Camino helps to open doors but that the individual must choose to walk through them to be transformed in some way. Pilgrimage does not "make one" a better person. Personal change is often a long-term process of trial and error.

MEMORY: GOING BACK IN THE MIND

In the beginning I was asking myself if I walked to Santiago at all. I didn't remember things. After a while (from February on), I all of a sudden remembered certain landscapes, certain villages on the Camino. I still am in that phase. In the shower, in the tram, at work I suddenly feel the wind, the temperature, the smell. They are very precise memories.

Swiss, male, age 28. Reached Santiago in November 1994.
Written March 1995.

I am still on the way to Santiago. Nearly every day in my thoughts I am on one of the stages of the Camino and sometimes nights too. Roncesvalles, Puente la Reina, Hontanas, Nájera, Frómista, Carrión de los C., Sahagún, León . . . in my mind's eye I walked and walk the way once more and once more, a beautiful feeling.

Anton, German, age 59. Reached Santiago in October 1994.
Written February 1995.

But sometimes after my daily "why to do that" [transcribing his journal from the Camino], I persist in playing [transcribing]. And I live again some moments, and I live again the Camino, and I think it is worth walking in one's head, worth living again.

Guy, French, age 43. Round-trip from Le Puy. November 1994.
Written November 1995.

The Camino is still present in my heart.

German, male, age 30. Reached Santiago in September 1994.
Written November 1995.

One of the most profound ways that the Camino affects and remains with pilgrims, once the physical journey has been completed and the immediate return phase passes, is through memory. As a memory the Camino is not only a mental process but also a sensory experience. Lee, the former American professor, felt his body turn into a "sensorium" through contact with the Camino.[22] These sensations, taken in through all the pores, are evoked not only by markers or memory aids such as photos but also by smells, sounds, or simply quiet moments. During the journey an internal space is created which in the postpilgrimage is revisited.

As a memory the Camino exists on at least two levels: that which is shared and re-created for an audience and that which exists privately for the pilgrim, the place that is revisited and remembered, bringing back the journey's discoveries. The first level surfaces immediately with the arrival home in the process of interpretive retelling. Pilgrims develop a narrative of their favorite stories and odd encounters to describe the journey. The narrative's content depends on the audience. The metaphor of an onion is not inappropriate to describe this process. It is rare to arrive at the many-layered core, a place often foreign even to the pilgrim. Yet here is often where the Camino continues to exist: "in my heart," "a place in our souls which we continue to visit," "in my head," "this little home within myself."

Even if the Camino does not remain a daily memory, it is clear that this inner space created through the total sensory nature of the journey leaves an indelible mark in the memory. This point was sharply reinforced when I delivered a lecture on the reincorporation of the pilgrimage at Harvard University.[23] Besides the usual audience of eight, the theme attracted twenty additional people who were completely unfamiliar to the lecture's organizer. In the minutes before I began to speak two members of the audience told me that they had made the pilgrimage. One was a man in his forties who walked the Camino in 1985, and the other was a woman in her mid-forties who made the Camino by car in 1989. The woman in particular was eager to share her experiences and immediately invoked a memory of the "Celtic village" in Cebreiro. On completing the lecture I was surprised to find the comments did not focus on the reincorporation but on the journey. The above-mentioned woman immediately countered in an animated and critical way that what she remembered was the prominence of Santiago Matamoros both as an iconographic image and as an important political figure for the Galicians. She illustrated her point by invoking the images of him on top of the Rajoy Palace stomping on dismembered Moors and swooping down on the Plaza del Obradoiro. She also mentioned that his presence dominated the cathedral's main altar where he sat mounted, sword raised (while Santiago Matamoros does top the altar, the friendly seated saint is what dominates).

A man in his forties, who came in late, stated emphatically that this was not the Camino he remembered. He explained that he made the pilgrimage in 1979 and began a passionate discourse on his solo, isolated journey with no refuges, conjuring vivid images of the landscapes, his thirst, acts of kindness by nuns, the scorching heat of the meseta, and the solitude.

In both instances these participants did not respond to the central theme
of the lecture, reincorporation and postexperience; they instead focused
on the journey. What was particularly interesting was how the memories
of the Camino were reproduced in the seminar as if they had recently occurred. The Camino clearly left a strong imprint on these two people who
needed to share publicly and to reaffirm their memories as different from
those that I presented, turning them from attendees at an academic talk
to participants once again on the Camino. Furthermore, the interest the
lecture's theme produced and the passion and even anger at having their
memories contradicted or transformed in some way through my presentation led me to conclude that even if the Camino were not present in
one's daily life, the pilgrimage often continues to live close to one's heart.

The power of the pilgrimage, as an experience absorbed through all
the senses, is demonstrated by how memory is invoked through body
and place. Travel through areas where the pilgrimage passes can take one
suddenly back to the Camino. One woman from Lugo in Galicia described how she suddenly found herself remembering the Camino through
her body while driving over parts of the Camino. She said the experience "fue grabada en mi cuerpo" (was recorded in my body). As she was
driving she identified particular physical states she experienced while
walking with the places she passed. She then realized how much she took
her body for granted in daily life, explaining that on the Camino all sensations are felt more intensely. Consequently, during the Camino she became much more attentive and attuned to her body, telling me joyfully
about several end-of-the-day group massages. She acquired a nickname
among her new pilgrim friends that related to the massages. In this unexpected return her memories resurfaced, reminding her of the greater
unity of spirit and matter she felt she had acquired while walking and
wished to renew.

Another instance of unanticipated mental return to the Camino
through passing over its landscapes produced a profound sense of ending and arrival for Ursula, a twenty-eight-year-old German graduate student. Traveling by bus through several villages and cities of the camino
francés a year and a half after completing the pilgrimage, she began to
recognize landscapes and then suddenly began to see herself and the group
she had traveled with through a series of vivid memories in those places.
The memories conjured the painful struggles while walking. Looking
from the bus window, she saw herself naive and with a host of unanticipated changes waiting for her on the road ahead. Then her gaze turned
back inside the bus and she realized how far she had come during that

period, the brave steps she had taken and overcome away from the Camino, thanks to the strength it had given her. Ursula then recalled that at this point on the bus her tears began to flow uncontrollably. They were tears of joy, relief, and arrival. Moving eastward (instead of westward) in a bus, she felt herself more profoundly in Santiago—as the ultimate point of resolution or personal center—than she ever did arriving by foot. In this way unanticipated arrivals and endings can continue to surface via memory and place often independent of time.

KEEPING THE PILGRIMAGE ALIVE

The pilgrimage, according to one English pilgrim, is "a state of mind, a way of life, a condition of the heart," that is, a set of thoughts and interpretations, actions, and feelings or sentiments.[24] And it appears that the pilgrimage does continue to exist on these levels in varying degrees according to each pilgrim's personal and social circumstances. Memories mediate their expression and guide current fields of feeling, thought, and action. Unlike the two former pilgrims who attended my lecture at Harvard, many people actively work to keep the Camino and its influences a part of their lives through memory aids, communications, associations, and repetition.

MEMORY AIDS

By "memory aids" I mean those objects that pilgrims bring home from the Camino, such as the staff, the credential, metaphors, diaries, and photos, which help to illustrate the experiences lived and to keep them real in daily life. Writing to me in February 1995 after completing the pilgrimage in September, a twenty-six-year-old South African man, now living in England, said, "The memory of the Camino is as vivid as though I'd arrived at Santiago de Compostela yesterday. The *Compostela* and credential hang proudly on my wall, and it is with enormous pleasure that I admire them each morning." I had the opportunity to visit him a month later. On entering his room I noticed that the *Compostela* and the credential were hanging from his otherwise blank wall by safety pins. For him the Camino ("a personal high, driven by an inexplicable force") is kept close through these objects. On other home visits I made in England, Germany, and Spain, I found many other credentials, *Compostelas* (carefully framed and hanged), staffs, scallop shells, and photos openly displayed both for guests to admire and for pilgrims to remember and share.

Figure 39.   An English couple review their photos from the pilgrimage at home in England. Note the framed Compostelas *(right).*

Pilgrims also shared with me numerous photos and photo albums documenting their journeys. At times it is possible to witness a transformation of values. In one case the first photos were of places, and as the journey progressed the subjects reflected more the social aspects of the pilgrimage. While cameras are important for some pilgrims, others consciously choose not to bring them or take fewer photos than expected because they want to remember the pilgrimage in a different way or do not want to worry about the equipment. A number of pilgrims reported that their cameras malfunctioned or even that they lost them on the road. Many took this as a sign to reflect. A Brazilian man suggested that the "road was controlling the images." And when a German lost his camera at the beginning of the journey, it set the tone: he knew he would have to rely on words when he returned home rather than let the pictures speak for him, as he normally would.

Another type of memory aid exists on the level of metaphor. Pilgrims often express the desire to bring the Camino home by translating the metaphor "life is a pilgrimage" into their own lives, feeling that being a pilgrim becomes a lifelong process not limited by the boundaries of the way. Needless to say, life as a pilgrimage is an ample metaphor. An Italian woman described living daily life on the Camino thus: "[It means] to have some kind of detachment toward possessions, work, life. . . . Now

I look for silence, I would like to move within silence. I feel that my journey has started and the Camino has given me the *initiation*." For a thirty-three-year-old Spanish woman who began to live in a religious community a year before making the Camino and whose life already is dedicated to the "search for God, prayer, and her interior life" the pilgrimage gave "the intent to live the here and now with gratitude, happiness, and intensity." The Camino reaffirmed her faith, made her feel it more profoundly, and gave her lessons to take home. Now, while in the community, memories of the Camino surface to apply to her life. Being a pilgrim is something she grew to feel inside: "Without moving I continue to feel like a pilgrim every day."

Finding silence and peace in solitude, living and appreciating the moment, and making life less complicated are all ways that participants try to bring the Camino as pilgrimage home. Feeling oneself a pilgrim through personal and social encounters during the journey also marks the experience in the memory of the postpilgrim as more than a holiday adventure. It is described as an internal experience rather than an external one. Postpilgrims want to continue journeying, believing that a vital part of their identities is as pilgrims on the Camino.

The pilgrimage as metaphor is sometimes translated to voluntary activities. A twenty-six-year-old nonpracticing Catholic pharmacy student from Madrid originally made the pilgrimage to escape from his suffocating personal problems. In fall 1996, more than a year later, he wrote to me: "This summer I was in Guatemala working at an orphanage, and the experience felt similar to the Camino. I learned to appreciate simple things that normally you think you'll always have: food, water, health, love. The orphans also marked me. In some ways, it was also an internal journey of who I am and what I want to be, of what my fundamental values are and what the values are of the people around me." Another Spanish man in his late forties decided, while walking to Santiago, to quit his job and go to India to work among the poor, which he did for a year. Translating the experiences of the Camino to other life situations is another way in which participants keep the memories alive.

Metaphoric memory aids are often highly personalized. Some pilgrims return with internal images (e.g., a coiled spring of potential energy) that symbolize the Camino's influences. Ursula described returning from the Camino with two images, a fountain and a steel bar. The fountain represented what had been tapped by the lack of stress, the distance from the source of her problems, the novelty of being anonymous, and the sensation of being alone and open to experiment. The steel rod symbolized a new sense of strength that was lodged firmly in her body, entering her head and leaving through her feet. Both of these images played a central role in her return home where the pressure to turn off the fountain (the spring of self-discovery) was strong. She found that each time she attempted to turn off the fountain and ignore what she felt to be true from the pilgrimage a darkness and a sense of dying inside replaced the lightness and flow of the fountain. These images gave her the strength to make difficult decisions and to act to change her life, which was no longer compatible with what she had confirmed and found on the Camino.

In essence, despite the often-stated desire, it is difficult to continue to live one's life as a pilgrimage. For this reason pilgrims often seek the Camino through association membership and leadership, correspondence or visits with pilgrims, maintenance of friendships, repetition of the experience, or even returning to the Camino as an hospitalero.

COMMUNICATIONS

Pilgrims often continue to keep the Camino alive by reading further on related themes or reproducing their own experiences through various creative activities such as writing a book, compiling a collection of poems or drawings made while walking, or public speaking. A German priest wrote to me more than a year after returning, "The Camino I made last year is still present, not only because I've a little chapel dedicated to St. James in my parish or [because] I have given two interviews in different radio programs. No, the Camino is still present in my heart. . . . You see I am still a pilgrim."

Many more pilgrims state a desire to write memoirs than actually do, but occasionally limited editions are published for friends, family, or associations.[25] Some diaries or narrative accounts reach wider audiences and inspire others' journeys.[26] Other forms of writing or artistry may emerge during the Camino or in the post-Camino to express, process, and remember again the journey. Guy wrote that he finally understands why one of his French companions during the Camino would often pause, write furiously, and then keep going silently, ignoring the rest of the group. This companion wrote a play while walking, and he invited Guy to its one-day performance in France.

In another instance a painter from Barcelona who found inspiration and the desire to work while making the Camino for the second time filled more than seven drawing books of one hundred sheets on the journey (I sent one home for him when I was a hospitalera). His desire to use basic colors in what he called a "primitive" way was a product of the rejuvenation he experienced while making the pilgrimage. While his use of color and flowing style did not continue after his return home, his inspiration and desire to work did. He, too, began an illustrated book.

Another expressive form that pilgrims use in the reincorporation is the letter. I maintained (and still maintain) a correspondence with many pilgrims in which the ideas and feelings of the Camino continue to be worked through. In these letters pilgrims often discuss the correspondence they maintain with other pilgrims. On several occasions pilgrims thanked me for giving them the opportunity to express sentiments that have not been given voice in daily life through letter writing. A Canadian graduate student wrote,

> I'm sorry I didn't respond right away. I meant to but somehow kept putting it off, just as I put off my intention to write down my memories and feelings about the trip. Even now with the help of my sparse journal I'm reluctant to write—the inadequacy of language, the fear of reducing feelings to cliché. I desperately want to convey the sense of a magical, overwhelming journey, filled with trial and triumph, love and despair. Even as I write these words they fall flat and cannot express my belief that the Camino is a unique experience perhaps beyond the understanding of anyone who has not traveled it.

Her ambivalence about putting down on paper the often-inexpressible sensations of the journey is common. Ambivalence often leads to non-action and even a sense of guilt for not following through on something that is of great personal significance. Others manage to continue the connections despite having to cross linguistic barriers. While the whole group may not remain in contact, corresponding with one or two companions often plays a crucial role in keeping the pilgrimage alive.

Either on or off the Camino, pilgrims maintain their informal international pilgrimage groups through individually planned visits, yearly reencounters on the Camino, or group reunions in a neutral location. Jonás, who found his sense of self while cycling in 1994, repeated the Camino experience a year later by walking. In this second experience he developed strong bonds with a group that formed along the way and had an important intimate relationship. This group of ten now meets twice a year in different locales of Spain to renew their friendships. One English pilgrim called "a wonderful example of the spirit of the Camino" a pilgrim's reunion organized by a German schoolteacher. She invited the pilgrims she had met to a simple cooperative in Germany to share a weekend of celebration at an open public meeting.[27] In early 1998 Stephanie, the American who after her successful first pilgrimage in 1995 repeated in 1996 and 1997, made an open invitation to Santiago pilgrims in the U.S. Friends newsletter to come to her hometown in Virginia for a weekend "gathering." Explaining by letter, she said that it could not be a reunion since they had never met; instead it would be a "gathering of people who have shared an experience—to most of us an extraordinary experience." For her, even a few people would make it a success. Another informal group, composed of Spanish, German, and French pilgrims, plan to meet at the cathedral the last day of 1999 to ring in the new year, the new century, and the new millennium.

Expectations of maintaining contacts can also disappoint. I spent three grueling days in Roncesvalles waiting with a cyclist from La Coruña who had been planning for a year to meet "by chance" the French friend he had met the year before. The Spaniard, an electrician, had formed a completely unexpected friendship with the French professor and had the "time of his life" during their two-week journey. Staying in touch by letter, he knew that the friend would pass Roncesvalles on a certain day. He waited and waited. The disappointment and stress produced tears and a ground littered with cigarette butts. Finally, because his time was limited, the Spaniard left. Later he reported that his friend had nearly died in a car accident and thus could not make the pilgrimage. The second pilgrimage was a disappointment; the new group could not compare to his first friendship.

As we have seen, the Camino opens the pilgrim to a new social world in which relationships that are normally unlikely because of class, age, gender, language, or nationality, are the order of the day. Pilgrims often say that many of their closest friends are other pilgrims. These may not be the pilgrims with whom they made their journeys, but they are people with whom they have an innate understanding; others who can understand the pilgrimage as a "state of mind, a way of life, and a condition of the heart." In this way they share a common "culture of the Camino."

It is quite common for homecomers to retell their journeys in a variety of public settings—church groups, high schools, associations, and even the local jail in San Sebastián, Spain. Radio and television programs as well as newspaper interviews are other avenues for verbal presentations. On arriving in Santiago pilgrims may be interviewed by the local papers, *El Correo Gallego* and *La Voz de Galicia,* which carried nearly daily stories of pilgrims and their arrivals to the city between 1993 and 1996. Celebrity status can begin before the return home.

ASSOCIATIONS

Pilgrims often begin to feel part of an "imagined community" while making the Camino. This imagined community links pilgrims, through their
bodily actions and a geography of pilgrimage routes, to past, present,
and future travelers of the way.[28] To make literal the imagined community pilgrims began to form communities or societies of pilgrims in
their local areas to keep those bonds alive. Friends of the Camino and
ecumenical confraternities began to form on a wide scale in the early
1980s. The driving force behind their organization and formation was
usually homecoming pilgrims who wished to maintain a connection to
the pilgrimage and to other pilgrims. The desire to help pilgrims prepare for their own journeys, friendship, the desire to share the impact
and positive outcomes with others, and the need to be with others who
intuitively understand what it means to be a Santiago pilgrim encouraged the associations.

From small grassroots groups to organizations of as many as 1,500
members, the associations are found in most European countries, including Germany, Belgium, Italy, Holland, England, Norway, Ireland,
Switzerland, France, and Spain. In addition there are associations in the
United States, Canada, Brazil, and New Zealand; and several are now on
the Internet. In Spain the expansion and development of associations has
taken place at an astronomical rate since the late 1980s. Whereas in most
countries there are as many as three associations, in Spain there are many
informal ones and at least twenty affiliated officially with the Spanish
Federation of Associations of Friends of the Camino de Santiago. The
Spanish associations are not located only where the Camino passes but
in all parts of the country, including Madrid, Valencia, and Murcia. Each
small Spanish association is city- or region-specific and is not always composed of former pilgrims. Some of these associations are organized like
middle-class social and historical societies or walking clubs. Each group
maintains "control" over the Camino in its area, possibly organizing small
talks on pilgrimage-related themes, acting as information centers for potential pilgrims, or participating in the maintenance of refuges in their area.

The growth and expansion of the associations have also brought greater
sophistication, for example, sponsorship of international conferences,
book publishing, and networking with the Council of Europe. Membership becomes a way for pilgrims to continue connections, develop new
friendships, assume leadership responsibilities, fight the isolation they
may feel as homecomers, contribute time or money to the pilgrimage's

Figure 40.   A members' meeting of the Confraternity of St. James, London. Photo courtesy of Peregrino *magazine.*

preservation, help others, renew their positive Camino sentiments and values and share experiences. At the same time association membership also allows the continued enactment and unfolding of an identity experienced in the Camino. Many of the numerous association bulletins publish firsthand accounts, allowing pilgrims to express in their native languages their memories and stories.[29] Returning pilgrims can also participate in associations through annual meetings, pilgrim preparation, organized local pilgrimages, local and international conferences, and rites of reincorporation. On the latter point, the Friends in Guipúzcoa, Spain, give return pilgrims scallop shells, and in Belgium the Vlaams Genootschap van Santiago de Compostela (Flemish Friends Society of Santiago) has, since its founding in 1986, given return pilgrims terra cotta scallop shells (one color for cyclists, another for walkers). In addition, it publishes numerous firsthand accounts in its quarterly bulletin, *De Pelgrim* (The Pilgrim), and since 1995 has held fall meetings for pilgrims who have completed the journey.[30] Members are also asked to submit a copy of their *Compostela* to the association—"a beautiful collection" commented one long-term member. The English confraternity asks its members to contribute chronicles of their journeys, which are kept on file in the main office. And the Guipúzcoa association occasionally pursues the question, open from a religious perspective, "*¿El Después?*" (Afterward?) in its bulletin, *Actividades Jacobeas* (Jacobean Activities).

Figure 41.   Pilgrim Preparation Day held by the Confraternity of St. James in 1995.

The success of the associations since the 1980s demonstrates how the Camino continues to exist in the postexperience and produces positive social change. Other associations, both Spanish and non-Spanish, actively promote the support of the refuges by sending volunteers to become hospitaleros. English pilgrims support the refuge they created with the Bierzo Friends association. And the Italian confraternity sends its volunteers to the refuge it established in the meseta. Other associations send their members wherever the need may be; for example, the Swiss group sends its members to Belorado. The Camino would not live actively in people's lives if it were not remembered and then acted on.

While transnational border crossing does occur, national differences are also reflected in and replicated by the associations. Although there is a sense of supranationalism, or "Europeanism," among pilgrims, the associations often foster nationalism by focusing on routes within their countries and the histories of pilgrims from their areas. In Spain, for example, long-standing parallel concerns of center and periphery relations in politics are also seen in the associations. This sense of *cada uno a su bola* (each one to his own thing) rings true of Spanish society in general and parallels the rapid proliferation of associations and resistance to centralization. France is another interesting example. Despite its placement at the heart of Europe and the large number of French pilgrims, the lack of French presence among volunteers, refuge builders, conference

*Figure 42. A prospective pilgrim reads the sign "Help Future Pilgrims . . ."
at Pilgrim Preparation Day.*

participants, and associationism is noticeable. This absence can be explained by a strong orientation to the routes within France and the desire to attend to what is close to home. In addition, the once-pathbreaking
Paris office remains more oriented toward the academic side of the pilgrimage than toward assistance and correspondence with or for pilgrims.
The relatively young regional branches tend to be just that, regional—
focusing more on local activities than on international concerns. There
are exceptions, and some active local leaders take the initiative, such as
in the case of the Amis de Saint-Jacques des Pyrenees-Atlantiques, which
has invited Swiss, German, and English associations on joint walks. In
Switzerland and Belgium, two associations serve the language needs of
their distinctive communities, not without some tension. England maintains a strong central office in London and relies on a strong spirit of
volunteerism among its participants, yet some claim that their refuge in
Rabanal is "little India." Rather than have an open membership, like the
English confraternity, the Italian Confraternita de San Jacopo di Compostella in Perugia inducts only sponsored pilgrims into the association on
return from Santiago at a ceremony in which they are given a membership document and black pilgrim's cape. The German assocations and
confraternities have various orientations but no national leadership.

REPETITION: GOING BACK IN BODY

Wim wrote to me in February 1995, six months after reaching Santiago, "When I met you in Belorado we discussed your question as to whether I would do it again or not. . . . I said I wouldn't and discussed my point of view afterwards repeatedly with others. The reason is that I found it such a unique and great experience that a second time for me would mean chasing feelings that can only be there because everything is so new and so different. . . . Having returned I am no longer sure of that. I now can imagine doing it another time just for the good feeling it gave me."

James J. Preston calls the power of a sacred place to attract devotees "spiritual magnetism."[31] The pilgrimage often seems to have this effect. It continues to attract pilgrims to relive and repeat experiences. One of the dangers of the pilgrimage is the feeling of becoming a perpetual wanderer, perhaps going home physically but never feeling like one has arrived in Santiago.

Among those who wish to repeat the pilgrimage, the meanings that the return has are highly individualized. The sense of well-being that one feels while on the Camino is precisely one of the prime movers to repeat: the desire to relive a positive experience or to experience "another opening." As with Wim, the desire often stems from the positive memories and good feelings the Camino gives participants. His original ambivalence about returning was lost once he returned home and put the experiences in perspective. He commented that he noted how Dutch pilgrims seem to get the "pilgrimage bug" and often begin to plan other, longer journeys—to Rome and Jerusalem. In the spring of 1997 he himself set out for Rome on foot. He had found work meaningful to him but still found the time to continue his walking.

The Spanish phrase *estar enganchado,* meaning "to be hooked" or addicted, is frequently used to describe (self-referentially as well) "serial" pilgrims—those who repeat or maintain their connection to the Camino. Supporting this claim, Stephanie wrote after her 1995 pilgrimage, "*It's addictive*—I'm leaving June 18th to walk 2 more weeks alone!" Some Spaniards return to the Camino to recharge the batteries (*recargar las pilas*): the pilgrimage is literally energizing. The idea of the Camino as the *ruta de terapia* (therapy route) also supports the idea that the Camino, because of its positive influences, can be like a drug. The danger is that as a drug its impact becomes soporific and the pilgrimage a habit (familiar, well-known, and safe) rather than a stimulant for self-exploration. The Camino does become a habit for some participants, especially those who live near the road. While interviewing the president of a local Spanish association who is a pilgrimage aficionado I asked, "Are you doing the Camino again this summer?" as if it were a perennial summer plan. The author of a published religious guide, he responded that he probably would be making the Camino for a week by bicycle. Repetition also leads to habit. For others, the repeated return may be a source of renewal, a sense of going home to one's "new community," an escape, a way to "keep the spark alive." For some religiously oriented pilgrims, making the pilgrimage can be a way to serve as a witness of faith: one's act becomes the testimony of God's presence in the world.

Some pilgrims wish to return with family and friends to share the Camino with them. Roy, who had a run-in with bulls in Sahagún, wrote to me two years after he finished his seven-week walk about the summer car-and-mobile-home trip (7 weeks, 7,000 kilometers) he took with his wife retracing his steps in the summer of 1996: "I visited the plastic *refugio* of the Jato family in Villafranca del Bierzo. In 1995 I was pretty ill at this *refugio*. Now I had the chance to thank Mrs. Jato and I brought her some flowers. I was happy about that. Mrs. Jato recognized me right away. My visit was a surprise!" Being able to return to give thanks, the good feeling of being recognized and being able to share the Camino experience, is clear in his words. Pilgrims are often amazed at the Spanish people's generosity to Santiago pilgrims. A common anecdote that pilgrims tell is of being invited to a home for a meal, and despite insisting on compensating the people for the meal, they are usually flatly refused or charged a pittance. Pilgrims are left with a series of un(der)paid or unreturned debts that often have no financial basis, tying pilgrims to the Camino in a positive way. How is it possible to calculate the value of an unexpected smile on the eve of discouragement which transforms the day of despair into achievement or hope? And how do you repay a priceless, (apparently) freely given gift? Pilgrims often realize that they can never repay directly or help the person who smiled or listened. The gift of listening or the smile may be passed to another person on the Camino or in another context altogether.

Pilgrims who discover a particular interest relevant to the Camino may remain connected to it through their work, for example, an academic specialty or the construction of refuges or improvement of the Camino infrastructure. Numerous professional careers have developed from the Camino. By giving two weeks or a month of personal time working in a refuge, hospitaleros have the opportunity to interact with a wide array of pilgrims, share in their experiences, assist those in need, and receive the pleasure of having helped another complete his or her way. One hospitalero from Burgos commented, "The only thing that moves us to do what we do is a sense of gratitude for what the Camino has given us in comparison with the little that each of us can give of himself. From this sense, the ability to understand pilgrims' problems is born."[32] Some also claim to become better pilgrims. One outcome of the receipt of a gift of food, time, or an unexpected smile in a moment of need is the desire to return this same type of generosity in one's home context. Such pilgrims feel compelled to share the generosity they experienced with others in their own communities. Some former pilgrims donate money to refuges.

A number of pilgrims repeat the journey because they felt that something was missing from the first or even second time. Overall they describe the journey as positive, yet they are ambivalent. These pilgrims hope that the sense of failure and dissatisfaction will be relieved if the return to the Camino is made "one more time" under the "right circumstance." The Camino becomes the search for the elusive Holy Grail, always just one step ahead yet inaccessible.

When I was an hospitalera in Hospital del Orbigo in the summer of 1994 I met a young man from Madrid who was making the Camino for the second time. His first pilgrimage, with his mother in 1993, lasted a week. Through a combination of unexpected physical challenges, personal contacts, and a new sense of achievement he reached Santiago triumphant and thirsting for more. He knew he wanted to go alone and for a longer time. His second journey in 1994 began in Burgos and was a very positive experience; it was physically easier and more socially enriching. Normally shy, he opened up, and he made a close new friend. Yet in the return to Madrid he still felt dissatisfied and wanted more— direction in life and a certainty about himself. He strongly believed that there was something in the Camino that he was not finding despite his desperate search. He went to the Silos spiritual retreat and was particularly moved by the story of another young man's decision to enter a monastic order on finishing the Camino. I met him in Madrid in 1995 to discuss his third pilgrimage. Meanwhile, he had begun to read guidebooks as well as esoteric books and kept in close touch with friends he had made. He explained that he would plan his journey carefully this time. He wanted to travel a greater distance and spend more time. He planned to do the "whole thing" alone from Roncesvalles, hoped to re-

ceive a staff from Pablito, and would speak only to people when necessary. In his attempt to control the outcome of the Camino he missed
what others often find brings them discovery—that experiences unfold
rather than are artificially constructed. His latest Christmas card, in
1996, stated, "Only children know what they are looking for." He
wanted the Camino to "make him" understand rather than interact with
it in an unforced way.

The positive experiences, however, tend to outweigh the negative and
continue to grow. Helped by the many gifts given and received on the
road pilgrims return both mentally and physically. As participants continue to "come back for another opening," as one woman put it, the
Camino's spiritual magnetism is spread in ever-widening arcs.

TIME, SPACE, AND PLACE

As we have seen, within the culture of the Camino there exists the commonly held idea that the longer the journey, the greater its impact on the
individual's life. It is generally those who make the longest journeys who
support the idea of time/distance relationships, an idea that is further
strengthened by the current ideal of authenticity. I have discovered in my
research that contrary to this idea, what appears to be more important
is what the pilgrim brings to the Camino (state of mind, motivation) and
how the Camino is remembered and acted on in the postexperience. Are
the gifts opened and reciprocated? or lost behind the door with the staff?
or in the closet with the backpack? Long journeys can be made, but the
experiences may remain festering at home or seem too overwhelming to
implement. The gap between desire to change and fear of action is too
great to be bridged. Or the idea that change must be radical to be a success haunts pilgrims, who feel the Camino's messages slipping away like
grains of sand in their hands.

In discussing the relationships between time and place, one geogra-
pher suggests that "while it takes time to form an attachment to place,
the quality and intensity of experience matters more than simple dura-
tion."[33] Using the example of love, he argues that it can occur "at first
sight" or may never develop into more than friendship despite a longtime relationship.[34] The same is true of the Camino. A week on the Camino may immediately and radically shake some pilgrims' sense of reality on the road and at home. For others, a journey of four months may
produce infinite opportunity for meditation and reflection yet confusion
and aimlessness back home.

Effects may also be latent, only surfacing months and years after the Camino is made. A twenty-eight-year-old Swiss man wrote to me in December 1995, more than a year after he made the Camino:

> I remember when I wrote to you last time, I said that the Camino didn't change me. Now I must say that it did. The subject I thought about most while walking was my close and less close friends and my family. Of course I didn't choose this subject on purpose. At that time I wasn't aware that this would have an effect. The reason why I thought at first that the Camino didn't have an effect on me is simply: I couldn't *use* the conclusions I had made on the Camino until I was back into regular life with all the people that surround me. Or maybe I couldn't *make* the conclusions until I was back in regular life with my surroundings.

Twice this man refers to how the Camino acted on him as if he were a spectator to the pilgrimage's processes. It was in the return home that he found his role again and was able to place the two realities that he has lived side by side, a comparison not possible during the Camino. When we met in Santiago in October 1994 he was also skeptical then of the Camino's impacts, mostly feeling pleased that he had accomplished the hard-won goal. He also did not consider himself a pilgrim, yet the pilgrimage obviously continues to work its way into his life. The long hours of unforced, uncontrollable thoughts lived on the Camino came to light only in the return. Knowing the value of friendships and family and what they mean to him is now central.

The time/place discussion also relates to the part-time pilgrim. The subjective element that is brought to the Camino as well as the places in which the pilgrimage is enacted play a vital role in the meanings the Camino can have over a long period. The part-time pilgrim is in a constant state of coming and going, of beginning and ending the journey, and in this way has the possibility of keeping the Camino present and undone, in ways different from the pilgrim who makes the journey in one long stretch. What I have discovered is that for some part-time pilgrims the pilgrimage has a way of living continuously and growing in daily life, and the long distance is somewhat irrelevant to the cumulative experience.

George first began the Camino in France with his wife in 1990. He keeps a journal of experiences, and his first entry begins as follows: "We are setting out on this pilgrimage to mark the 25th year of our marriage—though in planning and preparing for the walk the idea of pilgrimage has caught my imagination strangely. It seems quite fitting to do it in a non-confessional spirit—no point in pretending to a faith we don't have—

but with respect for the faith, and the many motivations, of our prede-cessors." On an impulse they decided to make the journey together in portions to accommodate a work schedule.

Five years later, reflecting on the first beginning, George commented that the Camino came to represent in part an opportunity to renegoti-ate a possible spiritual life. In his journeys he not only discovered his poet's voice, but cautiously yet movingly he began to pray, an act he never before engaged in. He says that he feels that he is always on the road, whether at home in London or at his summer home in France. I asked him if the Camino was in abeyance during his times at home. He re-sponded in the negative, saying that it was actively churning inside him, growing and transforming him. On the eve of finally getting to Santiago in 1997 he commented, "It's been an eight-year project." During a home interview in January 1995 he shared with me the following piece of po-etry that he wrote in October 1994 after a summer's portion of pilgrimage which beautifully expresses his own landscapes of discovery—creative, spiritual, and reaching across personal and social borders.

> Steering an erratic course
> Between the joy of solitude
> And the pleasures of friendship
> This part-time pilgrim finds
> Some cardinal points on his compass:
> The power of submission
> And the drain of deceit;
> The generosity of poverty
> And the need for pain;
> The giving of grief
> And the mystery of faith;
> Joy built on hardship
> And beauty on foundations
> As evanescent as the wind.

ARRIVING AT THE BEGINNING

Keep Ithaka always in your mind.
Arriving there is what you are destined for.
But do not hurry the journey at all.
Better if it lasts for years . . .
  —*Konstantino Kavafis,* Collected Poems

Concluding a book is similar to arriving in Santiago: It's a relief to have made it, it's a bit anticlimactic, and there's disappointment that it has to end. Conclusions, though, also resonate with going home, with taking time to stop and look back at what has come before and attempting to draw the disparate stories of the long journey together. In retracing one's steps one moves both on and off the road once again.

As I write these conclusions, almost five years have passed since I first set foot in Santiago. Like many others, I came to the pilgrimage by chance. I found myself at Santiago's doorstep in a moment of unanticipated personal transition. I began the journey as a researcher but experienced many things described in this book: confirmations of myself, an opening of my eyes to different perspectives, personal doubt and crisis, a sense of liberation from the strictures of regimented time. I realized from the road that my life was governed by an "imagined future," an oasis where time was abundant and where I did not feel constant stress to always do and be more. My academic life reinforced my sense of dissatisfaction and inadequacy to "do it all." The Camino allowed me, at least briefly, to step off the treadmill and put my unhealthy relationship to time in perspective. How can I flow with, rather than against, time?

In that first journey I also felt that bottled-up parts of myself were suddenly tapped. Once open, there was no way to reclose the bottle. As I went home my greatest wish was to be able to reincorporate the positive elements of the road into my relationships with my husband and my work, not to create upheaval. I cannot really explain how or why, but something inside of me snapped or broke free while walking. I sensed a truth about myself that I could no longer ignore. I did not go on the pilgrimage to change, nor did I want to create a rupture in my life, but that was one of the results.

Making a dramatic change in one part of my life, I learned, does not guarantee that the rest will fall into place. I still struggle with time, often giving more value to doing rather than being. I have had the unusual experience of having these issues constantly before me. Sharing the journey with countless people also gave me the opportunity to reflect on my own experiences, the ups and downs, feelings of discouragement at having lost the way, and triumphs. In a sense I have not had the chance to get off the road since 1992. I made the pilgrimage in 1993 and returned to Spain for my field research in 1994 and 1995, and since then I have been writing, which brings me back to people and places of the road.

Now I am at the margin of my academic life. I feel relieved to realize that I wrote this book more from the passion that I have for the Camino and the debt I feel toward those along the way who helped me, shared their lives and stories with me, and became my friends than from fear generated by the "publish or perish" mentality requisite to advance an academic career. I have found, however, that in closing one door, over time others may open. The most unexpected gift of the Camino walked out of the forest one day and came to the door at Roncesvalles where I was working as an hospitalera. First friendship, then love followed in Santiago. The Camino has given me a great deal.

THE MEANINGS OF MOVEMENT

Throughout this book I have argued that through movement pilgrims make statements about themselves and society. Among the hundreds of thousands that come to Santiago each year in pilgrimage to the tomb of Saint James, and more in Holy Years, an ever-increasing group eschew modern ways of reaching the shrine in favor of making a long human-powered journey. This minority group of pilgrims who walk, cycle, and occasionally go by horse or with a pack animal tend to be middle-class, educated, white, urban Europeans who are attracted to the pilgrimage as both an inner and outer journey. Their motives are multiple and layered and evolve both over the course of the long journey and in the return home. Foot and cycle pilgrims frequently bring to the Camino their own, often vaguely defined personal struggles or find themselves at a point of transition. Often the inner journey is set in motion well before the external one begins. Most pilgrims consciously reject other models of travel or ways of expressing devotion already familiar to them in favor of the human-powered effort. These pilgrims tend to see themselves as different from those who go by bus and car, not because of motives, but because they believe bus and car pilgrims miss the essence of the road. Moreover, tensions relating to styles of movement are important and help to explain why cyclists may feel marginalized within the contemporary pilgrimage. They are part of a liminal category—neither one nor the other. Reading between the lines of difference, foot and cycle pilgrims implicitly reject modernity, technology, speed, superficial connections, and consumer society.

In the implicit, and often explicit, critique of modern society there is a concomitant valorization of "contact," felt to be either lost or hard to achieve in a fast-paced world characterized by mass communication and an apparently increased callousness toward human life on political and social levels. These types of contact are varied: with people, with the road, with the past, with nature, with the self, with silence and solitude, with less, with the spiritual and the religious. At the heart of this desire for contact is often an unspoken lack that pushes the person out of home and on to the road. On some level a wish for transformation—perhaps of both the self and society—or at least clarity and insight exists. For these reasons I call the modern pilgrimage a journey of the suffering soul rather than a journey of the suffering body, as journeys to popular Catholic shrines associated with miraculous cures, such as Lourdes, might be characterized.

These various contacts (and hoped-for transformations) are made fundamentally through the body and its movement through time and space. The proverb "Seeing is believing, but feeling is the truth" seems to have some applicability. Most people recognize "Seeing is believing" but do not realize that at some time during oral transmission the second part was dropped.[1] It appears that in the modern pilgrimage foot and cycle pilgrims recuperate the second part of the message: the pilgrimage can be seen and believed from the window, but the truth of the way is felt on the road. The pilgrim's body is not only a conduit of knowledge but also a medium of communication, a means to connect and make contact with others, the self, the past and the future, nature. The body can also be used as an agent of social change ("cause pilgrims"), as a way to protest the fast-paced, disheartening aspects of modern society, and as a way to peacefully ask for change. Pilgrims are noticed, and on some level many want to be noticed: perhaps they are making a cry for help, a show of grief, a testament of faith, a plea against resignation and personal and social stagnation, a statement about an alternative way of living, or a public protest. In this way pilgrims not only pray with their feet but also speak with or through their feet or their bicycles.

Through the movement of the body, through learning new rhythms and perceiving with all the senses, various meanings of the journey begin to emerge which also relate to the life-worlds of the participants. Throughout the journey pilgrims are confronted with personal, physical, and mental challenges as well as unexpected acts of kindness and patience. Pilgrims encounter new sights, sounds, and ways of feeling and perceiving the world and often develop surprising friendships. Each day's journey becomes filled with anecdotes and stories that become models for future action. Pain and the limitless horizon may lead one to a greater sense of humility. Being invited into someone's home may serve as a lesson in generosity and lead to a greater faith in humanity. Receiving unexpected gifts can lead to one's own desire to give. Being unable to sleep because of thirty snoring people reminds another of the ludic. Feeling God's presence in the sunset over the sea brings another closer to his religion. Surviving a difficult day lost can bring greater self-reliance or the knowledge that there are no accidents. Singing at the top of one's lungs in the middle of the meseta may give another a sense of freedom and wild abandon. Sleeping on the floor reminds another of how easy it is to live with less. Making new friends gives another a feeling of sociability and belonging. Each story becomes part of the pilgrim's journey which can later simply be recalled or applied to another life situation.

It is a mistake to reduce the meaning of particular landscapes or types of experiences to a single interpretation. The pilgrimage is a "realm of competing discourses" in which each person's life-world (personal, social, cultural, etc.) influences what he or she finds, values, criticizes, or rejects. The meseta, for example, is not just a metaphor for the journey through the desert and for crisis, which is a typical interpretation. Instead, it affects each person uniquely—as an experience forgotten to modern people, silence, frustration, a hiding place, loneliness, the site of intense physical pleasure, freedom, an encounter with God. Part of the Camino's enormous appeal as a symbol is its flexibility to accommodate various interpretations of its spaces and encounters yet still retain its basic structure.

Feelings of one's potential and a sense of renewal can also emerge during the pilgrimage and at the same time reveal more clearly the everyday lacks that pilgrims suffer. Despite the pain, fatigue, and other difficulties that one encounters while making the pilgrimage, the interpretation of these experiences as meaningful sometimes leads to feelings of physical, spiritual, personal, and social renewal—which is why some pilgrims call it the therapy route. The body often unexpectedly surpasses the expectations of the pilgrim. Some feel new respect for their bodies and want to care for them better in the everyday. Pilgrims often report the appearance of a hitherto unknown creative side—artistic, oral, written, spiritual. Feeling oneself more strongly connected to the senses pilgrims may express a desire to work with their hands, to create something of their own rather than the abstracts of their daily lives. Some pilgrims realize on the Camino how alienated they are from their bodies, their products, and their society. The desire to decrease the sense of alienation in daily life may motivate an interest in craftwork or making life more simple. Others, realizing an internal void, discover a desire to develop their spiritual lives. From these new visions of the self and others, while making the journey pilgrims often express the desire to make a decision, to take action, or to be less materialist, to be more generous with others, to bring their spiritual life into daily practice. Some pilgrims make more radical decisions—to quit a job, to change careers, to move, or to alter a relationship. The confidence and strength that come while walking and cycling lead many to want to bring these feelings back to daily life.

Others experience disappointment, but few feel unmoved. Instead of transformation and clarity, more questions than answers arise. For some, the Camino simply provides good memories and a sense of accomplishment, which can be sufficient. Others are haunted by the inability to make it to Santiago or to find solutions, for example, to personal crises, social failure, or unexplained pain. Some come to the Camino believing that the "therapy route" will give them the quick fix or the spiritual insight they crave yet feel frustrated when it seems that only others end up with the solutions. Some accept the lack of discovery as "not being their time" and repeat to find what is missing, or they may reject the Camino itself.

I observed in chapter 1 that many pilgrims are attracted to the Camino for its natural environments and its connection to the past. I suggested that a "sentimental longing for feelings and things of the past" permeated the Camino. Frequently, pilgrims refer to the past and feel connected to it through walking and cycling. Some pilgrims describe the Camino's energy and report feeling the inexplicable presence of others who made the same journey. Again, basic human movement brings many people closer to what they feel is real about the past and the present. Walking and the road are tangible. Believing that one can have experiences through walking that are lost in the modern world helps some pilgrims to feel more connected to the present and themselves. Understanding how pilgrims imagine the past can help us understand what pilgrims believe the present lacks. Many, in their daily lives, feel estranged from or out of touch with others, meaningful work, spiritual life, the self, place, and community. While making the Camino pilgrims often feel a reconnection to these values by creating a personally negotiated link to the past—a past characterized by greater faith, a sense of community, innocence, and sensuality. Through their nostalgia pilgrims create and find within themselves and others these values as well as friendship, appreciation, and generosity. Ironically, although pilgrims often feel that these values are lost in the past, their source is the present. Therefore, what is sought does exist in the present, or it would be impossible to "revisit." Some pilgrims are able to recuperate in the Camino, at least temporarily, values that appear to have been paved over by modern society.

In analyzing authenticity claims it is important to see how the development of this community, whose membership is gained through shared experience, can lead to exclusivity: those who truly buy into the project make it most "authentically." Pilgrims who find something authentic in interpreting their actions and the past in these ways often feel protective of it; they do not want it to be desecrated by others outside of the culture of the Camino. Thus when new pilgrims enter the community (which is imagined and in a constant state of regeneration and flux) who seem to lack "authentic" values or whose journeys appear to tarnish the meanings of the Camino, some pilgrims fear that what they have found will be diminished.

In "nature," pilgrims report that their perceptions of time and place are radically altered. Many come to feel that in daily life their senses are deadened by the overstimulation of electronic (often violent and graphic) images and the repetition of urban spaces. Through "cutting out the noise," by slowing down, by subjecting oneself to the pains of the physical body, pilgrims frequently find a heightening of the senses and an appreciation for the minute (e.g., focusing on spider webs when before they were just annoying, seeing individual blades of grass, feeling oneself in a particular place, realizing that time does not have to be governed by the clock). Those accustomed to these sensations through hiking and outdoor activities may take on a different perspective through the historical dimension, the directionality, and the social context of the pilgrimage. In this way the breaking down of normal ways of perceiving allows some pilgrims to begin to interpret their experiences and encounters in different ways. Some are opened to feeling a mystical union of the self with God and nature. Others connect more directly to their own pasts and the dead. Some pilgrims believe that the Camino acts to help the individual break patterns of behavior. Trying new things (food, language, lighting a candle), experimenting (with limits, rhythms, a relationship), and risking (sharing with others, trusting, confessing) also open pilgrims to seeing themselves and others differently and may provide a needed catalyst for change. Many pilgrims, at least temporarily, learn that alternatives exist. But the fundamental question of whether one is able to alter one's deep, underlying structure in the return is more difficult. Does the Camino provide merely superficial insight, or does the combination of practice, feeling, and thought lead to action and change?

REINCORPORATION

The paradox of the arrival is the perpetual beginning at its doorstep. In Santiago the physical arrival is paired with the expectation of a metaphorical new beginning that one "should" embark on at the same time as one arrives. Santiago is a city of joy, celebration, and boasting. The tears of accomplishment, the relief of fulfilled vows, the laughs of shared Camino moments with what seem to be old friends, the pride of achievement— all coalesce into a festive ambience. The city is also the point of unfinished business, limbo, a threshold between the past, the present, and the future. At times the stagnation, doubt, and weight of uncertainty are pungent and oppressive. Weeks and months of intense experience must be quickly reintegrated into normal society. Strange encounters, new friends, questions long held at bay, all become pressing. The questions of the Camino—Where do I eat? Where do I want to sleep?—are replaced by the realities of living—How am I going to get my train ticket home? When shall we meet again? What decision am I going to make regarding the priesthood? While in Santiago, the pilgrim has several choices: go home, remain, or continue the journey. Most choose the former. Very few remain, though the rare person does stop and become dedicated to the pilgrimage. Others decide to keep going a bit farther, to ease the transition home. Many reasons impel pilgrims to keep going: to search for unattained inner resolution; to celebrate an esoteric, Celtic, or initiatory ending at the sea; to feel the geographic finality of the coast that is lacking in Santiago; to prepare for the return home; to explore sites linked to legends of the pilgrimage.

Once begun, the pilgrimage appears to be a continuous process, at least on the level of memory, if not of action. The arrival in Santiago marks the beginning of the next phase: the pilgrim's translation of the stories to home life, which may seem difficult or as unlikely as the legend of the apostle's own translation. How does one bring together two distinct realities, life on and off the road? The challenge is complicated by how the inner journey appears actually to be a series of inner journeys. Pilgrims may feel exhilarated on a physical level yet not feel that their spiritual questions have been resolved. Or perhaps the journey was meant to be a time of personal reflection on a love relationship, and instead of greater clarification the pilgrim felt distracted by body pains, a resurgence of unpleasant childhood memories, or an unanticipated spiritual awakening. The simple pairing of an inner and an outer journey is too narrow a metaphor to understand contemporary pilgrims' experiences.

The inevitable return home after the goal or destination is reached is a crucial part of the process. Many pilgrims feel unprepared to return home, and rarely do pilgrims have rites of reincorporation to ease the transition. Returns are often abrupt, made in isolation, and homecomers may have little or no time to process the events and stories of the road before returning to work. Many find the return home to be difficult and requiring a transition over time. The homecomer is often a "familiar stranger" to those around him or her. Those in the home context may view the returnee with new eyes—with new respect, curiosity, surprise, concern, pride. Home life may not seem as relevant as before leaving. Pilgrims seek closure or perspective on the journey through retelling, which allows them to reinterpret, re-create, and revisit the events. Most find, however, that those in the home context, while sympathetic, have no frame of reference with which to understand the experiences and the stories of chance encounters, union with nature, new friendships, or spiritual awakening. Memories produced through making the pilgrimage are mental and sensual. Pilgrims do not just remember the Camino, they often speak of going back with their senses and feeling as if they are on the road again. They may use metaphors or stories to help recall events and significant moments to help keep the pilgrimage alive.

CHALLENGES OF REINCORPORATION

The vast majority of pilgrims claim that the pilgrimage is a positive experience that they want, in some way, to integrate into their daily lives. Many find on the Camino reaffirmation of their values or of an aspect of their personalities that needed testing. Going home, in this case, can bring a joyous sense of well-being, renewal, and appreciation for what is. A sense of physical well-being, pride in one's accomplishments, and being part of a larger community often remains with pilgrims, influencing other aspects of their personal and social lives, at least in the immediate postreturn. Pilgrims also retain the stories of the journey, with which they may continue to guide some small parts of their lives such as learning not to waste water or trying to live more in the here and now.

Some pilgrims, however, slip back into the quotidian without being able to make a connection between the two realities, home and the Camino. Pilgrims describe several challenges that impede integration: the problem of compromise, day-to-day realities, and the strength of old habits. Once having had one's eyes opened to alternative ways of seeing, feeling, and acting, it can be difficult to close them again. In going home pilgrims may capitulate to the compromise of social pressure, compartmentalize the realities, or struggle to integrate the two.

Despite a desire to incorporate the alternative ways of being and knowing learned in the Camino, the reality, for example, of supporting a family, may outweigh the realization of personal exploration. Or, despite learning the value of living with less, one's job as a salesperson may be dependent on others consuming more. How does one reconcile these dissonant realities? Some capitulate to and accept the social pressures that encourage maintenance of the status quo. It may be too painful or too difficult to bring the two realities into line. The familiar habits and pressures of home life may effectively snuff out the spark that the Camino represents. If the energy gathered from the Camino feels lost with the return to a consumeristic, alienating society, pilgrims usually at least retain the memory of having lived another reality, known themselves and their society in another way, and experienced other rhythms.

Others find that they are able to compartmentalize the two realities and accept an unhealthy lifestyle, an emotionally unfulfilling relationship, or a job that leads to personal alienation or maintain hierarchical or sexist relationships at home or work, justifying the decisions by claiming "the Camino is not real life." Some pilgrims, then, are pilgrims only walking or cycling. It is just another part of their identity, a reality among many others. These tend also to be the pilgrims who are most concerned with others' authenticity because on some level they realize that they do not "really live the Camino" in the day to day: they have a lover on the road and a family at home, attend Mass and pray during the pilgrimage but not in the everyday, live austerely in the Camino yet maintain a rich lifestyle at home, discover nature in the Camino but not out their back doors, enjoy being helped and treated with hospitality but do not think to offer help when the need arises. For some, the pilgrimage is a bracketed experience and the Camino can come to be like an oasis or a distant island that is journeyed to but not brought home.

Others struggle and work to keep the pilgrimage alive and actively seek to apply the lessons of the Camino to their personal, social, and familial lives. Some make immediate, life-changing decisions on returning home. Many of these latter pilgrims do find positive personal transformation but feel that the journey is never quite over, which is positively valued ("to always be on the move internally," as one said). Time is an important factor. Realizations of how the journey affects daily life and how integration is possible often requires reflection, retelling, interaction with other pilgrims, and repetition.

Those who want to keep processing the events and struggle to keep the spark alive can join Friends associations, maintain contact with their Camino "group" through letters and reunions, repeat the experience, become hospitaleros, or find ways to take their jobs to Spain. Repetition always exists as a possibility to recharge the batteries, to renew the feelings, to search for new openings, or as a way to again live "life on the road." Those who tend to compartmentalize the Camino may return to the pilgrimage and play at this other reality again, enjoying their special status as pilgrims. Often these pilgrims take pride in the number of times they have made the pilgrimage, as if somehow their authenticity is increased through repetition. Many former pilgrims, especially those under thirty years of age, do not join associations, preferring to maintain contacts via letters and reunions in which they rehash the journey and the subsequent turns life has taken.

The initial walking or cycling journey may be just the beginning of a much longer series of inner journeys in which the participant retains the feeling of being a pilgrim even though he or she is not on the road. Some may sense that they have moved beyond the Camino as a physical journey but that it remains with them in other ways. Making the pilgrimage on foot or bicycle serves as a voluntary and informal rite of initiation into a society of pilgrims—which can be both an imagined and a real community. Unless religiously motivated, most participants do not generally think of themselves as pilgrims before they begin but often come to see themselves as such through developing an identity as a member of a large supranational group of pilgrims (past, present, and future). The community is not bound by geography, nationality, motives, a liturgy, or a leader. Rather pilgrims are connected by experience, movement, and sharing a common culture of the road.

Others want to literalize in daily life the feeling of community they acquire while on the road. This literalization of community is precisely what motivated the formation of many Friends groups. Some associations are specifically oriented toward pilgrims; others maintain a multiple orientation toward all aspects of the pilgrimage (local history, routes, churches, medieval studies) and pilgrims as well (preparation, rites of departure, and reincorporation).

Part of this sense of community is the idea of the "new Europe." One of the clichés of the Camino's reanimation, especially since the 1980s, has been the creation of the new Europe via the Camino's past as the seed from which Europe grew. From the pope to all levels of state and regional government, this idea has been used to generate support for the protection of the Camino's architectural and artistic patrimony. From the point of view of the Catholic church, the reanimation of the Camino is an ideal way to evangelize Europe's youth through returning to its Christian foundation and center of faith. In an attempt to create a cultural base for the "European identity" wished for by the European Union, the Council of Europe and many of the Camino's "experts" have vigorously sought historical evidence to link the routes and the peoples. Individual pilgrims and associations have also sought similar goals to create a more united Europe for the future. Despite movements toward union signs of disunion are also apparent in associationism, which reflects a continuing alliance to national communities and identities.

Analysis should reveal not only the explicit but also the implicit. Part of the search for a unified "European" identity may erase some national differences, but it also creates walls and divisions: if there is something European, then there is something that is "not European." Going to the roots of Christian Europe leads one immediately to the Crusades and, what is more relevant here, to the Reconquest of Islamic Spain by Christian forces ("soldiers of God"). Santiago's identity as Moorslayer is a violent one and illustrates another aspect of the roots of Christian Europe— a Europe forged by intolerance and bloodshed. The modern pilgrim erases or at least sidesteps Santiago Matamoros by believing that he represents the past; that is, he is not relevant to the present. But the "past" is where many want to go. Thus "memory" of the past is always selective. It is also important to remember that the idea of a common European identity is largely an ethnically white movement by a politically white society, possibly threatened economically and socially by being "invaded" or "overrun" by immigrants from the south (largely Islamic countries) who may be nationals but who do not share "European cultural roots." Thus one reading of the pilgrimage of the "past" is that of a white, Christian Europe—a place to which some would like to return.[2]

PILGRIM'S PROGRESS

What can we say about the relationship between pilgrimage and tourism? The study of the Camino's contemporary reanimation illustrates that there is no simple way to mark the difference between these two complex phenomena. Rather, attempts to understand the meanings of movement and analyze participants' categories—how they are used, who is excluded and included, and why—may be more productive. Those who walk, cycle, use a pack animal, or go on horseback almost always consider themselves pilgrims, or peregrinos, and use this term. Participants in the modern Camino are also encouraged by the social environment to identify themselves as pilgrims. Rather than simply claim pilgrimage as faith and tourism as frivolous, it is important to look more deeply into the life-worlds and values that shape travelers' journeys.

Most observers of pilgrimage, assuming that its central motivation is religious, want to know the place of faith and belief in the contemporary Camino. As a realm of competing discourses, the Santiago pilgrimage accommodates a host of opposed orientations and belief systems. In the modern pilgrimage one can be an "authentic" pilgrim and not be religious, that is, not have faith or believe in God or in miracles central to Catholic doctrine. This may seem to be a contradiction, but it reflects the prevalence in Euro-American society of being a pilgrim in a metaphoric sense. The metaphoric pilgrim seeks an inner way or alternatives to the breakdown of modern society, overwhelming social and personal problems, or the alienation of daily life. The trend toward "seeking alternatives" that can be seen in the proliferation of eclectic religious and spiritual movements as well as alternative and ecotourism movements reflects a general sense of late-twentieth-century cultural dissatisfaction. The modern pilgrimage to Santiago is ecumenical, even though its symbols and infrastructure have a distinct religious history and meaning.

In what appears to be a desacralization of pilgrimage by alternative and competing interpretations, many, especially the religiously devout, fear the loss of its essence: faith, belief, community, communion, and religious and spiritual sentiment. In general the proliferation of individualized spiritualities is interpreted as the rejection of religion and, by analogy, the loss of community and a sign of further social fracture. Yet it appears to be more accurate to say that for participants faith and belief actively live and grow in the contemporary pilgrimage. Faith and belief, however, may have various orientations and manifestations. Some pilgrims rediscover the sacred in their lives and in the Church and regain faith in themselves and humanity through the Camino and its encounters. Some already practicing believers—Catholics, Anglicans, Protestants—find a renewal of faith in God, Saint James, or their church. Others find themselves drawn away from their church as a result of the pilgrimage yet feel stronger in their faith in God.

A curious outcome of the pilgrimage relates to the power of the gift. Pilgrims often feel a strong sense of debt and allegiance to the Camino. Unlike the trend of many privatized religiosities, which do not seem to foster group consciousness, one interesting consequence of the pilgrimage seems to be a sense of being positively linked and even obligated to an imagined community of Santiago pilgrims and the "Camino" as a concept. Rather than being held together by a liturgy or a leader, pilgrims may feel loyalty and allegiance to one another via the shared journey. The symbols of the journey are shared as meaningful, but the meanings of the symbols are individualized; each person extracts something unique from the Camino. It appears that the pilgrims' diffuse set of beliefs and motivations strengthens the bonds of the community. Although there are people and institutions which attempt to control the Camino and its meanings, there is no exclusive voice that mandates authenticity. Among the competing discourses of what it means to be a pilgrim and how to enact the role pilgrims generally find more liberty than control and the possibility to feel and take from the experience whatever is relevant to their own lives. Moreover, pilgrims often develop a sense of gratitude to the Camino that is directed at many points along the road. The debts and power of the gift are spread out among many, over a vast landscape. There may be specific moments and people on which they are focused, but it is usually the experience taken as a whole that is remembered. A series of meaningful experiences—moments in nature, pain, small gifts of good cheer in a dismal moment, quenching of thirst—produce the whole. Some feel grateful for faith, for having the best experience of a lifetime, for having a space in which to grieve, for giving another new

perspectives, for relieving the stress of a high-pressure job. It may be one
or a combination of all of these.

Some pilgrims want to give back to the way—by being hospitaleros,
by donating money, by volunteering time in an association, or by introducing others to the road, way marking the road, giving another a shell,
making another journey for those who cannot go.

Earlier I posed the question of whether the influences of the pilgrimage
are superficial or endure in a lasting way. In examining the reincorporation I tried to understand how the pilgrimage affected both individuals and the societies from which they come and to which they return.
In terms of the larger institutional forces, it is clear that the official words
of the Catholic church and governmental agencies that support the pilgrimage's reanimation are typically self-serving. There is no doubt that
the pilgrimage's reanimation has produced social and economic change
among the villages and towns through which the Camino passes. At
times positive connections between pilgrims or hospitaleros and villagers
have created greater links between disparate peoples, or the development of social services, or revitalized local economies. Some negative
repercussions are also visible, for example, the loss of fountains in Galicia, the villagers' fear of economic competitiveness from refuges, and
the literal overrunning of small villages by hundreds of pilgrims in the
summer months, which in some cases has exacerbated existing social
tensions. The recuperation of historical civic and ecclesiastic architecture can also be seen as a positive social ramification, yet the desecration of other places, such as Monte del Gozo, is disheartening. The associationism and creation of transnational links between pilgrims
appears to be an outcome specifically designed to counteract the loss
and disintegration of community felt by many middle-class Europeans.
And some pilgrims have used their journeys for the benefit of those who
cannot go.

On the personal level participants describe how the Camino provides
opportunities to live, at least temporarily, another reality and to discover
alternative ways of perceiving and acting in the world. The issue of where
the locus of change lies—the individual or the Camino—has a bearing on
how the Camino continues to influence pilgrims' daily lives. Some few
people experience a sense of illumination or conversion, which provides
an immediate cause for a radical shift in home life. Some repeat the Camino
to renew the "Camino reality." Others are content to compartmentalize.

Thus it is possible to see both superficial and enduring changes. Many,
at least temporarily, taste something different but are unable or unwill-

ing to integrate the Camino reality as a deep, personal, structural change. The simple act of making the decision to go and follow through with a dream may be sufficient and the greatest achievement. Most pilgrims, however, find that deep personal transformation occurs over time through action and reflection, that the Camino may have provided the catalyst, but they work to integrate the Camino and daily reality. In a sense one chooses to be changed.[3]

Fieldwork on the Road

Finding our feet, an unnerving business which never more
than distantly succeeds, is what ethnographic research
consists of as a personal experience; trying to formulate
the basis on which one imagines, always excessively, one
has found them is what anthropological writing consists
of as a scientific endeavor.

   —*Clifford Geertz,* The Interpretation of Culture

Clifford Geertz uses the metaphor of "finding our feet" to describe the
personal nature of ethnographic research. It is a metaphor that is particularly relevant to the study of pilgrimage. I began my pilgrimage, as
an anthropologist, with my feet, as do pilgrims. As a field site the Camino
presents a number of challenges methodologically. First, unlike most anthropological studies conducted in fixed locations, both the Camino itself and the population of pilgrims are in a constant state of flux. When
the pilgrimage is completed, the pilgrims return to more than sixty countries. Second, pilgrimage is process and pilgrims often discuss how their
motives evolve over time. And third, pilgrims frequently find themselves
at a loss to articulate this process while doing the Camino and may only
realize its importance after they return home.

   To attend to these challenges I needed to adapt my fieldwork to experience the Camino in an array of ways and places. The Camino is not
bound to one place or time; rather it is a set of multiply constructed meanings in a variety of locations, and my work became what George Marcus
has called a "multi-sited" ethnography.[1] The obvious starting point was
to make the pilgrimage. I returned to Spain in the summer of 1993 for a
period of nine weeks to make the pilgrimage with a group of Americans—
professors and students—as an initial form of participant-observation.
I was looking forward to the physical dimension of the Camino as well
as anticipating that living its historical topography would be both ped-
agogically and personally rewarding. On a personal level I was drawn

to pilgrimage, not for any religious sentiment, but (as I discovered with many pilgrims) for the opportunity it provided to break from the quotidian. Despite my naive attempt to remain the objective observer along the Camino, I was surprised to find myself deeply moved during the experience and my life shaken by its influence when I returned home.

The next summer I returned to Spain for thirteen months to experience one year's cycle of the pilgrimage at various locations in Spain and in several other European countries. When I made the Camino in 1993 it stunned me to encounter a Dutch woman temporarily living in the Navarrese village of Belorado, attending to the needs of the pilgrims in the local refuge. In 1994 I contacted the priest who organized the volunteer hospitaleros and, on request, he assigned me to work in four refuges along the camino francés (Roncesvalles, Belorado, Burgos, and Hospital de Orbigo) from August 1 to September 9 and then from October 1 to October 15. In four of the ultimately six refuges in which I served as an hospitalera in 1994 and 1995, I worked with partners from Spain (a thirty-three-year-old female government worker, a sixty-year-old retired woman, and a twenty-seven-year-old male law student), the Netherlands (a forty-nine-year-old female teacher and a fifty-year-old male Reiki healer), Germany (two professional women in their midthirties), and the United States (a woman studying the literary and historical aspects of the Camino). Except for the retired Spanish woman, all were former pilgrims.

I spent many hours mopping floors, discussing techniques for removing hair from showers, and learning more vocabulary in Spanish on plumbing than I know in English; all the time amplifying my definition of fieldwork. I also passed countless hours engaged in rich conversation or participating in the rhythm of the pilgrims' lives—tending blisters, cooking an evening meal, listening to the day's stories, asking probing questions, strolling in the village or city, writing postcards and journals. It was demanding yet rewarding work that required mental energy and stamina. The day is quite long, there is little time to rest, and the waves of pilgrims at the height of summer rarely ebbed. By the end of fifty days I was both mentally drained and supersaturated with the stories of hundreds of pilgrims.

Besides the contacts with pilgrims, I developed relationships with (mostly older) locals who lived nearby or had a connection with the refuge. Being hospitaleros has given foreigners a role in the communities where refuges are located and has allowed unexpected encounters between people who would normally never meet because of national, linguistic, age, or class differences. One day while picking vegetables in the garden of a villager in Navarre, he stood up and commented to me and the new German woman who had just arrived, "Ay, here we are in this small village, three people, three nations, three languages, and we are all communicating." The Camino had brought the world to this man who has never been outside of Spain.

To enrich my research base I spent the winter of 1994–95 in Santiago to understand the pulse of the city in the off-season. I had already spent two summers in Santiago, and I wanted to know how the city lived the Camino and experienced pilgrims as well as who the pilgrims were who braved the way in the winter. Furthermore, it was the logical place to be with pilgrims as the geographic goal was reached and they began the turn for home.

On arrival most pilgrims congregate in the old part of Santiago. I, too, spent much time there with them. I interviewed business owners up and down the important main walkways that fan out from the cathedral plaza to get a sense of the political-economic context of the pilgrimage in Santiago, a city in perpetual state of welcome. The experiences of locals in relation to pilgrims and tourists in general further interested me. Most vital to my research was the time spent with pilgrims in their arrivals and departures from Santiago. The fourteen-year administrator of the Pilgrim's Office, Don Jaime García Rodríguez, and his staff kindly allowed me to frequently come to the office to inquire about arriving pilgrims and also gave me access to information and records. Don Jaime found it odd, however, that a young, non-Catholic American woman would be interested in studying pilgrimage, a response that was typical among Spaniards.

In the fall of 1994 I decided to focus on the postpilgrimage experience while living in Santiago. During the research in five sites along 750 kilometers of the camino francés that summer I had the opportunity to observe and discuss with pilgrims how the experience of being a pilgrim unfolded within them. Each day was its own cycle of beginning and ending, arrival and departure. Santiago became an intensified version of this process as pilgrims began to come to terms with reaching the geographic goal. Follow-up research with a dispersed population is difficult. I decided to use the same methods that pilgrims themselves use: correspondence, in-house visits, and participation in activities of Friends of the Camino associations in Spanish and non-Spanish contexts. I traveled to Germany, England (twice), and various parts of Spain (Madrid, Barcelona, Zaragoza, Seville, the northern coast).

A NOTE ON METHOD
AND REPRESENTING THE CAMINO

My research was unorthodox, flowing and ebbing with the currents of the Camino. Reflecting the informal atmosphere of the pilgrimage, as an hospitalera I did not press my role as anthropologist through lengthy, formal interviews. The Camino is not just thought and done but also deeply felt. It is an experience of the senses. My conversations with pilgrims delved into motivation, group formation, personal discoveries, and hopes for the future. Among the hundreds of pilgrims with whom I spoke and shared I exchanged addresses and followed up with them.

I did not use questionnaires. In the context of my role as an hospitalera I felt it important that my work as an anthropologist not intrude into the experience of the pilgrims, though I found this to be impossible. Just as I had found it odd to encounter a Dutch woman in a small Navarrese pueblo, so too did the majority of pilgrims find the presence of a young American woman a surprise. This surprise and the openness fostered by an ethos of communitas in the Camino led inevitably to an explanation of my project (and many other themes less neutral, such as American domestic and foreign affairs or the television series "Baywatch," a favorite among young Spanish men). Most pilgrims were curious about the study and willingly spoke at length. My research benefited tremendously from pilgrims' self-reflection. Many were eager to share their experiences with me, and some wanted to know how others dealt with the same issues. Others thanked me for listening and helping them to work through their Camino experiences. In December 1994, April 1995, and December 1995 I wrote to pilgrims in an open-ended fashion, asking about the journey and the return home. In addition I conducted numerous interviews off the Camino in England, Germany, and Spain and spoke with both long- and short-term postpilgrims (some had made the Camino just a few months earlier; others had made the Camino thirty years earlier). I still maintain a regular in-depth correspondence with a number of pilgrims.

The Camino, as a distinct space, is similar to small-scale communities in which gossip flows freely. Communications move backward and forward in the message books found in the pilgrims' refuges as well as in verbal reports of delayed pilgrims, and faster-moving cyclists. Yet, paradoxically, it is an ever-changing community whose few fixed members are not pilgrims themselves. At times during my fieldwork experience people recognized me as "La Americana" or the "American writer/anthropologist" before we met. My own incorporation into the culture of the Camino also translated into the postpilgrimage. A pilgrim friend e-mailed me in December 1995 to tell me that at a recent meeting of the Confraternity of St. James in London an Englishwoman included me in her presentation of her summer's journey. Another English pilgrim sent me a draft of his postpilgrimage reflections and asked my advice on where to send it for publication. The following bit, extracted from the opening paragraph, caught my attention because of the questions it raises about representation. He wrote,

> Along the way I encountered traditional Catholics, sincere atheists, and honest agnostics. The way like the Europe of the nineties is pluralist—no longer the possibility of Catholic supremacy. . . . Here, there were people of faith and people of none, students from Brazil, a parish group from Germany, journalists, unemployed Spanish workers and even a Californian anthropologist spending a year studying the phenomenon of pilgrimage. Strangely, an agnostic in her year's study had become more Catholic than those she studied. Counselling one of them in his lack of faith, she admitted that in extremis she spoke to St. James!

These comments address the important question of representation and ethnographic authority.[2] In his account I am part of his reflections and his vision of the "pluralist" Camino. I find myself described by place (not American, but Californian), by belief (agnostic and Catholic, and, I suppose, honest), and as curiosity. While I am amused by the representation, I am surprised by the inaccuracies and the use of details out of their original context, producing a sensationalized result. I admit that I did speak to Saint James occasionally, but it was due not to any budding religiosity but rather a sense of wonder and amusement at how my life had managed to become intimately entwined with Saint James's own audacious history. In my ethnographic representation I strive to use pilgrims' own words, yet I know that this version is a "partial truth" limited by memory, ways of remembering, and personal bias. During a taped interview this same pilgrim remarked that I was not "value-free" in my approach. His comment provoked a quick question in reply, "Who or what is?" One pilgrim suggested to me, "Just tell us about ourselves," and this became my goal.

Finally, all of the translations in the text are mine, except as noted. There are numerous quotations without any citation. These come from letters in my possession and interviews. Most of the non-Spanish letters were written in English, and I have translated the Spanish pilgrims' letters. The pilgrims' names in the book are fictitious, but the people and their stories are not. I use the real names of pilgrims whose work is published.

APPENDIX B

The Twentieth-Century Reanimation

In the 1840s the British travel writer Richard Ford sounded the death knell for the Camino: "Pilgrimage, the oriental and mediaeval form of travelling is passing away even in Spain. The carcass remains, but the spirit is fled."[1] It is unlikely that Ford could have imagined the vibrant reanimation of the pilgrimage one hundred fifty years later. "Reanimation" means the act of giving new life. My use of the term responds to Ford's idea of the Camino's lost spirit and counters with animism—the idea that all things, both phenomena of nature and the inanimate, have a soul or a life force. There is no doubt that the Camino has been given new life in the twentieth century, and those who are ardently attached to the pilgrimage would probably attribute the changes to the indomitable "soul" the Camino possesses, surviving the winds of change, the capriciousness of human loyalty, and transformations to its roads and ways.

One can discern since the tenth century continuity in the symbols and players important to the rise of the shrine—Santiago as a pilgrim and as a warrior saint, ecclesiastical and political influences, wealth and power, faith—yet discontinuity in their uses and meanings. A crucial early development in the cult's return to prestige occurred in 1879 when the saint's remains, hidden for two centuries, were unearthed. Pope Leo XIII proclaimed their authenticity in his 1884 papal bull, *Deus Omnipotens* (All-Powerful God), and set the stage for a renewed interest in the art, history, and literature of the pilgrimage during its medieval heyday. The discovery took place during what came to be called the Marian Age: the florescence of a cult devoted to the Virgin Mary through a series of apparitions at Lourdes in 1858 which were supported by a receptive Church eager to develop and control popular religious expression.[2]

Moving quickly to the 1940s, a continued academic and a new political interest began to focus on Santiago. The American Walter Muir Whitehill began the tedious job of transcribing the *Codex Calixtinus* in the cathedral's archives during the late 1920s and early 1930s. The Spanish Civil War (1936–39) delayed its publication and accessibility until 1944.[3] After the grueling Civil War, Santiago Matamoros became a politically potent symbol to advance the nationalist policy of Spain's new fascist leader, Generalísimo Francisco Franco. The Camino also reopened as a peaceful zone, no longer crisscrossed by the bloody Civil War. Out of this moment Franco consciously allied himself with Santiago Matamoros and identified himself, like the bellicose Santiago, as the savior and unifier of Spain. "The Francoist style of religiosity, later disparaged by the liberal, Vatican II priests as 'National Catholicism,' was based on the public display of faith in processions, solemn masses, and elaborate ceremonialism reminiscent of the Counter-Reformation church."[4] Consistent with this theory, even before the end of the Civil War Franco made a public petition to reinstate the Voto de Santiago (nullified in 1931 under the Second Republic)[5] and to reinstate Santiago as the patron of Spain.[6] On July 21, 1938, during a decisive Civil War battle at Brunete, Franco petitioned for the patronage to be returned. On July 25, the saint's feast day, the battle was won. He (apparently) called this "the second Clavijo," invoking the image of a crucial Reconquest battle in which Santiago appeared as Matamoros. This linking of Brunete and Clavijo illustrates Franco's use of Santiago Matamoros to equate himself and the Nationalists with the maintenance of an essential Spanish identity inexorably connected to Catholicism.[7] Under the Franco regime Spain was considered "La gran reserva católica de Occidente" (The great Catholic reserve of the West). In essence, Franco proclaimed himself the second savior and the Nationalist movement the second great salvation of Spain.

Though Franco used the Matamoros image to bolster and toughen the state, he also initiated research into the pilgrimage itself. Under the Franco government came the publication of two lengthy texts on the history of the pilgrimage. In honor of Santiago's martyrdom 1,900 years earlier the Institute of Spain sponsored a contest in 1943 that produced Luciano Huidobro y Serna's three-volume *Las peregrinaciones jacobeas*

(1949–51) and later the classic three-volume *Las peregrinaciones a Santiago de Compostela* (1948) by Luis Vázquez de Parga, José María LaCarra, and Juan Uría Ríu. Concurrently, the Archicofradía of Apóstol Santiago (the head confraternity of St. James) in Santiago began to publish the magazine *Compostela* in honor of the 1948 Holy Year and the renewed interest in the cult. The same year, La Peregrinación Mundial de los Jóvenes a Santiago (the World Youth Pilgrimage to Santiago) was organized and repeated during consecutive Holy Years to honor the Church and the Spanish state.

Broken and fractured by the chaos of war and the demonstration on a mass scale of man's inhumanity to man, post–World War II Europe entered a period of serious social reflection. The late 1940s also marked the beginning of a period of relative peace in Western Europe and the increased mobility of middle-class Europeans seeking leisure opportunities in the warm Mediterranean. During this period a political search began to unite Europe through its shared past. The Camino, with its history in the roots of Christian Europe, provided the ideal way to transcend political difference and integrate a continent through the sound of pattering feet rather than the beat of war.

The thought of war was also on the minds of the few pilgrims of this period who walked to Santiago. In 1945 three young Spaniards decided to walk to Santiago with the desire to reach the apostle's tomb "to give thanks for the gift of Christian faith that He transmitted to us and with hope that He would help us to discover the way that we should follow to work in the construction of the Kingdom of God, a New World, especially for the marginalized poor." Unlike pilgrims of the 1990s, they went without any preparation, without maps, sleeping bags, or special shoes. The three found poverty in the villages and realized that the people had forgotten the pilgrimage; they were looked at with fear, especially in Galicia where the people "suspected that [they] were members of the anti-Franco guerrillas, the *maquis.*" They encountered two other groups of pilgrims: three German soldiers and five Spaniards. The Germans had escaped from Allied concentration camps and now walked to Santiago to plead for protection. The young Spanish men (four from La Rioja and one from Galicia) were part of the Blue Division, a Spanish volunteer unit, mostly Fascists, that fought on the side of the Germans. Having survived "healthy and free in the battle of Stalingrad [they] vowed to go Santiago to thank the Apostle." They arrived together in faith, tattered by war, to hope for something better.[8]

The 1950s and early 1960s marked the rebirth of confraternities of

St. James in the form of Friends of the Camino associations in France and Spain, continued political interest by the Spanish government, and an expansion of academic interest in the historical and artistic aspects of the Camino. In 1950 a group of French academics formed a Friends of the Camino group (Société des Amis de Saint-Jacques de Compostelle) in Paris whose purpose was to investigate and restore the vast cultural patrimony linked with the Camino in France since the tenth century. This early association focused on the medieval aspects of the pilgrimage, the pilgrims, iconography, literature, French folklore, and the role of French monastic orders in shaping the pilgrimage and its routes.[9]

In Spain the 1954 Holy Year sparked a series of group youth pilgrimages focused on developing faith in God and *la patria* (the fatherland or homeland). This interest paralleled a general proliferation within the Spanish Catholic church of *cursillos,* or religious retreats and group meetings focused on the development of one's interior faith based on concepts of fundamental/authentic Christianity.[10] Many equestrian pilgrimages made by those with state military connections went to Santiago to pay respect to Santiago the Apostle and Patron of Spain and to uphold the yearly offering on the saint's day that was reinstated by Franco. In 1956 *Compostellanum,* the rectory of Santiago's academic journal, was published, and a few years later the Centro de Estudios Jacobeos (Center of Jacobean Studies) was founded to focus more specifically on the cult of Saint James and its history.

Academic interest abroad continued. Walter Starkie, who made three pilgrimages to Santiago between 1924 and 1954, commented in 1957 on the "pampered pilgrim," marking a crucial moment in the development of the ethos of the modern pilgrimage: "Pilgrims today are even more gregarious in spirit and more robotlike than they were in my younger days, thirty years ago, and such attention has been paid to their personal fads and fancies by the confraternities who supervise their prayers and the tourist companies who plan their journeys that no unforeseen adventure happens. . . . Nevertheless, even today, there are still in every country a number of lonely pilgrims who forsake the rapid-moving supervised pilgrimage and make the long journey guided solely by the myriads of wandering souls in the star-dust of the Milky Way."[11] In this bit of nostalgia and social commentary Starkie sets up a distinction between the pilgrimage by bus or car and the pilgrimage by foot. Though still considered pilgrims by him, the hint of mass transit and large groups taints the authenticity of what seem to be to him tourist-pilgrims.

The development of the tourism industry played a significant role in the reanimation of the Camino.[12] In the 1960s Spain began to diversify its economy through tourism at first designed to attract foreigners to a Spain that was considered "a country of Europe, but not 'European.'"[13] South of the Pyrenees was an exotic attraction of colorful folk, flamenco music, gypsies, bullfights, honor, and religion. Foreign tourism in Spain grew astronomically in this period. In 1951 Spain received 1.3 million foreign tourists. In 1963 the number jumped to 11 million, and by 1978, 40 million flocked to Spain.[14] Tourism also changed between the 1960s and the 1970s—from exotic to solar Spain, attracting northern foreigners to the sunny, Mediterranean coast in droves. At the same time a budding appeal for tourism related to the past did not escape the attention of the then minister of information and tourism, Manuel Fraga Iribarne (the current president of the Xunta of Galicia). He actively promoted tourism related to the Camino and sought to improve the infrastructure of routes and to preserve monuments especially around the Holy Years of 1965 and 1971. Under Franco, Fraga was responsible for implementing the *parador* system.[15] In the early 1960s, through the Ministry of National Education, Franco established the Camino de Santiago as a *conjunto histórico-artístico* (historic and artistic entirety) with its own board of trustees under the protection of the state. This act recognized the Camino's patrimony and the desire to both protect and exploit it as a historical resource.[16]

The desire to protect the historical and artistic patrimony of the Camino also marked the expansion of the tourism and travel industry in the West on a wide scale, where the past became "a foreign country with a booming tourist trade" and middle-class Europeans could enjoy leisure time through the democratizing benefits of mass transit.[17] The focus on history and nature, as well as a general "revitalization of European rituals," in the 1970s emphasizing nostalgia, heritage, and play coincided with the movement to preserve the European patrimony and to recover a past and a "collective memory" believed to be slipping away.[18]

From the 1950s through the 1970s many pilgrims (I use the word intentionally) went to Santiago by car, following the Camino de Santiago signs posted in the early 1960s by the Spanish government along National Highway 120. Some pilgrims of the 1980s and 1990s (especially non-Spanish) recount tales of going to Santiago in their teens by car in the 1950s and 1960s. The early promotion opened the Camino to a wide array of mobile tourists. In 1962 the French magazine *Eclair* published an article, "*Sur les chemins de Compostela à l'age de la 'gazolina'*" (On the Roads to Compostela in the "Gasoline" Age), which recounts a car trip; Franco's highway signs are clearly visible in the photos accompanying the article.

In Estella, Spain, the first Friends associations, Los Amigos del Camino de Santiago, formed in 1959. Like Les Amis of Paris, they focused on medieval aspects of the Camino and subsequently launched an academic magazine and founded the Center of Jacobean Studies as well as the long-running Medieval Studies Week. In 1972 they sponsored the conference "Europa en el Camino de Santiago" (Europe in the Road of Saint James) and six years later, "Camino de Santiago, Camino de Europa" (Road of Saint James, Road of Europe). This earliest and most influential group in Spain sought to revitalize the route by joining forces with European walking clubs (the European Association of Foot Tourism) and Spanish mountaineering associations to promote European unity and patrimony through revitalizing the network of pilgrims' footpaths.[19] The Camino became the ideal way to realize these goals.

The Estella group developed a reanimation plan by making the Camino on foot. In 1963 three of the founding members decided to walk from Estella to Santiago "to ascertain the conditions that the Camino was in with a specific interest in lodging, communication, routes, paths, awareness." "It was in this way," the group continued, "after an exhaustive study and analysis, we began to work vigorously on the 'repristinization' of the Camino Francés."[20] They did not just walk as pilgrims of the twentieth century, but instead they wore the medieval garb, long capes and scallop shells. What they discovered was that the pilgrimage route did not exist in the public memory (or the fantastical "collective memory," as some call it) as they imagined, and in fact they were occasionally mistreated or taken for vagabonds. Their pilgrimage became not only a contemporary act of revitalizing the Camino but also a play of history and identity—reliving the way "as it was."

In 1965 a twenty-one-year-old American student also made the pilgrimage on foot in both France and Spain. In letters home he recounted feeling that modern times were not oriented toward the pilgrimage. In France especially the people did not remember the pilgrimage or what a pilgrim was and he was frequently taken for a vagabond. In Spain he received advice on begging (how to extend his hand and where the best places were) from a tramp who did not recognize him as a pilgrim. On reaching Roncesvalles he felt he had arrived two hundred years too late. He did receive help in Estella, share lunch with several priests near Burgos, and spend the night at an active eleventh-century episcopal college in León. After lunch with the novice priests and a group sing, he com-

mented, "This is a real palace, and being old, puts you back as a real pilgrim." Both he and the Estella group originally sought remnants of the
medieval Camino in the present—going with little money, following the
routes, hazarding the way—but found more of a tourist route than a devotional route. The American student wrote while close to Galicia, "The
pilgrimage is big business in this area. But not many real pilgrims (probably virtually none, but not even many practicing fakes like us)." In
essence, both were looking for vestiges of the medieval pilgrimage but
were confronted by the modern reality. At the same time, their actions
served to help "reawaken" "public memory" of the pilgrimage among
village folk.[21]

In the 1960s and the 1970s the Camino's main appeal was as a cultural and historical way linking the modern to the medieval. A series of
exhibits and publications boosted interest in the pilgrimage. In honor of
the 1965 Holy Year the Ministry of Tourism published a guide for the
car traveler to Santiago complete with legends, information on routes,
an introduction associating the development of the Camino and the forg-
ing of the European spirit, and information about the Galician coast.[22]
Moreover, Les Amis made their first association pilgrimage by coach from
Paris to Santiago "to visit the tomb of St. James" during the 1965 Holy
Year.[23] In 1977 the French journalists Pierre Barret and Jean-Noël Gurgand walked to Compostela in fifty days and wrote their personal account with parallel text from medieval pilgrims' journals.[24]

Meanwhile, at the end of the 1960s, the Catholic Church in Spain
was in upheaval with the changes wrought by the new doctrines of Vatican II. Reforming Vatican II priests now balked at the public displays
of Franco's National Catholicism, calling instead for an end to "the notion of religion as a monopoly and accept[ing] the existence of an open
market for religious ideas."[25] Religion became contestable. Those parts
of the Spanish Catholic church that still supported National Catholicism continued the encouragement of the pilgrimage with fanfare and
offerings. Moreover, the Church generally preferred what it could control and a large-scale pilgrimage such as the Camino de Santiago could
lead to a religious practice outside of its realm.[26] Still, the Delegación
Nacional de la Juventud (Spanish National Youth Delegation) organized a national pilgrimage to Santiago and published for the 1971 Holy
Year the *Ritual del peregrino,* a pamphlet explaining the pilgrimage and
its history, ceremonies, and liturgy for pilgrims as well as daily prayers
and hymns. The message was clear: the pilgrimage should be oriented
toward the development of faith through meditation, mortification, and

piety, keeping in mind the medieval journey.[27] At the same time an alternative movement of esoteric knowledges that combined car tourism began to take off in France in the late 1960s and early 1970s and made its way to Spain via Louis Charpentier's *The Mystery of Compostela*, in which he calls the Camino the "Great Work" of the medieval alchemists. Driving in one's car over the great work, New Age pilgrims could unravel the esoteric knowledges hidden in secret symbols of the cathedrals and churches of the way. On the grassroots level, the Movimiento Mundo Nuevo (New World Movement) based in San Sebastián has since 1971 continuously organized religious pilgrimages to Santiago, for the development of Christian and human values among young people.

Though always a pilgrimage, in its mid-twentieth-century reanimation, the Camino began to be promoted by the state as a tourist way, as an "alternative" to mass tourism and the apparent superficiality of seaside travel.[28] In 1982 the Estella group suggested that the revitalization of the Camino is a form of "cultural tourism economically superior to that of mass tourism and has a further advantage: it doesn't deceive the tourist. Instead its recuperation will promote Christian Spain, that is, Western Civilization."[29] As an alternative the tourist is reoriented toward the cultural and historical heritage of the pilgrimage route. The tourist is not disappointed in Catholic Spain, where the heart of the religious and cultural Occident is found.

A sharp transition occurred in the 1980s and 1990s when participants began to reject the car in favor of walking and then cycling the route. In Spain during the 1980s a new type of tourism began to develop which moved away from a focus on "quantity" and toward one on "quality," at least superficially, in what one researcher calls "ecological-cultural" tourism. The focus came to be on making Europe Spanish—"el modo de ser y vivir español" (the way to be Spanish and live like a Spaniard) and on noncompetitive sports, the outdoors, and a "tolerant and plural Spain" that allows a psychic restoration from the workaday world.[30] The valorization of nature, the rejection of mass tourism, an emphasis on inner discovery, and a desire for physical leisure activity could all be found on the Camino. In the early 1980s the desire to make the Camino under one's own power (walking and cycling) in the "traditional way" began to increase with greater force, especially among non-Spanish participants. No longer were car pilgrimages the vogue as they had been in the late 1950s and 1970s. Instead, the long human-powered journey began to replace the easy car journey.[31]

The long-distance pilgrimage did not become popular among Spaniards until the late 1980s. Differences in values relating to leisure, the tradition of local rather than national pilgrimages, and the ambivalence about Santiago and his relation to Franco created indifference to the Camino. "The devotion to Santiago is more international than strictly Spanish and perhaps more Spanish than Galician," suggested one anthropologist writing in the late 1970s.[32] Moreover, Santiago was often associated with the "official" or state devotion, and pilgrimages to his tomb were often sponsored in dioceses or made in honor of a Holy Year (more out of obligation than devotion). With Franco's death in 1975 and the transition to democracy in the early 1980s, Santiago was not embraced quickly by Spaniards more familiar with Saint James the Moorslayer than with Saint James the Pilgrim. A popular Galician verse of the time expresses this ambivalence:

Eu ben che decía, nena,
que non foras a Santiago,
que che iba meter medo
ver un home nun cabalo

[I already told you, girl
not to go to Santiago
that it was going to scare you
to see a man on a horse][33]

With Franco's death much of the financial support and political momentum of the Camino was lost. In April 1979 the president of the Friends in Estella announced the cancellation of the seventeenth annual Medieval Studies Week because the usual government funding was reduced to a pittance.[34] In the post-Franco socialist era Spain had become more and more secularized politically.[35] In the transition to democracy the socialists were not apt to maintain a close tie to Franco's symbolic alter ego, Santiago. By 1985 the government promotion of the pilgrimage was significantly less than it had been during the Franco period. Despite the national government's relative silence on the subject of the Camino during the 1980s, interest on the microlevel, especially from beyond Spain, continued to surge.

Friends of the Camino associations began to spring up in the 1980s on a wide scale all over Europe, based loosely on models of the late medieval pilgrims' brotherhoods. Former pilgrims, enamored of the pilgrimage and lacking rites of reincorporation in their own communities, motivated the growth. The societies often focus on the study of the medieval Camino and the marks it left in their communities (e.g., roads, churches, pilgrim's hospitals). Some associations also conduct pilgrim preparation and organize pilgrimages as well as rites of departure or reincorporation for the returnee.[36] The associations are generally ecumenical, highlighting the changing nature of the pilgrimage in the late twentieth century. Besides publishing their own bulletins, cooperation between associations resulted in route rehabilitation and a number of international conferences since the 1980s dedicated to the specific study of the pilgrimage in its many dimensions. For example, in 1983 the Centro Italiano di Studi Compostellani (Italian Center of Compostelan Studies) hosted the international symposium, "The Pilgrimage to Santiago de Compostela and Jacobean Literature." This conference was followed in 1985 by the I Encuentro Jacobeo (First Jacobean Meeting), held in Santiago, as well as the Ghent exposition "1,000 Years of European Pilgrimage." In 1987 the second international conference of Jacobean themes took place in Jaca, Spain, and was sponsored by the newly formed National Coordinator of Associations (which came to be the Spanish Federation of Associations of Friends of the Camino in 1992). At this conference the issue of the pilgrim's credential and the development of refuges was actively debated. The federation was formed as a centralizing force in the rapid reanimation of the way. It receives money from participating associations and primarily from the Spanish Ministry of Culture and the sale of publications of the federation. Not surprising, there is some resistance to centralization by a number of Friends groups that object to the bureaucratic aspects the federation brings to the road. Since 1987 the number of transnational encounters of associations has grown and continues to influence the reanimation of the pilgrimage in its contemporary form. Under the direction of the Australian (by adoption) Kosti Simons, Pilgrims International formed in 1984 after his own conversion experience and 111-day barefoot walk to Santiago from Paris. He made three ecumenical pilgrimages in the 1980s with pilgrims from all over the world. These associations also organize interassociation activities: the Friends of the Camino in Navarre is closely linked with the Acquitaine group over the border in the south of France. The English confraternity made "Le Walk" as an interchange with another French association. This same French association now plans a similar encounter with one of the German associations.

On the religious front, the state-oriented National Catholicism that had once been characterized by a "theology of fear" changed its orientation to a "theology of love." Comments one anthropologist, the "current dis-

Figure 43. *A 1996 assembly of the Fourth International Congress of Jacobean Associations, an aspect of the Camino off the road. Photo courtesy of* Peregrino *magazine.*

course in Spain about the 'theology of love' stems from the church's relinquishing of a monopoly over faith and its acceptance of a market for religious ideas. Younger priests now say that they make an 'offering' of the faith to people, and everyone is free to take it or leave it. Since religion has become contestable, since one can say yes or no, many in Spain today, especially the young, are saying no to religion and declaring it irrelevant to their lives—even as the new 'young church' struggles to make it relevant."[37] With the decline in attendance at religious services, an aging and declining population of religious professionals, and an increasingly politically secularized Europe, the Catholic church interpreted the revitalization of the Camino as a positive return to the sacred and an ideal means of cultivating faith among European youth. One pilgrim's magazine states, "[Through recognition of Santiago as a] symbol of unity between all the countries of Europe . . . the Camino will help [break down barriers between races as well as allow a] rediscovery of the religious and human values that are at the foundation of the Camino's origins."[38]

A constant theme in ecclesiastic literature of the 1980s and 1990s is that youth, converted by the Camino, will become the new evangelizing force in Europe in the year 2000. Despite this acknowledgment, the Catholic church in Spain has been slow to act on the reanimation and its tremendous opportunity for evangelization, other than to claim from the pulpit the essential vitality of religion in a politically secularized nation. Since becoming a nonconfessional state with the transition to democracy, a proliferation of new religious movements and distrust of cults swept through Spanish society in the early 1980s and 1990s, reflecting the idea that many young people find religion irrelevant. In 1993 the archbishop and president of the Spanish Episcopal Conference, Elías Yanes, accused politicians of "aspiring to secularize" the Camino and stated that the Camino's success "continues to be a religious happening of the highest order" in all of Europe and above all with youth.[39]

One way the "young church" can market and make religion relevant to young people is to link it to the modern pilgrimage—a shared cultural and religious journey. In 1988 the bishops of the parishes of the camino francés from Roncesvalles to Santiago produced the *Carta Pastoral* (Pastoral Letter), which puts into perspective the contemporary reanimation of the pilgrimage as it relates to a return to religiosity as a response to modern social problems. Using the metaphor of Christ as the Way, the Truth, and the Life, they encourage group and diocesan pilgrimages to foster and develop the religious elements of the journey and to teach Catholic religious principles to the *catecumenal* (the person preparing for the baptism and First Communion or conversion) through the physical journey. The journey and its trials provide models to see the hand of God in all acts, to live in a Christian community, to pray and to learn lessons of humility, brotherhood, generosity, and love. It becomes an "itinerary of faith" and an example of the "theology of love."[40] The presence of the official Church is most strongly felt in Santiago when pilgrims arrive at the cathedral, attend the Pilgrim's Mass, and go to receive the *Compostela*. The Office of Welcome is run by a delegate of the cathedral's canons. Pilgrims frequently register surprise that the cathedral does not seem more oriented toward the international faithful as are other major centers of pilgrimage (i.e., Lourdes and Fátima). This surprise often extends to the general lack of attention given to the spirituality of pilgrims along the route. During the Third Pastoral Meetings of priests of the Camino in 1996 the question of what initiatives priests of the way currently were taking to attend to pilgrims' spiritual needs surfaced. Acknowledging that a great potential exists to offer a place to pray, a place for reflection, or a place to propose questions and answers to pilgrims which will guide them toward faith and an interpretation of their experiences within a religious framework, these priests also recognize that "at times they lack perseverance in attending to pilgrims and in some cases lack interest."[41] Recognizing these needs, the Junta Central del Año Jacobeo 1999 formed in October 1996, and in 1997 the archbishop of Madrid announced the formation of an episcopal delegation dedicated specifically to the Camino and the spiritual requirements of pilgrims.

Perhaps the most persuasive promoter of the pilgrimage within the Catholic church is Pope John Paul II, who visited Santiago in the 1982 Holy Year and in 1989. In his visits, as in his other worldwide "pilgrimages," he emphasized the importance of Europe building and linking foreign peoples through the common bonds of faith. In the European Act of 1982 at the Cathedral of Santiago, the pope declared, "My vision extends over the immense network of routes that unite all the cities and nations that constitute Europe and I see that since the Middle Ages the Caminos have all led and now lead to Santiago de Compostela." The pope's second visit to Santiago in 1989 attracted thousands of young Catholics, introducing them to the pilgrimage and the notion of Europe building. Many of these youths who arrived by bus, in organized pilgrimages sponsored by local parishes, were inspired to return in coming years as pilgrims on foot or bicycle, explaining in part the overwhelming number of pilgrims in their late teens during the 1993 Holy Year. The pope specifically planned his visits to reach Catholic youth, organizing the 1989 World Youth Day in Santiago, which drew hundreds of thousands of young people to the city. An example of a mass pilgrimage in the context of Santiago was the 1993 seven-day march of nearly two thousand Spanish youths along the camino francés with the archbishop of Madrid leading the way.[42]

Outside of the official Spanish hierarchy of the Church, a number of priests living on various parts of the Camino made significant contributions to its reanimation. Through improving infrastructure, providing spiritual guidance and lodging, publishing information, and organizing pilgrimages, these priests attempted to maintain the sense of Christian hospitality that is the foundation of the Camino. Many of them have devoted their lives to the preservation and reanimation of the Camino and, above all, the care of pilgrims. Don Elías Valiña of Cebreiro is recognized for his instrumental role in reanimating the pilgrimage and caring for pilgrims through an award (given to an association for its work to promote and protect the pilgrimage) named in his honor. Additionally, the presence and powerful influence of priests and lay followers of the conservative Catholic religious movement Opus Dei all along the Camino concerns some associated with the pilgrimage who are suspicious of their involvement, secrecy, and insidious power. There are also divisions within present-day parishes and religious orders on whether modern secular yet spiritual pilgrims should be given the hospitality usually reserved for the religiously motivated.

The development of the European Union (EU) has significantly altered economic, political, and social borders in Europe. In Spain, EU membership as a primary foreign policy goal was realized in January 1986 on the heels of whirlwind societal transformation in the post-Franco democratic transition.[43] The reanimation of the Camino de Santiago pilgrimage through its heritage conforms precisely to the fiction of a unified European culture area and identity that the EU wishes to promote.[44] This is precisely what occurred on a transnational political level. In 1985 UNESCO named Santiago a World Heritage City, and in 1987 the cultural branch of the European Union, the Council of Europe (within the Architectural Heritage Program), decided to adopt the pilgrimage route as the premier "European Cultural Itinerary." Continuing its mission in 1988, the council organized a congress (in conjunction with the German Jacobean Studies and the German Committee for Monument Protection) in Bamberg, Germany, to study and protect the pilgrimage routes of Europe. The secretary general of the Council of Europe, a Spaniard, stated on this occasion, "One could hardly find a phenomenon closer to the very essence of the Europe we wish to build than this pilgrimage movement, whose routes, above and beyond the religious dimension, which was the pilgrims' profound motivation, have remained a meeting place, a medium of exchange, a means of communication and a source of solidarity which is the basis and origin of our own identity."[45] Suddenly, a Europe fractured forty years before is now characterized by a distinct "identity" whose foundation is union. Not only is it Europe, but it is "our identity," an identity that somehow erases national boundaries in favor of a loftier European identity located somewhere in the collective memory embodied in the pilgrimage routes. Moreover, the pilgrimages routes are understood to contain a "set of values and a fund of shared experience recorded for all time in our collective memory, representing the indivisible heritage of all European countries."[46]

The council funds signposting projects and the identification of routes and works to support preservation of monuments related to the pilgrimage. The council also supports a "committee of experts" whose president is the heart and soul of the very active Italian Friends of the Camino Association and research center of Jacobean studies. The "experts," who are drawn mostly from European academic circles, meet quarterly to advise the council on policy matters relating to the restoration of the

Camino. Their power is often substantial as their advice determines the funding of projects by both the Spanish Ministry of Tourism and the council. There is no representative of the Church on the committee.

All of this attention to the pilgrimage routes wrought changes for the pilgrims as well. From the 1960s through the mid-1980s pilgrims found shelter in barns, on church floors, in abandoned school rooms, in fields, in charity centers, or in monasteries. In the late 1980s this free-for-all began to change.[47] A wide range of religious and secular groups began to establish pilgrims' refuges. Then people (mostly former pilgrims) began to volunteer to maintain the refuges during the summer months. For the 1993 Holy Year the governments of Castile-León and Galicia provided base camps for the thousands of pilgrims on the road. Numerous guidebooks in various languages were published, and the way marking in some parts of the route looks more like graffiti than simple arrows. Since the 1993 Holy Year pilgrims have begun to complain that the Camino "wasn't like it used to be." How quickly things change.

Finally, in the late 1980s and the early 1990s the Spanish goverment began to understand the full impact of the pilgrimage's reanimation. Despite interest from within the country on the grassroots level, neither Church leadership nor the socialist government picked up the ball and ran in the 1980s. Instead, Holy Year 1993 took Spain by surprise. In 1993 millions came to visit Santiago and more than one hundred thousand walked at least 100 kilometers or cycled at least 200 kilometers to receive the cathedral's document of certification. In a last-minute attempt to capitalize on the resurgence of interest in the way the Galician government invested millions of pesetas in the ill-conceived Plan Xacobeo 93, a plan to make the Camino a tourist trap par excellence. Pelegrín, a Disneylandized version of the modern pilgrim, became the Xunta's standard-bearer and began to march across Spain inviting citizens of all walks of life to become pilgrims for a day in Santiago. Behind the movement to attract pilgrims to Santiago was a thinly veiled attempt to draw them to Galicia and the coastal zones for a pleasure weekend. The Xunta rapidly published guides on gastronomy and routes and created an infrastructure of refuges maintained by public money. The 1993 Holy Year came on the heels of the 1992 Olympics in Barcelona and the World Expo in Seville. Busloads of curious arrived from all parts of Spain looking for Spain's third fair. Few knew what Xacobeo meant or who Pelegrín represented. The director of Xacobeo 93 and adviser to the president, Jose Carro Otero, told me this Holy Year anecdote that he heard frequently. A Spanish visitor would arrive at the stunning Plaza del Obradoiro, full

Figure 44.   This sign in Galicia—Attention! Pilgrims' Crossing—and others found the length of the camino francés are clear examples of government involvement with the pilgrimage.

of Santiago's finest civil and religious architecture, look around, and then stop a Santiago native and ask, Where do you buy the tickets for Xacobeo 93? Ill-conceived marketing turned the pilgrimage into a spectacle. The pilgrimage became marketable in the 1990s on the public front as well. Images associated with the pilgrimage are being used to sell a wide variety of products—milk, furniture, even telephone service. Hundreds of bars and eating establishments with the name El Peregrino or El Camino de Santiago or El Bordón or Ruta Jacobea have sprung up. The pilgrimage has become big business in the public sphere as well. Even Iberia, Spain's national airline, got into the act: in the mid-1990s the company began to offer reduced one-way fares from Santiago for pilgrims bearing the *Compostela*.

The Spanish state (under PSOE, the Spanish Socialist party) entered the fray in the late 1980s, supporting what was unthinkable in 1982. In the last several years before the 1996 government transition to the Partido Popular (Popular party), Carmen Alborch, the Spanish minister of culture and president of the Consejo Jacobeo (Jacobean Council), made a number of appearances in Santiago and along the Camino. During her term in office a task group consisting of representatives from the Min-

istries of Public Works, Business, and Tourism as well as the seven autonomous communities through which the Camino passes was formed to
realize the economic potential of the Camino as well as conserve its patrimony.[48] As part of the recuperation of the Camino government ministers and the royal family found it politically expedient to present themselves as pilgrims and do parts of the pilgrimage on foot, further linking
the state and pilgrimage. These are often well-publicized media events.
The Jacobean Council met in 1997 to request money from the central government for improvement projects leading up to and beyond the 1999
Holy Year. The members of the council, though, seem to be out of touch
with contemporary pilgrims. One project, fortunately shelved temporarily, was to convert the Monte del Gozo into an amusement park "for the
pilgrims' enjoyment before reaching the Galician capital."[49] The pilgrimage and the image of the pilgrim as everyman are being used as a
stepping-stone to greater European expansion and economic development.

In contrast, the city of Santiago, in conjunction with the Xunta and
the state, created a campaign for the Holy Year called Compostela 93.
In this program Santiago is eliminated from the title and symbology. Instead it is the city itself that is emphasized. Stylized lines are used to represent the cathedral in advertising, emphasizing only the key edifice and
the name *Compostela*. There is an implicit rejection of Santiago the saint.
The following quote illustrates the city's manipulation of Santiago's cultural patrimony: "Today the celebration of the Cultural Capital of Europe in Santiago will help to intensify the relationship between the culture of Galicia and the peoples of Europe, thus serving as reminder of
their intimate 1,000-year relationship and to consolidate it in the future."[50] Underlying the city's embrace of the Holy Year was its grand
plan to become the Cultural Capital of Europe for the year 2000. This
goal was achieved in November 1996 after a long campaign that relied
heavily on the Camino and its thousand-year heritage linking the end of
the medieval world to the rest of the civilized world (Europe, that is). Santiago's relationship to Spain is less important than it and Galicia's direct
link to Europe. The socialist mayor, Xerardo Estévez, embraced this message by proclaiming that the Camino "was and continues to be the seed
of the united Europe."[51]

Neither the Xunta nor the city plan to be taken unawares for Holy
Year 1999. The Xunta began plans for Xacobeo 99 in 1994 and continues to work for a compromise between tourism and pilgrimage. For
Xacobeo 99 Pelegrín is joined by Pelegrina, a pink version of the same,
but with huge "feminine" eyelashes—a move toward equality? The pres-

ident of the Xunta, Manuel Fraga, also announced his dream to see for "the Holy Year of 1999 the creation of a virtual [reality] Camino de Santiago, that like the Jacobean route will be made by thousands of cyberpilgrims from the five continents simultaneously."[52] The city remains focused on developing its status as the cultural capital of Europe and its mayor continues to invest millions of pesetas in contemporary art and architecture around rather than in the historical district, where such an investment is sorely needed. The Spanish Federation of Associations of Friends continues strong. Each year more pilgrims walk and bicycle the Camino, joining the informal society of pilgrims extending across the centuries.

Beginning in the 1950s and 1960s the pilgrimage developed as a touristic and cultural way called the Camino de Santiago based on political reconstruction and a budding nostalgia for preserving medieval European patrimony. During this portion of its current revitalization performance of the journey was not paramount. The reanimation took an unexpected turn in the 1980s and 1990s when the act of making the pilgrimage as a long-distance physical journey based on models of the medieval past became popular on a wide scale. The pilgrimage has not become reanimated as a strictly religious journey but has been amply interpreted as an ideal way to enjoy "leisure with meaning" for middle-class, urban, educated, and largely male Europeans. In this milieu the role of the pilgrim not as solely a religious traveler but as a more generalized seeker, wanderer, and adventurer became popularized and an ideal way to realize personal and social goals.

NOTES

INTRODUCTION

1. See Appendix A on my fieldwork and Frey 1996, the dissertation on which the present book is based.

2. *El Correo Gallego,* March 12, 1997.

3. Throughout I use *Camino, road,* and *way* interchangeably. I do not intend "Camino" to be understood as a "Way" in the sense of a path to enlightenment unless it is specifically identified as such. I use both "Saint James" and Santiago" to refer to the apostle. It is common for pilgrims to refer to him in their native language (French Jacques, Italian Jacopo, German Jakob, Catalan Jaume). All are derived from the Latin Sanctus Iacobus, as is the word *Jacobea/o* (as in Ruta Jacobea, Año Jacobeo, etc.). Likewise, I refer to the city of Santiago de Compostela as both Santiago (the most common usage) and Compostela.

4. On the history and reconstruction of the routes in France and Spain, see, for example, Oursel 1984; Passini 1984, 1988; Soria y Puig 1993.

5. On the Camino as an economic exchange route, see Cohen 1976, 1980. There are more miles of routes in France than in Spain with their own wealth of historically important chapels, reliquaries, bridges, hospices, and cathedrals. Each of the four famous points of departure in France had its own name based on where the road passed: Paris to Tours, *via turonense;* Vézelay to Limoges, *via lemovicense;* Le Puy, *via podense;* and Arles to Toulouse, *via tolosana* (Melczer 1993: 24–27).

6. On Marian apparitions, see Zimdars-Swartz 1991, and on Lourdes, specifically, see Eade 1992.

7. On various occasions I have heard observers dismiss the pilgrimage because they find it ludicrous to believe that the apostle's remains are in Santiago; they see the cult as just one more sham fomented by the Catholic Church to pull the wool over the eyes of innocent followers. As an anthropologist I am not interested in proving or disproving the site's authenticity but in the fact that mil-

lions of people have traveled and continue to travel to this green corner of the world. In the end when one looks at the meanings of pilgrims' journeys, the issue of whose bones they are becomes irrelevant.

8. Three of the four gospels contain details on the life of Saint James: Matt. 4:21–22, 17:1–13, 26:36–46; Mark 1:19–20, 3:17, 5:37, 10:35–45, 14:32–42; and Luke 5:12, 8:51, 9:28–36. See also Acts 12:2.

9. Melczer 1993: 10–11. See also Acts 1:8.

10. See Melczer 1993: 30–31; Sánchez-Agustino 1993; Vázquez de Parga, LaCarra, and Uría Ríu [1948] 1993: 187–88.

11. Davies and Davies 1982: 220–21.

12. Archaeological excavations of the nineteenth and twentieth centuries demonstrate that the zone where Saint James's remains are located (what is now below the main altar of the cathedral) is also the final resting place of Roman and pre-Christian souls, supporting the *compostium* definition. See Guerra Campos 1982 for a discussion of the archaeological excavations in the Cathedral.

13. See Uría Maqua 1993; Clissold 1974.

14. Castro 1954: 135–36; Castro's emphasis.

15. Ward 1982: 112. It was as a result of this miracle that the name Santiago (and later *¡Santiago y cierra España!* or Santiago, and close Spain!) became the Spanish battle cry.

16. For a further discussion, see de Lozoya 1969: 400; Gárate Córdoba 1971; Mitchell 1988. Much of the "New World" was conquered under the banner of Santiago, resulting in such place-names as Santiago in Chile and Ecuador (see Myers 1991).

17. See Melczer 1993: 67–69 for an interesting discussion of this theological and iconographic anomaly.

18. Davies and Davies 1982: 53. See also Kendall 1970; Sumption 1975.

19. Holy Years, or Años Jacobeos, occur when July 25 (the saint's feast day) falls on a Sunday. According to Catholic doctrine, an indulgence "is the remission of all or part of the debt of temporal punishment owed to God due to sin after the guilt has been forgiven. . . . A plenary indulgence remits the entire payment of punishment due up to the point when it is gained, while a partial indulgence remits only part of the punishment" (Clouse 1978: 508).

20. See the excellent introduction and English-language translation of the miracles in Coffey, Davidson, and Dunn 1996.

21. For further details, see Vázquez de Parga, LaCarra, and Uría Ríu [1948] 1993: 172–79; Melczer 1993: 28–35.

22. Melczer 1993: 38–44.

23. Pilgrims from a number of countries wrote travelogues, among them, William Wey (1456), Edme de Salieu (1531–33), Herman Künig von Vach (1496), Jacobo Sobieski (1611), and Domenico Laffi (1666, 1670, 1673). See, respectively, Wey 1992; Bronseval 1970; Künig von Vach 1989; Sobieski 1878; Laffi 1997.

24. Davies and Davies (1982: 221–22) suggest that the "skepticism that sounded the death knell of the popular medieval pilgrimage to Compostela" is evidenced in one of the *Colloquies* of Erasmus, entitled *The Religious Pilgrimage*.

25. See Plötz 1989: 100–4 for a good overview of the pilgrimage's decline; see also Vázquez de Parga, LaCarra, and Uría Ríu [1948] 1993: 111–17.

26. Valiña 1986: 132.

27. Appendix B is an account of the pilgrimage's twentieth-century reanimation.

28. Both quotes from Gergen 1996: 80. See also O'Reilly, O'Reilly, and O'Reilly's (1997) edited volume on travel as a transformative experience.

CHAPTER 1. PILGRIMS TO SANTIAGO

1. *Pilgrim* stems (via the French *pèlerin*) from the Latin *peregrinus* (from the verb *per agrare,* "to travel," "to visit" [Romero Pose 1993: 12]), meaning a wanderer, one who travels in foreign lands or a religious traveler to a holy place. It also signifies in Spanish that which is "rare, special, extraordinary, never seen" (De Ochoa 1917: 1089). Following the same etymological links *pilgrimage* (Spanish *peregrinación* or *peregrinaje*) comes from the Latin *peregrinatio,* signifying travel to distant or foreign lands (ibid.). The understanding more commonly held is its religious definition: a collective or individual journey to a holy place. In essence, pilgrims are travelers who leave their native land and are, conversely, strangers in the lands through which they travel. When used in the religious sense, the journey is intimately linked with a spiritual journey of faith (Romero Pose 1993: 13).

2. See Chidester and Linenthal's (1995: 10) discussion of how bodily actions consecrate and desecrate sacred spaces.

3. *Compostela* 1994: 36–37.

4. Turner and Turner 1978: 240. See also Nolan and Nolan 1989; Eade and Sallnow 1991.

5. As Caucci von Saucken (1993: 163) observes, the Spanish *romería* and the German *Wallfahrt* share structural and motivational similarity. Both are "brief pilgrimages that are often made in a day, occur on fixed days as part of a particular celebration, and with the majority of the village participating."

6. *La Voz de Galicia,* January 15, 1996.

7. These pilgrims-for-a-day are reminiscent of the type of inversions experienced by tourists who can become a "peasant for the day" or, conversely, a "queen for the day" through receiving service labeled as "royal treatment" (Gottlieb 1982).

8. Carro Otero 1993.

9. Iriarte 1993b: 6.

10. Pfaffenberger 1983: 61. Early researchers of tourism looked to pilgrimage for analytic models because it appears that both sacred and secular movement share structural similarities. Both pilgrimage and tourism involve a journey in which the normal social rules are suspended or inverted and the movement away from home is temporary, and both are usually possible only when one has discretionary income, leisure time, and social sanction (Smith 1992: 1). Graburn (1983, 1989), for example, understands tourism as a "sacred journey," that is, an individually created ritual in a secular world. MacCannell ([1976] 1989: 43) suggests that tourism is ritualized behavior for the middle class seeking authentic experiences that are missing from their own worlds; it is a modern form of pilgrimage in which the sacred stops are replaced by monuments and attractions.

Secular travel and pilgrimages appear, at times, to invoke similar kinds of reverence (Horne 1984). In a variety of contexts nonsacred centers have been transformed into points of reverence, for example, Heritage Village, USA (O'Guinn and Belk 1989), and Graceland (Davidson, Hecht, and Whitney 1990). Some historians of Western medieval travel look to medieval pilgrimage in Europe as the source of modern mass tourism, characterized by large-scale movement, hostelry and infrastructure development, generally unrestricted passage for the pilgrim, the central role of economics in experience, and the frequent mixture of sacred and profane elements (Theilman 1987; Cohen 1976; Constable 1979). Herrero Pérez (1994) has asked the question, why do nonbelievers make the pilgrimage? and concludes, in part, that the modern Camino is a secular ritual that allows participants to feel part of something larger—history, nature, Europe—but not necessarily something religious.

11. Adler 1994: 3; Adler's emphasis.

12. "Performed in a set-apart, extraordinary symbolic space [like the Camino de Santiago], rituals can act out and embody perfectly the way things 'ought to be'" (Chidester and Linenthal 1995: 9). And moving within a sacred space "focuses crucial questions about what it means to be a human being in a meaningful world" (ibid., 12).

13. Longrigg 1994: x.

14. The Catholic hierarchy in Santiago is interested in the religious motive (see *Peregrinación en 1996* 1997), and the federation is interested largely in pilgrim satisfaction (see *Encuesta '96* 1997). According to the federation, of the roughly 26,000 pilgrims who were given credentials in 1996 to begin the journey, 3,500 (3,000 Spanish and 500 foreign) were sent questionnaires after they returned home asking for biographical information, a rating of satisfaction with the journey, experiences of the Camino through the different autonomous communities, and motives. Of the 3,500 sent, 41% responded: 82% called the experience very positive, 17.5% called it positive, and only one said it was a bad experience. The two most important motives (respondees could pick more than one) were spiritual (24%) and contact with nature (18%). Results from both the cathedral's Pilgrim's Office and the federation are published annually (since the mid-1990s) in the magazines *Compostela* and *Peregrino,* respectively.

15. By age, 0 to 15 (7%), 16 to 20 (20%), 21 to 25 (16%), 26 to 30 (13%), 31 to 40 (18%), 41 to 50 (13%), and older than 50 (13%). The average age is 30. In terms of profession, by far the greatest percentage of pilgrims (45%) are students, a large increase from previous years and inflates the numbers of pilgrims between the ages of 16 and 25. The high percentage of white-collar workers (*profesiones liberales*) (12%), professors and teachers (11%), priests (2%), and technical workers (13%) attests to the generally high level of education found among pilgrims. I have translated *profesiones liberales* as "white-collar workers" because the direct translation, "liberal professions," does not hold significant meaning in American English but refers to occupations that require an advanced education, such as architects, engineers, and even doctors. I use "blue-collar workers" for the Spanish *obreros* and "service workers" for *empleados.* These terms are not exact translations but are intended to give a sense of the general composition. Despite this heavy leaning toward some degree of higher educa-

tion, there are also service workers (8%), wage laborers (6%), and housewives (*amas de casa*) (3%). During the winter months seasonal workers make the pilgrimage as an inexpensive way to travel and pass the off-season.

Besides a generally high educational level, most pilgrims come from urban areas. Among the Spanish pilgrims (71% of the total), 25% come from the autonomous community of Madrid and most from the city itself. In fact, the Madrid Friends of the Camino group is way marking a route from the St. James Parish Church in Madrid to link to the camino francés at Astorga. The other autonomous communities with the highest portions are the Basque Country, Galicia, Valencia, Castile-León, and Catalonia (*Peregrinación en 1996* 1997).

The long-term perspective shows a steady increase of pilgrimages to Santiago beginning in the early 1970s and then increasing significantly after the 1982 Holy Year. A register of pilgrims, begun in the Pilgrim's Office in 1953, was lost. In 1970 they began a new register to chart those arriving by foot and bicycle. Modest numbers were reported throughout the 1970s, with the number of arrivals peaking at 471 in the 1971 Holy Year and bottoming at 29 and 13 in the post-Franco years of 1977 and 1978, respectively. It is hard to assess the accuracy of these numbers as a figure of 6,000 was also reported in the *Memoria del Año Santo 1971* for the same period in 1971 (Feinberg 1985: 194). In the early 1980s a more equal number of non-Spaniards and Spaniards made the Camino. After 1985, when Santiago was named by UNESCO as a center of human patrimony, and 1987, when the Camino became the Council of Europe's First Cultural Itinerary, the number of foot and bicycle pilgrims began to increase by 20% and more a year. In 1987, 2,905 pilgrims received *Compostelas*. Four years later in 1991, before the "massification" of the 1993 Holy Year, 7,274 pilgrims received *Compostelas*: 69% were men, 40% students, and 67% Spanish.

The Camino appears to be becoming an international web linked by millions of steps and tread marks. In 1983 pilgrims hailed from eight European countries, in 1994 from 33 countries, and in 1996 from 63 countries. In 1997 the *Compostela* was awarded to 25,719 pilgrims, with the percentage figures remaining constant. As more pilgrims make the pilgrimage and spread the word, the field of participation grows larger and larger.

16. Artress 1995: 15.

17. Father José Miguel Burgui (1993, 1997: 26–29) has written specifically on the theme of pilgrimage and youth, basing his comments on his experience leading groups on foot along the Camino.

18. In *The Celestine Prophecy,* one of the many popular accounts of spiritual awakening via a spiritual or physical journey, Redfield comments, "For half a century now, a new consciousness has been entering the human world, a new awareness that can only be called transcendent, spiritual. . . . It begins with a heightened perception of the way our lives move forward. We notice those chance events that occur at just the right moment, and bring forth just the right individuals, to suddenly send our lives in a new and important direction. Perhaps more than any other people in any other time, we intuit higher meaning in these mysterious happenings. We know that life is really about a spiritual unfolding that is personal and enchanting" (1993: Author's Note).

19. Though the terms "pilgrim" and "pilgrimage" are often associated with a physically enacted journey, in contemporary usage they are also commonly used metaphorically for any difficult spiritual or secular journey that takes one to foreign places of the self or place. One of countless examples is Bolen's *Crossing to Avalon* (1992), which is called by its reviewer an "arduous journey to inner destinations." Bolen describes becoming a pilgrim in her search for the Holy Grail and at the same time achieving spiritual and personal enlightenment and healing. "It is in these wanderings that 'we find what really matters to us and can reach the core or center of meaning in ourselves'" (Foster 1994). Pilgrimage as a metaphor for any kind of personal journey entails displacement from self or home and often combines a linking of movement and change. How one chooses to enact this metaphor, whether it is inside or outside of a religious tradition, through literal or metaphorical movement, varies with the individual.

20. Badone 1991: 535.

21. Norris 1996: 19.

22. Bellah et al. 1985: 220–21.

23. Luhrmann 1989; Badone 1991.

24. Alonso Romero 1993: 87.

25. Aviva 1996: 65. See the two narrative accounts by Americans who use the theme of the stars or Milky Way to frame their pilgrimage: Feinberg 1989 and Stanton 1994.

26. Melczer 1993: 31, 149. See also Luis Buñuel's film *La voie lactée* (The Milky Way), which narrates the journey (through time and space) of two "pilgrims" from Paris to Santiago.

27. A similar Order of Santiago developed in Spain and remained an influential force until the fifteenth century, using the image of Santiago Matamoros and the red cross (composed of swords) as the standard. During its ascendancy the order's economic and political power was substantial. Both knights and servants of God, the members of the order also built castles and other structures along the pilgrimage routes and at other points in Iberia crucial to the Reconquest. The most famous of these castles on the camino francés is in Ponferrada. In part because of their economic power and claimed secrecy these orders were said to be the holders of esoteric knowledges and in some cases were violently persecuted (Alarcón H. 1986: 125–39; Vázquez de Parga, LaCarra, and Uría Ríu [1948] 1993: 304–10).

28. While cycling to Santiago in 1997 I encountered a trio of Brazilians who, as they marched along keeping time with their staffs, chanted a phrase I could understand only as I got closer: "Paulo Coelho es maricón, Paulo Coelho es maricón" (Paulo Coelho is a fag . . .). When I asked them about this surprising defamation they remarked that reading his book had motivated their journey but now they were sorely disappointed by the discrepancies between his text and their lived experience. They were convinced that Coelho had never walked the road since he never spoke of the physical trials (of which they were acutely aware), only of the spiritual ones.

29. Mooney 1996: A47.

30. *El Correo Gallego,* January 5, 1997.

31. Post 1994: 97, quoting Houdijk and Houdijk 1990: 30f.

32. On pilgrims' songs, see Echevarría Bravo 1967 and Moser 1985; on the miracle of the Hanged Innocent, see Coffey, Davidson, and Dunn 1996: 68–70, 139 n.553.

33. Graburn 1995: 165. A striking characteristic of the reanimation of the Camino is the appeal to nostalgia and "feelings and things of the past." There is a valorization of and nostalgia for nature and humankind's connection to it (see Alvarez Gómez 1993), the quaint, and the technologically obsolete. Shaw and Chase (1989: 2–4) suggest that nostalgia as a social phenomenon surfaces under the following conditions: (1) in societies with a linear worldview, (2) when the present is deemed deficient, and (3) when the past is readily available through buildings, monuments, or images. It has also been suggested that "nostalgia celebrates an ordered clarity contrasting with the chaos or imprecision of our own times" (Lowenthal 1989: 30).

34. Feinberg 1985: 239.

35. Geary 1986: 169. In the "Return of the Middle Ages" Eco (1986) analyzes the romanticization of this period in modern Western society and its use as a search for roots felt to be lacking in the here and now. Following Eco we must ask which Middle Ages (he identifies ten uses in contemporary renderings) or which past? In the Camino of today it often seems that only two periods exist—the "medieval" and the current. Stafford (1989: 33–37) calls this a "nostalgia for pre-modern society" in which medieval society is viewed as being "superior" because human relationships and work were more satisfying than they are today.

36. See Dennett 1987 for multiple sclerosis; Graham, Paternina, and Wright 1989 for hospices.

37. *El Correo Gallego,* February 16, 1997.

38. Ibid., August 20, 1996. See also Piñeiro 1997. This middle-aged man from La Coruña also appears in *Guiness* for his record 62-day walking pilgrimage from Munich to Santiago de Compostela (2,300 km) in 1993. The book is directed at those who want to be or have felt the need to be "authentic pilgrims"—without money, with little clothing, and with austerity.

39. The penitential pilgrimage plays a vital role in the history of the Santiago pilgrimage of the Middle Ages. The first book of the *Codex Calixtinus* includes thirty-one sermons. The seventeenth sermon, known as the *Venerada Dies,* or A Day to be Honored, takes up the theme of the penitential pilgrim and the salvation found at the saint's altar in the cathedral on completion of the journey (see Coffey, Davidson, and Dunn 1996: 8–56; Moralejo, Torres, and Feo 1992: 188–234). A criminal or sinner was sent to wander as a holy outcast (sixth- to twelfth-century Europe) or to a specific shrine such as Rome, Jerusalem, or Santiago (tenth through twelfth centuries) as a form of penance (Merton 1967: 98–105). "One of the most powerful motives for going on pilgrimage was simply to get rid of an overwhelming sense of guilt, and penances often took the form of a pilgrimage prescribed by a priest" (Davies and Davies 1982: 29). Sins would be expiated at the altar of the saint on the completion of the pilgrimage and partial or plenary indulgences granted depending on whether it was a Holy Year. On the medieval penitent pilgrim and penitence system, see Lea 1968; Sumption 1975; Vogel 1963.

40. This information is taken from Swinnen 1983 (then the Ghent prison director) and a 1992 Oikoten brochure that is translated into English by the organization.

41. See Post 1994.

42. George added that he used the term "walking wounded" with "bitter irony" because of its link to the World War I "system of military-medical triage—the wounded being classified into those who could walk back from the front; those who were worth stretchering out, because they could be patched up and sent back; and those who weren't worth the attempt, who were therefore left to die."

43. Stanton 1994: 1.

44. Lavie, Narayan, and Rosaldo 1993: 1. Pilgrimage, like other ritual performances, provides a space for personal transformation to occur. This comes from the idea of pilgrimage as a process, or as a rite of passage, characterized by three phases: separation from society, a liminal or marginal period in which social norms are inverted, and finally reincorporation into daily life (Van Gennep [1909] 1960). The marginal period is often characterized by heightened feelings of social cohesion or communitas (Turner 1967, 1969), though not always (e.g., Sallnow 1981).

CHAPTER 2. JOURNEY SHAPING

1. Rodríguez Fernández 1995: 18.

2. In journey shaping pilgrims draw on various models of pilgrimage found in the Christian tradition. In his worldwide overview of pilgrimage, Morinis (1992: 10–13) outlines a typology of "sacred journeys": *devotional,* whose goal is "encounter with, and honoring of, the shrine divinity, personage, or symbol"; *initiatory,* which "have as their purpose the transformation of the status or state of participants"; *instrumental,* in which there are "finite, worldly goals" such as cures; *normative,* which are part of the ritual calendar; *obligatory,* required as penance or by faith; and *wandering,* in which there is "no predetermined goal."

Examples of each of these six types can be found in Christianity and, to a lesser extent, in the Camino. Abraham's wandering pilgrimage (to the Promised Land to fulfill a promise) was used paradigmatically as a model for the holy ascetics and hermits (Romero Pose 1993: 14) and was taken up passionately by early Irish Christian monks (Merton 1967: 94). Many hermits populated the Iberian Peninsula and became popular visiting points for pilgrims on their devotional journeys to Santiago. Other long-distance devotional pilgrimages inspired visits to the sacred centers of Jerusalem and Rome. In Christian teachings the pilgrimage is linked metaphorically to the spiritual and daily journey to the heavenly or eternal Jerusalem. These pilgrimages originally drew pilgrims to venture from the safety of home and country to journey to the known end of the earth in devotion to Christ/god and Apostle James. The ideal of wandering, illustrated by the Christian monks, motivates many contemporary pilgrims who seek in the journey an ambiguous metaphorical goal and hope to find some kind of enlightenment (personal, religious, or spiritual) on the way to the geographic goal.

3. Longrigg 1994: xi–xii.

4. Winchester 1994.

5. Mrs. Cleaver, from the television series of the 1960s, "Leave It to Beaver," represented the model U.S. mother and homemaker. Never with her pearls off or a hair out of place, June Cleaver happily fulfilled her domestic responsibilities and showed unfailing devotion to her husand and two sons.

6. Testimonial book, Roncesvalles, July 17, 1993.

7. Neillands 1985: 21.

8. Schaad 1994: 57.

9. Iriarte 1993a: 8.

10. Testimonial book, Roncesvalles, August 22, 1993.

11. Raju 1996: 29.

12. Adler 1994: 4; Adler's emphasis.

13. Raju 1996: 33.

14. Among other long-distance travelers or drifters ways of dressing and the backpack are often markers of their status outside of the community through which they travel and help them identify one another as well. See Teas 1988: 40; Cohen 1973.

15. Melczer 1993: 58.

16. Vázquez de Parga, LaCarra, and Uría Ríu 1993: 136.

17. See Coffey, Davidson, and Dunn 1996: 23–26 for a translation of the *Veneranda Dies* sermon, which specifically outlines the meanings and purposes of the pilgrim's garb, including the staff and the shell.

18. Mandianes 1993: 134.

19. Haab 1996: Pt. 2: 25, 26.

20. Pablito is from Azqueta, a small village in Navarre. He dedicates part of his time to making walking sticks for pilgrims. He goes to the Pyrenees in the springtime searching for young hazelnut trees, which he cuts and prepares for pilgrims. His use of the hazelnut is based on the Grimm legend in which the mother of God goes to the forest and hides behind some hazelnut trees when she is frightened by a menacing snake. She says that since the tree has been her protector, it should be the protector for all mankind (*Azqueta* 1993: 27–36).

21. Rodríguez Tero 1997, 21.

22. French 1974: 1.

23. Fernandez originally brought attention to the idea of consensus and variation in "the meanings people attribute to the religious symbols they accept and use" and their influence on group members' behavior: "Ritual can achieve integration on the social level, between participants who on the cultural level—the ideological level of beliefs, rationales, interpretation of symbols—in fact, lack consensus" (1965: 912). Stromberg (1981: 544) adds that participants "agree on the meaningfulness" of symbols rather than their specific content, which, he argues, allows participants to act on them socially.

24. Schieffelin (1993: 272) explains the dialectical relationship between participant and symbol like this: "the participants are engaged with the symbols in the mutual creation of a performance reality." The performance reality is making the journey (which is a process), and the symbols of the journey both influence and are influenced by participants.

25. Giving a hug to the apostle literally refers to the act of hugging the back of the statue of Saint James behind the altar in the cathedral. One accesses the

saint via a staircase that circles around the back of the altar. See also Feinberg 1985: 300.

26. Neither landscapes nor spaces are value-free. Landscape is not only topography and monuments but includes other aspects of the environment that influence the stories that pilgrims develop along the way in relation to others, to places, and to themselves. Besides the physical and monumental landscapes, social landscapes also exist. People can also be "places," that is, pauses in movement (Tuan 1977: 6). Just as a pilgrimage may be made to both a location and a person believed to embody the sacred, landscapes are made up of both human and nonhuman features that influence the creation of the journey's story and meaning, which "transforms an abstract homogenous space into place. . . . Places help to recall stories that are associated with them, and places only exist (as named locales) by virtue of their emplotment in a narrative" (Tilley 1994: 32, 33).

27. Chidester and Linenthal 1995: 15. Because the Camino is such a large space with an ever changing population and new routes, it is hard to control. Whoever controls the landscapes, the routes, the participants, and the hospitaleros on some level controls the way. "Space is found in any exercise of power" (Foucault 1984: 252).

28. The normalization is somewhat controversial. In Spain other associations produced credentials for use by their own members, but the Spanish federation has strongly discouraged this practice, claiming that local associations will have less control over its distribution. Others claim that the credential is in essence a touristic ploy and ought to be abandoned completely. The credential is in part supposed to answer the question, Who is an authentic pilgrim? As it is clear in its twentieth-century manifestation, it is difficult to ascertain who or what is authentic, let alone who has the authority to judge. In addition, the control of space is also at issue. Researchers Chidester and Linenthal (1995: 19) suggest that appropriation and exclusion are "two strategies most often employed in attempts to dominate sacred spaces by advancing special interest of power or purity." The pilgrim's credential and the *Compostela* are two examples. The federation named itself representative of the Spanish groups, and the Navarrese Friends (among others) are criticized for not joining. The Navarre group, for example, is not opposed to charging a minimal fee to pilgrims for maintenance of refuges, but the federation balks because money taints the "purity" of the way and debases the Camino as frivolous tourism.

CHAPTER 3. LEARNING NEW RHYTHMS

1. Tuan observes, "If we think of space as that which allows movement, then place is pause; each pause in movement makes it possible for location to be transformed into place" (1977: 6). Time can be conceived as motion or flow (i.e., it is linear or circular) and place as a "pause in the temporal current" (ibid., 179).

2. Iriarte 1993a: 9.

3. Hoinacki 1996: 14–15.

4. As a concept, landscape comes from fifteenth-century Dutch art as a particular way of "seeing" and capturing or preserving the natural world (Bender 1993: 2; Cosgrove 1984: 22; Hirsch 1995: 2). Anthropologists have generally

used the idea of landscape as a "framing convention" for ethnographies or as a way to understand the meaning given to land by people (Hirsch 1995: 1) or to map myth on the surface of the land (Cosgrove 1993: 281). Geographers focus more on the physical environment, perhaps neglecting its personalization (Hirsch 1995: 5). Both tend to use landscape to create an empirical composite picture. Since the 1970s and 1980s the focus on landscape as a concept moved from one of an "abstract" (container, surfaces, universal, objective, external, neutral, atemporal, coherence) to a "'humanized' or meaning laden space" (medium, densities, specific, subjective, relational, strategy, empowered, temporal) (Tilley 1994: 7–8). In the early 1990s a number of works in the anthropological literature addressed the need to forefront landscape as a non-neutral, politicized space (Bender 1993), as a vital way to access cultural knowledge and memory (Küchler 1993: 85), and as a means for theorizing the relationships among place, time, and space (Hirsch and O'Hanlon 1995). In *A Phenomenology of Landscape,* Tilley argues that, to grasp the meanings that both spaces and landscapes have for participants, it is imperative to understand how they are experienced, how they mark people, and how they are socially produced. In his view spaces are subjective social products rather than value-free "containers for action." Moreover, "because space is differently understood and experienced it forms a contradictory and conflict-ridden medium through which individuals act or are acted upon" (1994: 10). The Camino is one such space. For an excellent case study of how people understand natural landscapes, "the importance they attach to named locations within" them, and the stories they tell about them, see Basso 1984.

5. Hoinacki 1996: 14; Hoinacki's emphasis.

6. Ibid., 37–38.

7. In the study of pilgrimage landscape and sacred geography tend to be conflated. Rather than look at how pilgrims experience and understand sacred geography, the focus tends to be on the social meaning of dramatic features associated with the sacred center (Morinis 1992: 24–25), as a nonproblematized feature of the sacred whole (Eade and Sallnow 1991: 8–11), or as a backdrop to movement (Coleman and Elsner 1995: 212). Sacred landscapes are subject to a variety of interpretations by pilgrims, who are nonetheless influenced by the system in which the pilgrimage operates (the "constraining" function of sites) (Tilley 1994: 209).

Pilgrims do not merely pass through or over the Camino but are constantly interacting with the symbols, landscapes, and people of the way. Even if a pilgrim moves through a sacred landscape in a processual manner, interactions with the symbols are both social and personal. For example, a pilgrim may stop at a place on the ritual path because it is the common practice, but in this place the pilgrim may make a prayer, marking the sacred with a personalized memory. The sacred stop is not just where a pause was made on the ritual path but is part of giving place meaning. Landscape is not only a "backdrop" but also a central part of pilgrims' experiences.

8. Rodríguez Fernández 1995: 22–24.

9. Haab 1996: Pt. 2: 33.

10. See Haab 1992 for the German original.

11. Haab 1996: Pt. 2: 28–29.
12. Longrigg 1994: xiv.
13. Hoinacki 1996: 147.
14. Tilley 1994: 11.
15. Merton 1967: 92.
16. Rodríguez Tero 1997: 6.
17. See the Catholic interpretation of symbols in Rodríguez Fernández 1995: 21.
18. See James [1902] 1985 for a discussion of natural mysticism.
19. Post 1994: 91. See also Bakken 1994: 15–16 on the importance of nature and faith.
20. Haab 1996: Pt. 1: 23.
21. Starkie 1957: 1.
22. Hoinacki 1996: 147.

CHAPTER 4. LANDSCAPES OF DISCOVERY

1. On the idea that meaning emerges through the performance of ritual, see Bruner 1986: 11; 1994: 332.
2. Dunn and Davidson 1994: xi.
3. For a discussion of how people "author" or "craft" themselves, see Myerhoff 1993 and Kondo 1990: 48, respectively. The same occurs in the Camino. Through the creative process of interaction, reflection, movement, and experimentation pilgrims continuously reshape their identities.
4. Kruyer 1996: 23.
5. Ibid., 24.
6. Cariñanos 1992 (February 21).
7. Testimonial book, Roncesvalles, July 20, 1993.
8. Cariñanos 1992 (January 24).
9. Cuchi 1994: 30.
10. See the unique series of articles by Felix Cariñanos (1991–92), a well-known pilgrim, scholar, and *jota* singer from Viana whose nickname in the testimonial books is Telerañas.
11. Alonso 1994: 48.
12. Cariñanos 1991–92 (February 21).
13. Tuan 1977: 179.
14. See Vuijsje 1990. Herman, a Dutch journalist and sociologist, walked from Santiago to Amsterdam in 1989. His diary-style book relates his various experiences while going in reverse.
15. Hoinacki 1996: 186, 187–88.
16. Ibid., 39.
17. Gurruchaga 1993.
18. From a prayer read at the Pilgrim's Mass at the cathedral in March 1996.
19. Kruyer 1996: 23.
20. Hitt 1994: 108, 110.
21. Suárez Bautista 1987: 7.
22. Victor 1994.

23. Janin 1994: 9.

24. On the analysis of "techniques of the body," see Mauss [1936] 1973 as well as Bourdieu's (1977) subsequent use of his ideas with the concept of *habitus*. De Certeau's (1984) use of "tactics" and "strategies" for understanding the body in ordinary life is also relevant. For a general overview, see Bell 1992: 94–117 and Sullivan 1990.

25. See Douglas 1973.

26. La Fray 1997: 9.

27. On the interior journey of a young Spanish man who entered a monastic order after making the pilgrimage to dedicate his life to prayer, see Torres 1996.

28. Rodríguez Tero 1997: 6–7.

29. See also Haab 1996: Pt. 1: 28 on the idea of praying with one's feet.

30. *Carta Pastoral* 1988: sec. 33, quoted in García Costoya 1993: 78.

31. See García Rodríguez 1995: 6–9.

32. Fernández 1996: 10.

33. Eade and Sallnow 1991: 5; emphasis in original.

34. Bruner 1994: 400.

35. Diocesan Commission 1993: 3. Emphasis in original.

36. Arias Villalta 1996.

37. *Encuesta '96* 1997.

38. Pliego 1994.

39. García Azpillaga 1995: 27.

40. Iriarte 1993b: 10, 11.

41. See the Hanbury-Tenison account (1990) of a journey to Santiago from Roncesvalles by horse.

42. The sociologist Judith Adler writes, "The history of travel (like that of other arts) is best seen as a history of coexisting and competitive, as well as blossoming, declining, and recurring, styles whose temporal boundaries inevitably blur" (1989: 1372). Despite the current model of the authentic pilgrimage as a physical act, this positive valuation of movement is part of a debate about whether truth or enlightenment is found in sedentary contemplation or movement (see Adler 1992, 1994). A variety of orientations toward pilgrimage and movement are found in Christianity. For example, Adler illustrates this point through comparing two discourses on movement among different monastic orders. Underlying the philosophy that encouraged wandering movement and voluntary exile among early Christian ascetics, Adler suggests that a "practical psychology (lay) which encouraged literal FLIGHT as a response to temptation and its attendant anxieties, and an anthropology and metaphysics . . . which found in the figure of the exile and the stranger the true image of the human condition. The ascetic detached himself through literal movement, and renewed his detachment by moving again; he sought to flee temptation and to recreate himself, again and again, as a 'solitary,' a 'stranger,' and an 'exile' in the world" (1992: 411; Adler's emphasis).

Adler also shows how a parallel movement in monastic theology viewed movement as a form of temptation, which needed to be curbed rather than encouraged. Rather than seek enlightenment in the wild, the development of the interior space ought to occur within the confines of the stability of the religious order

(Adler 1992: 412–14). This same oppositional discourse regarding movement and enlightenment is expressed well by Leclerq: "The important thing was no longer to leave one's country but to leave oneself. . . . The monastery could be a desert where everyone would remain stable with the spirit of exile. Previously they practiced a *stabilitas in peregrinatione* [stability in pilgrimage]; now they discovered a *peregrinatio in stabilitate* [pilgrimage in stability]" (quoted in Constable 1979: 142). See also Ladner's (1967) excellent article on the evolution of the idea of *Homo viator* (man as wayfarer).

Another shift in the value of movement is found in the Grand Tour (popular from 1600 to 1800) in which travel was seen as the upper-class young man's ideal educational tool (Brodsky-Porges 1981). In this case, with the decline of pilgrimage during the Reformation, travel as primarily a holy adventure was transformed into travel as a secular educational adventure. Again, in the late nineteenth century another shift is visible among the romantic writers such as Emerson and Thoreau. Through Thoreau's ascetic Walden experiment he argues that the world and the important mysteries of life are not found through travel to exotic locales or visits to gurus but are present in each moment in each individual (e.g., Thoreau 1952: 267).

With the contemporary pilgrimage comes the reappearance of the positive valuation and association of mobility with personal discovery and enlightenment, whether it be oriented toward salvation (Middle Ages), education (Renaissance), or personal search (modernity/postmodernity). Through venturing out literally to the thousand regions that lie beyond home, under one's own power, it is currently believed that the physical journey will lead to greater understanding of one's own inner regions.

43. McLuhan 1964: ix.
44. Palli 1994: 8.
45. Alonso 1994: 47.
46. Haab 1993: 25.
47. Rodríguez Tero 1997: 6.
48. Uli Ballaz 1990: 104.
49. Horner 1993.
50. Pliego 1994: 39.

CHAPTER 5. ARRIVALS AND ENDINGS

1. Hoinacki 1996: 88.
2. Within the Western philosophical tradition human progress occurs in a line from less to more advanced. This idea also seeped into other patterns of thought and ways of organizing the world. The metaphor of pilgrimage is a prime example. The vast majority of Christian pilgrimages have a distinct starting and end point; the end point is usually related metaphorically to reaching enlightenment, self-discovery, the Eternal Jerusalem, or the ultimate goal. Rather than circular, as is common in the Hindu, Buddhist, and Shinto traditions, the Christian pilgrimage frequently takes a linear form. Rarely is the return mentioned, partly because the Christian worldview focuses more on getting there. Moreover, there is an implicit assumption that while walking forward one is also making progress,

getting somewhere, advancing internally. This assumption becomes internalized on the personal level as the need to be changing or transforming into someone or something better. At times personal transformation is equated with forward progression, and this partly explains why getting lost often can be traumatic and the lack of change can be interpreted as failure.

3. Mora, Tamargo, and Catalán 1993: 156.

4. Haab 1996: Pt. 2: 31.

5. See Myerhoff 1993 on how the physical journey parallels a patterned quality of the inner journey.

6. Valiña 1992: 119.

7. Hogarth 1992: 26.

8. Asturias, a neighboring region, is also known for its hórreos, which there tend to be square rather than rectangular. In Galicia size, structure, base type, and building material vary from zone to zone.

9. Eliade (1958: 382) discusses the "dialectic of sacred space" or the flip-flop between accessibility and inaccessibility of arrival to the center. He suggests that, paradoxically, the sacred center is often difficult to access, yet at the same time the centers are always present. One wants to both arrive and keep going. To achieve the goal, the ending, the center is to bring one closer to the self or perhaps back home and what was left behind or simply the end of a very positive break from daily life. Pilgrims could of course easily access Santiago, yet they choose to make a long journey.

10. Haab 1996: Pt. 2: 31.

11. Longrigg 1994: xiv.

12. Morán 1996: 263, 273.

13. Janin 1994.

14. Quaife 1994: 55–56. Among many locals from Santiago, "Monte del Gozo" is a double entendre, referring both to the several houses of prostitution that grace the slopes of the surrounding area and to the pilgrims' point of Jacobean climax.

15. Uli Ballaz 1990: 153.

16. There are several versions of the origin of the word *Lavacolla* and this as a place of ritual cleansing as described in the accounts of medieval travelers. The name may derive from the Spanish word *cuello*, meaning "neck." Another popular version points to the Latin origin of the name from *Lava-mentula*, with *mentula* meaning "phallus." It is also suggested that *colla* in Romance languages means "scrotum," allowing for the transition from *Lavamentula* to *Lavacolla* (Melczer 1993: 144).

17. Stanton 1994: 187.

CHAPTER 6. SANTIAGO

1. Hoinacki 1996: 272.

2. Henderson 1994: 102, quoting Morris 1964: 40.

3. Tuan 1977.

4. Feinberg (1985: 317) noticed these same reactions among pilgrims in 1982.

5. Guijarro Camacho 1996: 12.

6. Haab 1996: Pt. 2: 26.

7. Stanton 1994: 190.

8. *La Voz de Galicia,* May 13, 1993.

9. Storrs 1994: 82.

10. *El País,* January 2, 1994.

11. Taylor 1996: 11–12.

12. Feinberg 1985: 323. Her use of "reaggregation" is a reference to the third phase of rites of passage, when the initiate is reincorporated into his or her normal society. There are often "rites of reincorporation" or closure to help facilitate this process.

13. Hoinacki 1996: 272–73.

14. Morín and Cobreros ([1976] 1990: 204) also point to Compostela's double function as center of reception and diffusion, suggesting that it is a quiet place surrounded by poles of opposing movement.

15. Feinberg 1985: 318, 324.

16. Among pilgrims there are often connections and misconnections. This Frenchwoman decided before beginning the Camino that she wanted it to be a celibate experience, yet she felt strongly attracted to a German pilgrim whom she frequently encountered in the refuges at the end of the day. Over the course of the journey they developed an ambivalent, tense, nonsexual relationship that produced the restless night referred to in the text.

17. Selby 1994: 211–12.

CHAPTER 7. TO THE END OF THE EARTH

1. Unlike the fourteenth-century Compostelan Church, the present-day Church position adamantly denies the validity of continuing to Finisterre as an act of pilgrimage.

2. Stanton 1994: 192.

3. Ramón y Ballesteros 1976: 220–21.

4. Historically, pilgrims continued to the coast in the greatest numbers between the fourteenth and the seventeenth century (Pombo Rodríguez 1994). This increase coincided as well with western European map making and the rise in popularity of finding western or northern extreme points (Jacobsen 1997). Pilgrims (especially in the fifteenth century) continued from Santiago to Finisterre "to prostrate themselves before Christ," believing that without this sacred trip the pilgrimage to Santiago was not complete. The "Christ" reference is to the miraculous figure located in the thirteenth-century Church of the Virgin Mary in Finisterre which is said to not only sweat but also to have a beard that grew miraculously after the image was placed in the church (Ramón y Ballesteros 1970: 195). See also the late-seventeenth-century account of the Italian cleric Laffi (1997) as well as that of a fifteenth-century Armenian bishop in García Mercadal 1952: 452.

The site's history extends much farther back in time. In the eighth century Finisterre is associated with Christian mendicants who sought the extreme west believing that Celestial Paradise lay in the waters beyond. Furthermore, Santiago's proselytization of the peninsula is said to have occurred there, and it became a site of penitential pilgrimage early after the second millennium (to the hermitage of Saint William). Some contemporary pilgrims believe that the Christian presence in Finisterre superseded or incorporated Celtic and other pagan beliefs associated with fertility. This extreme point, the Nerio Promontory to the Celts, was for the pre-Christian and pre-Roman inhabitants the "threshold to the Great Beyond" or the "Celtic Other World." Not only are early Christian cultic practices associated with the zone, but a few modern pilgrims also speak of the possibility that the legendary Atlantis lies off Finisterre (Alonso Romero 1993: 86–87, 98–99).

5. I collected these quotes from the comments made by various pilgrims who went to the town hall.

6. Testimonial book, Finisterre, 1995.

7. Stanton 1994: 193.

8. Stanton 1994: 193.

9. Haab 1996: Pt. 2: 34.

CHAPTER 8. GOING HOME

1. Gold 1988: 1. As Melczer suggests, the circular quality of pilgrimages also "presupposes, on the level of human experience, nature's essentially cyclic mode of regeneration: the two-beat alternation of death and renewal or . . . even with the fourfold sequence of the seasons of the year" (Melczer 1993: 6).

2. Morinis 1992: 27.

3. Myerhoff (1993: 218) describes pilgrimage as a process, as "in/out/in-with-a-difference" (i.e., the pilgrim goes from being in society, then out of society, and then back in society but different). The difference is what the pilgrim must deal with in the reincorporation to daily life. Change, as a result of pilgrimage, is clearly seen in Islamic *hajj*, in which one of the five duties of a Moslem is to make a pilgrimage to Mecca. On return the pilgrim's secular status is elevated to *hajji*, interwoven into the socioreligious system as well as mandated by faith. The anthropologist Marian Ferme (1994) demonstrates, for example, how the homecomer in an Islamic Mende community in West Africa not only receives a socially conferred change in status (Al-hajji) but also can influence the future interpretation of local rituals through authority granted to the pilgrim whose visit to the sacred center makes him now the bearer of knowledge closer to the heart of the religion (see also Campo 1991: 139–65).

In contrast, the Santiago pilgrim makes the pilgrimage, not generally as an article of faith, as in the Islamic tradition, but as a voluntary act, except in the infrequent case of the penitential pilgrim or the pilgrim seeking to fulfill a religious vow. It is a private decision, embarked on for a wide array of motives and with few, if any, rites of departure or reincorporation. Consequently, the homecomer's return often passes unnoticed except by those closest to him or her.

4. One must ask, if the return is the test of the pilgrimage, as Morinis suggests, why is it so infrequently studied? This can be explained in part by the methodological challenge presented by the study of pilgrimage. The population's dispersion, especially a transnational population such as is the case with the Camino, makes follow-up work difficult.

Another relevant explanation is the overriding emphasis found in accounts and scholars' analyses whose dominant organizing paradigm influences the production of a linear narrative structure. The pilgrimage provides the ideal structure for producing the "linear, climactic, pyramidal plot" (Harbsmeier 1986: 69) in which the green pilgrim begins naively, encounters and overcomes unexpected physical and mental trials, and finally reaches the hard-won goal. A hazard of using performance metaphors in analysis is that in theater, after the climax and denouement are reached, the actors leave their roles and go home. Pilgrims may experiment with identity while performing the pilgrimage, but in the end it is much more difficult to bracket the experiences, as if they were theater.

5. McKie 1996: 25.

6. Coleman and Elsner 1995: 207. They imply that transformation comes from a confrontation with the "exotic," which only narrowly understands how pilgrimage can influence pilgrims' daily lives and visions of the self and others. The new and exotic may not have an external source but an unexpectedly internal one. And transformation may take place through experiencing the self powerless in the face of a raging storm on the meseta whether one is in a group or by oneself.

7. Prescott 1958: 256, 278, 275.

8. Schutz 1945: 369.

9. Ibid.

10. Ibid., 374–75.

11. Iriarte 1993a: 8.

12. Pilgrims returning from Compostela in the Middle Ages often brought with them the scallop shell (either natural or made from silver or jet from the Church authorized vendors on the Cathedral's north side) on their hat, cloak, or staff. The brotherhoods and guilds dedicated to Saint James sometimes received the return pilgrim to the community just as they sometimes sent them off—with money, prayers of the village, or a blessing. Many guilds (often shoemakers) and confraternities had Santiago as their patron but did not necessarily have a direct connection to the pilgrimage. It is misleading to assume that records of confraternities of St. James were always communities of former pilgrims (at least in Denmark and Sweden and the Upper Rhineland), though many were dedicated to assisting the returned pilgrim. Excavations at about sixty sites in Europe reveal that a number of pilgrims were buried dressed in their pilgrim's garb or with scallop shells (Röckelein and Wendling 1989; Krötzl 1989: 65–66; Quaife 1996; Plötz 1997).

13. "Life consists of retellings" [in which] "every telling is an arbitrary imposition of meaning on the flow of memory, . . . that is, every telling is interpretive (Bruner 1986: 12, 7).

14. Suárez Bautista 1987: 8.

15. Testimonios 1994: 13, 14. See also Burgui 1993.

16. Meintel 1973: 47.

17. Ibid., 54.

18. "The plain truth is that pilgrimage does not ensure a major change in religious state—and seldom in secular status—though it may make one a better person, fortified by the graces merited by the hardships and self-sacrifice of the journey" (Turner 1992: 37). Turner suggests that pilgrimage makes one a "better person" through the hardship and sacrifice endured. What is meant by being

a better person is not clear, nor is change defined. Both Turner and Morinis imply that change would mean religious conversion or elevation in social status as a goal, which is not usually applicable to the Santiago pilgrimage.

19. The expression *por cojones* literally means "for balls" (testes). If one does something "por cojones" one might translate it as "he had the 'balls' to do it."

20. Fernández 1996: 11. This article is supplemented by personal communication.

21. de Tandeau 1997: 12.

22. Hoinacki 1996: 147.

23. I gave a talk for the Iberian Study Group in March 1996 entitled "Reenchanting Europe and the Contemporary Camino de Santiago Pilgrimage," organized by Joaquín Fernández-Castro and Enrique Alonso.

24. This quote comes from a speech given by a pilgrim, Laurie Dennett, the chairman of the Confraternity of St. James in London.

25. See Post 1994.

26. See, e.g., Aebli 1991 (a German man who walked from Le Puy to Santiago in sixty days); Barret and Gurgand 1978 (two French journalists who walked to Santiago in 1977 linking the medieval pilgrimages to their own); Breitenbach 1992 (a German priest in his sixties who walked in the late 1980s); Caucci von Saucken 1990 (a young Italian man who walked from Roncesvalles); Coelho [1987] 1995 (the popular Brazilian author's esoteric search); Dennett 1987 (a Canadian woman who walked from Chartres to Santiago to raise money for multiple sclerosis); Feinberg 1989 (an anthropologist's 1982 diary account); Frijns 1995 (a Belgian man's impressions and reflections organized thematically rather than day by day); Hitt 1994 (a middle-aged American writer who walked from France in 1993 as a life transition); Houdijk and Houdijk 1990 (a middle-aged Dutch couple who walked from Ghent to Santiago in 1988 on temporary leave from their office jobs); Lamers 1987 (a Dutch astronomist in personal crisis who cycled from Utrecht in 1984); Neillands 1985 (an English travel writer who cycled from Le Puy); Selby 1994 (another English travel writer who cycled from France); Torres 1996 (a young Spaniard's account of his inner journey and subsequent decision to join a monastic order); Uli Ballaz 1990 (a priest's eleventh walking pilgrimage from Zaragoza); Whitehill 1990 (an American woman's account of her religious journey with her husband from Paris to Compostela in 1986). Almost one hundred first-person narratives of the twentieth century are annotated in Dunn and Davidson's (1994) comprehensive annotated bibliography, to which I refer the reader.

27. Durant 1990.

28. See Anderson 1983.

29. For example, the Swiss Les Amis du Chemin de Saint-Jacques Association Helvetique includes in its bulletin, *Ultreïa*, modern pilgrims' material in French, and the *Fränkische St. Jakobus–Gesellschaft* (the Würzburg, Germany, St. James Society) publishes *Unterwegs im Zeichen der Muschel* (Pathways in Search of the Shell), which includes personal testimonies.

30. See *De Pelgrim* 40 (1995): 9–35.

31. Preston 1992: 33. Jill Dubisch (1995) elaborates on Preston's idea in her study of pilgrimage and gender in Greece when she suggests how magnetism is

transportable, allowing the pilgrimage shrine to be carried across time and space, through the experiences of pilgrims in contact with the sacred.

32. Barcala 1994: 76.

33. Tuan 1977: 198.

34. Ibid., 184.

CONCLUSIONS: ARRIVING AT THE BEGINNING

1. Dundes 1980: 86.

2. See Verena Stolcke's (1995) excellent commentary on European integration, Third World immigration, and the use of "culture" rather than race to define and justify difference.

3. On this final note, see Rainer Maria Rilke's (1951: 222–23) *Sonnet to Orpheus,* which begins "Choose to be changed, enchanted / By the flame of the new / The dancing spirit, free / Adores the turning point" (II.12). I thank Howard Nelson for his translation from the German.

APPENDIX A. FIELDWORK ON THE ROAD

1. Marcus 1995. The few anthropological studies done on the Camino since the 1980s (Feinberg 1985; Haab 1992; Mouriño López 1997) all attempt to deal with these dilemmas. Each researcher made the pilgrimage herself (Feinberg as a result of her research interest; Haab to study ethnology after making the Camino; and Mouriño to supplement her research with the physical journey in Galicia and being an hospitalera). Furthermore, the three (Mouriño to a lesser extent) also made important connections with the Camino outside of Santiago. Both Feinberg and Haab lived in villages along the Camino to understand the host-guest relationships between pilgrims and the environs through which they pass. Finally, all three interviewed pilgrims on arrival in Santiago, using their personal experiences as a connection.

2. Clifford and Marcus 1986.

APPENDIX B. THE TWENTIETH-CENTURY REANIMATION

1. Ford 1855: 601. For a description of the Camino in the 1910s, see King's (1920) important three-volume work; and for a vivid portrait of Santiago, the cathedral, and life in the area in the mid-1930s, see Anderson 1939: 151–94.

2. Zimdars-Swartz 1991.

3. Coffey, Davidson, and Dunn 1996: xxvii.

4. Behar 1990: 86.

5. The *voto,* a mandatory yearly offering to Santiago in thanks for saving the peninsula from the Moors, like the patronage, was instituted after the 844 Battle of Clavijo.

6. Uría Maqua 1993: 35.

7. See Marcos-Alonso 1967: 125. On the alignment of Franco and Falangist speeches with Santiago and the legends associated with Santiago's militant side, see Bennassar 1970 and Mieck 1977. For an example of a 1943 foot pilgrimage

using this Falangist rhetoric and with Franco in Compostela to greet the pilgrims, see *Peregrinación Nacional de la Falange a Santiago* (1943).

8. García Azpillaga 1996: 27.

9. La Coste-Messelière 1965.

10. Orensanz 1974: 44–49.

11. Starkie 1957: 323–24.

12. See also Plötz 1989: 104–5.

13. Aguirre Baztán 1988a: 11.

14. Ramos García 1980: 538.

15. Paradors were the brainchild of Franco's Ministry of Tourism headed by Manuel Fraga during the 1960s. In an attempt to develop tourism they converted civil palaces (cities), castles (countryside), and abandoned monasteries into luxury hotels. The system is still an important source of touristic enterprise. There are a number of paradors along the Camino, the most important being El Hostal de los Reyes Católicos located in Santiago de Compostela on the same central plaza as the cathedral itself.

16. Feinberg 1985: 202–3.

17. Lowenthal 1985: xvii; cf. Graburn 1995: 161.

18. On the changing pattern of festivals in Europe, see Boissevain 1992; on European "collective memory," see d'Haenens 1988.

19. Beruete 1978.

20. Roa Irisarrí 1995.

21. See *Angeles del Camino* 1990. The American student's letters are unpublished and in his possession.

22. See Noticiario Turístico 1965. See also Goicoechea Arrondo 1971, another major tome dedicated to the history, art, and routes of the Camino, linked to the Estella association and motivated by the idea of a united Europe.

23. Année Jubilaire 1965, Primiére Pérègrination de la Sociétè des Amis de Saint-Jacques de Compostelle.

24. Barret and Gurgand 1978.

25. Behar 1990: 89–90; see also Payne 1984.

26. Orensanz 1974: 17.

27. Villares Barrio 1971.

28. See Lanfant and Graburn 1992: 90–92 on the idea of the "alternative" in describing travel.

29. Beruete 1982: 53.

30. Aguirre Baztán 1988a, 1988b.

31. Other social changes taking place in Europe also affected the increasing numbers of pilgrims. One Belgian researcher, Bart Van Reusel, commented to me on the development of the "pilgrimization" of sports at the World Congress of Sociology in Beilefeld, Germany, in 1994. He cited the organization SPORTA (Sport Apostolaat), founded roughly in 1945 by a priest who began working with the disadvantaged to get them cycling. It began as recreational sport from a religious perspective. Later the project evolved to include pilgrimages to Santiago (with the athletic component primary) in which participants would first receive Mass, a blessing, and the scallop shell. There is also the St. Jacques cycling club in Brussels. Many of the participants with an in-

terest in the pilgrimage are men in their fifties and sixties, at a point of life transition, educated, and middle-class. He suggested that being seen suffering was
important to some participants. Moreover, this movement parallels another Belgian phenomenon, Scherpenheuvel (Sharp Hill), in which faithful run up or walk
to the shrine and then enact the fourteen passions of Christ by making fourteen
circles around the top.

32. Christian 1978: 555.

33. Ibid. The man on a horse is of course Santiago Matamoros.

34. Beruete 1979.

35. Pérez-Diaz 1991.

36. Breitenbach 1992: 130; Vázquez de Parga, LaCarra, and Uría Ríu 1993:
247–54; Warcollier 1965: 85; Martínez and Novoa 1993: 82–84.

37. Behar 1990: 104.

38. Editorial 1988: 3.

39. *El Progreso,* July 18, 1993.

40. *Carta Pastoral* 1988: 33–34.

41. García Rodríguez 1996: 14.

42. The Italian scholar Paolo Caucci von Saucken (1993) notes in his article
on the contemporary Santiago pilgrimage that in other parts of southern Europe
and the Latin Catholic world highly organized "mass [foot] pilgrimages" of
Catholic youths are taking place in ever-increasing numbers. The phenomenon
began in Italy in the mid-1970s and is now well articulated in its goals: "the meditation on life understood as a pilgrimage. Modern man, for the organizers, continues to be *Homo viator* of the medieval form and the true fatherland to be returned to is the celestial Jerusalem" (Caucci von Saucken 1993: 165). In addition,
the pilgrimages are organized to follow this theme liturgically in groups.

43. Hooper 1987.

44. Shore and Black (1992: 10) observe that "it has come to be accepted
that the goal of an 'ever closer union' sought by the European Commission will
not be achieved by economic and legal means alone and that to forge a real -
'community'—as opposed to a mere 'common market'—is a task that requires
concerted action on the cultural front in order to promote a sense of belonging
and develop feelings of 'Europeanness' among the citizens of the various EC
Member States." See also Dietler 1994, an excellent article that shows how the
political goal of a united Europe is also constructed through the use of "Celtic"
identity.

45. Oreja 1989: 3.

46. Oreja 1988: 3.

47. See David Gitlitz's (1997) reflections on twenty-two years of making the
pilgrimage (since 1974).

48. López-Barxas 1994: 18.

49. *El Correo Gallego,* May 31, 1997.

50. Ibid., 17.

51. Mahía 1993: 7. See Roseman 1996 for a complete discussion.

52. *El Correo Gallego,* January 21, 1997.

REFERENCES

Adler, Judith.
  1989.   "Travel as a Performed Art." *American Journal of Sociology* 94:
            1366–91.
  1992.   "Mobility and the Creation of the Subject: Theorizing Move-
            ment and the Self in Early Christian Monasticism." In *Le
            Tourisme Internationale Entre Tradition et Modernité*, 407–15,
            Actes du Colloque Internationale, Nice, 19–21 November. Paris:
            URESTI-CNRS.
  1994.   "The Holy Man as Traveler and Travel Attraction: Early Chris-
            tian Asceticism and the Moral Problematic of Mobility." Sociology
            Department, Memorial University of Newfoundland. Manuscript.
Aebli, Hans.
  1991.   *Santiago Santiago . . . Auf dem Jakobsweg zu Fuss durch Frank-
            reich und Spanien. Ein Bericht.* 4th ed. Stuttgart: Ernst Klett.
Aguirre Baztán, Angel.
  1988a.   "Las tres etapas de turismo en España." *Anthropologica* 4(2ª
            época): 11–12.
  1988b.   "El turismo como restauración psíquica." *Anthropologica* 4(2ª
            época): 15–33.
Alarcón H., Rafael.
  1986.   *A la Sombra de los Templarios. Interrogantes sobre esoterismo
            medieval.* Barcelona: Martínez Roca.
Alighieri, Dante.
  1965.   *La Vita Nuova.* Trans. M. Musa. Bloomington: Indiana University
            Press.
Alonso, Ignacio.
  1994.   "Experiencias de un hospitalero novato." In *Hospitaleros en el Ca-*

mino de Santiago. Informes y Experiencias. Dossier 1994, 44–51. [Santo Domingo de la Calzada, Spain]: Oficina del Peregrino.

Alonso Romero, Fernando.

1993. *O Camiño de Fisterra. Versión en galego, español e inglés.* Madrid: Xerais.

Alvarez Gómez, Angel.

1993. "El naturalismo acompañante del peregrinar." In *Pensamiento, arte, y literatura en el Camino de Santiago,* ed. A. Alvarez Gómez, 101–42. Vigo, Spain: Xunta de Galicia.

Anderson, Benedict.

1983. *Imagined Communities: Reflections on the Origin and Spread of Nationalism.* London: Verso.

Anderson, Ruth Matilda.

1939. *Gallegan Provinces of Spain: Pontevedra and La Coruña.* New York: Hispanic Society of America.

Arias Villalta, Rafael.

1996. "Esotéricos y gnósticos, parásitos de la peregrinación." *Compostela* 9: 7–8.

Artress, Lauren.

1995. *Walking a Sacred Path: Rediscovering the Labyrinth as a Spiritual Tool.* New York: Riverhead Books.

Aviva, Elyn.

1996. "A Journey without End: Reflections on a Pilgrim's Progress." *The Quest* (Summer): 65–73.

Azqueta: Pablito y Micaela.

1993. *Actividades Jacobeas. Asociación de Amigos de los Caminos de Santiago de Guipúzcoa* 11: 27–36.

Badone, Ellen.

1991. "Ethnography, Fiction, and the Meanings of the Past in Brittany." *American Ethnologist* 18(3): 518–45.

Bakken, Arne.

1994. *A Journey to Nidaros.* Trans. M. E. Davies. *Pilgrimages—Past and Present,* no. 10. Nidaros, Norway: Restoration Workshop of Nidaros Cathedral.

Barcala, Alfonso.

1994. "Experiencias como hospitalero en el Albergue de Peregrinos de Castrojeríz." In *Hospitaleros en el Camino de Santiago. Informes y Experiencias. Dossier 1994,* 76–81. [Santo Domingo de la Calzada, Spain]: Oficina del Peregrino.

Barret, Pierre, and Jean-Noël Gurgand.

1978. *Priez pour nous à Compostelle.* Paris: Loisirs.

Basso, Keith H.

1984. "'Stalking with Stories': Names, Places, and Moral Narratives among the Western Apache." In *Text, Play, and Story: The Construction and Reconstruction of Self and Society,* ed. S. Plattner and E. Bruner, 19–55. Washington, D.C.: American Ethnological Society.

Behar, Ruth.
  1990.   "The Struggle for the Church: Popular Anticlericalism and Re-
           ligiosity in Post-Franco Spain." In *Religious Orthodoxy and
           Popular Faith in European Society,* ed. E. Badone, 76–112.
           Princeton: Princeton University Press.
Bell, Catherine.
  1992.   *Ritual Theory, Ritual Practice.* New York: Oxford University
           Press.
Bellah, Robert N., Richard Madsen, William Sullivan, Ann Swidler, and Steven
           Tipton.
  1985.   *Habits of the Heart: Individualism and Commitment in Ameri-
           can Life.* Berkeley: University of California Press.
Bender, Barbara.
  1993.   "Introduction. Landscape: Meaning and Action." In *Landscape:
           Politics and Perspectives,* ed. B. Bender, 1–17. Oxford: Berg.
Bennassar, Bartolomé.
  1970.   *Saint-Jacques de Compostelle.* Paris: Julliard.
Beruete, Francisco.
  1978.   Letter, May 4.
  1979.   Letter, April 5.
  1982.   "Significación histórica del Camino de Santiago. Principios y
           evolución." *Noticiario Turístico* 109: 51–53.
Boissevain, Jeremy, ed.
  1992.   *Revitalizing European Rituals.* London: Routledge.
Bourdieu, Pierre.
  1977.   *Outline of a Theory of Practice.* Trans. R. Nice. Cambridge: Cam-
           bridge University Press.
Breitenbach, Roland.
  1992.   *Lautlos wandert der Schatten: Auf dem Pilgerweg nach Santiago
           de Compostela,* 2d ed. Schweinfurt: Reimund Maier Verlag.
Brodsky-Porges, Edward.
  1981.   "The Grand Tour: Travel as an Educational Device, 1600–1800."
           Annals of Tourism Research 8: 171–86.
Bronseval, Claude de.
  1970.   *Peregrinatio hispanica. Voyage de Dom Edme de Saulieu, Abbé
           de Clairvaux, en Espagne et au Portugal (1531–1533).* 2 vols.
           Trans. M. Cocheril. Publications du Centre Culturel Portugais.
           Paris: Presses Universitaires de France.
Bruner, Edward M.
  1986.   "Experience and Its Expressions." In *The Anthropology of Ex-
           perience,* ed. V. Turner and E. M. Bruner, 3–30. Urbana: Uni-
           versity of Illinois Press.
  1993.   "Epilogue: Creative Persona and the Problem of Authenticity."
           In *Creativity/Anthropology,* ed. S. Lavie, K. Narayan, and R. Ro-
           saldo, 321–38. Ithaca: Cornell University Press.
  1994.   "Abraham Lincoln as Authentic Reproduction: Critique of Post-
           modernism." *American Anthropologist* 96: 397–415.

Buñuel, Luis, dir.
1968.   *La voie lactée.* France: Greenwich-Medusa.
Burgui, José Miguel.
1993.   *El camino a Santiago con jóvenes.* Madrid: CCS.
1997.   *Camino de Santiago. Alicante-Santiago de la Explanada al Obradoiro. Guía del peregrino a pie, en bici o a caballo.* Alicante: Excmo. Ayuntamiento de Alicante.
Campo, Juan Eduardo.
1991.   *The Other Sides of Paradise.* Columbia: University of South Carolina Press.
Cariñanos, Félix.
1991–92. *Testimonios de Peregrinos.* Pts. 1–12. Tierra Estella (Spain). Cultura December 20, January 24, February 7 and 21, March 6 and 20, April 17, May 1 and 29, June 12 and 26, October 21.
Carro Otero, José I.
1993.   "El Año Santo. Su significado religioso-eclesial." In *El Apóstol Santiago y su proyección en la historia. 10 temas didácticos,* 59–66. Santiago: Comisión Diocesana del Año Santo.
Castro, Américo.
1954.   *The Structure of Spanish History.* Trans. E. L. King. Princeton: Princeton University Press.
Caucci von Saucken, Jacopo.
1990.   *Da Roncisvalle a Santiago de Compostela sul Camino de Santiago.* Perugia: Confraternità di San Jacopo di Compostella.
Caucci von Saucken, Paolo.
1993.   "Formas y perspectivas de la peregrinación actual." In *Pensamiento, arte, y literatura en el Camino de Santiago,* ed. A. Alvarez Gomez, 163–79. Vigo, Spain: Xunta de Galicia.
Charpentier, Louis.
[1971] 1976. *El Misterio de Compostela.* Trans. R. M. Bassols. Barcelona: Plaza y Janés. Orig. *Les Jacques et Le Mystère de Compostelle.* Paris: R. Laffont.
Chidester, David, and Edward T. Linenthal.
1995.   "Introduction." In *American Sacred Space,* ed. D. Chidester and E. Linenthal, 1–42. Bloomington: Indiana University Press.
Christian, William.
1978.   "La religiosidad popular hoy." In *Galicia. Realidad económica y conflictos sociales,* ed. J. A. Durán, 551–69. La Coruña: Banco de Bilbao, Servicio de Estudios.
Clifford, James, and George E. Marcus, eds.
1986.   *Writing Culture: The Poetics and Politics of Ethnoqraphy.* Berkeley: University of California Press.
Clissold, Stephen.
1974.   "Saint James in Spanish History." *History Today* 24 (10): 684–92.
Clouse, Robert G.
1978.   "Indulgences." In *The New International Dictionary of the*

Christian Church, ed. J. D. Douglas, 508. Grand Rapids, Mich.: Zondervan.

Coelho, Paolo.

[1987] 1995. *The Pilgrimage: A Contemporary Quest for Ancient Wisdom.* Trans. A. Clarke. San Francisco: Harper. Orig. *O diário de um Mago.* Rio de Janeiro: Rocco.

Coffey, Thomas F., Linda K. Davidson, and Maryjane Dunn, trans.

1996.　　 *The Miracles of Saint James.* New York: Italica Press.

Cohen, Erik.

1973.　　 "Nomads from Affluence: Notes on the Phenomenon of Drifter Tourism." *International Journal of Comparative Sociology* 14: 89–103.

1979.　　 "A Phenomenology of Touristic Experiences." *Sociology* 13: 179–201.

Cohen, Esther.

1976.　　 "In the Name of God and of Profit: The Pilgrimage Industry in Southern France in the Late Middle Ages." Ph.D. dissertation, Brown University.

1980.　　 "Roads and Pilgrimage: A Study in Economic Interaction." *Studi Medievali,* Ser. III, 21(1): 321–341.

Coleman, Simon, and John Elsner.

1995.　　 *Pilgrimage: Past and Present in the World Religions.* Cambridge, Mass.: Harvard University Press.

Constable, Giles.

1979.　　 "Opposition to Pilgrimage in the Middle Ages." *Studia Gratiana* 19(1): 123–46.

Cosgrove, Denis.

1984.　　 *Social Formation and Symbolic Landscape.* London: Croom Helm.

1993.　　 "Landscapes and Myths, Gods and Humans." In *Landscape: Politics and Perspectives,* ed. B. Bender, 281–305. Oxford: Berg.

Cuchi, Asunción.

1994.　　 "Me temo que voy a repetir." In *Hospitaleros en el Camino de Santiago. Informes y Experiencias. Dossier 1994,* 30–31. [Santo Domingo de la Calzada, Spain]: Oficina del Peregrino.

Davidson, J. W., A. Hecht, and Herbert Whitney.

1990.　　 "The Pilgrimage to Graceland." In *Pilgrimage in the United States,* ed. G. Rinschede and S. Bhardwaj, 229–52. New York: Oxford University Press.

Davies, Horton, and Marie Hélène Davies.

1982.　　 *Holy Days and Holidays: The Medieval Pilgrimage to Compostela.* London: Associated University Presses.

de Certeau, Michel.

1984.　　 *The Practice of Everyday Life.* Trans. S. Rendell. Berkeley: University of California Press.

De Ochoa, Carlos, ed.

1917.　　 *Novísimo diccionario de la lengua castellana.* Paris: Librería de la Viuda de Ch. Bouret.

Dietler, Michael.
    1994.   "'Our Ancestors the Gauls': Archaeology, Ethnic Nationalism, and the Manipulation of Celtic Identity in Modern Europe." *American Anthropologist* 96(3) : 584–605.

Dennett, Laurie.
    1987.   *A Hug for the Apostle.* Toronto: Macmillan of Canada.

Diocesan Commission.
    1993.   *El Apóstol Santiago y su proyección en la historia. 10 Temas Didácticos.* Santiago de Compostela: Comisión Diocesana del Año Santo.

Douglas, Mary.
    1973.   *Natural Symbols.* New York: Vintage Books.

Dubisch, Jill.
    1995.   *In a Different Place: Pilgrimage, Gender and Politics at a Greek Island Shrine.* Princeton: Princeton University Press.

Dundes, Alan.
    1980.   "Seeing Is Believing." In *Interpreting Folklore,* 86–92. Bloomington, Indiana. Indiana University Press.

Dunn, Maryjane, and Linda Kay Davidson.
    1994.   *The Pilgrimage to Santiago de Compostela: A Comprehensive, Annotated Bibliography.* New York: Garland.

Dupront, Alphonse.
    1985.   *Saint-Jacques de Compostelle. La quête du sacré.* Paris: Brepols.

Durán, José Antonio.
    1990.   *Angeles del Camino. Poesía e experiencia contemporánea do Camiño de Santiago.* Series: Historias con data. La Coruña: Video Voz for TVG, S.A. Videocassette.

Durant, John.
    1990.   "A Reunion in Germany." *Confraternity of St. James Bulletin* 35: 29–30.

Eade, John.
    1992.   "Pilgrimage and Tourism at Lourdes, France." *Annals of Tourism Research* 19: 18–32.

Eade, John, and Michael Sallnow.
    1991.   "Introduction." In *Contesting the Sacred: The Anthropology of Christian Pilgrimage,* ed. J. Eade and M. Sallnow, 1–26. London: Routledge.

Echevarría Bravo, Pedro.
    1967.   *Cancionero de los peregrinos de Santiago.* Madrid: Centro de estudios jacobeos.

Eco, Umberto.
    1986.   "Return to the Middle Ages." In *Travels in Hyper Reality,* trans. W. Weaver, 59–85. New York: Harcourt Brace Jovanovich.

Editorial.
    1988.   *Peregrino* 1: 2–3.

Eliade, Mircea.
   1958.   *Patterns in Comparative Religion.* Trans. R. Sheed. New York:
             New American Library.
Encuesta '96.
   1997.   *Peregrino* 52: 28–31.
Feinberg, Ellen.
   1985.   "Strangers and Pilgrims on the Camino de Santiago in Spain: The
             Perpetuation and Recreation of Meaningful Performance." Ph.D.
             dissertation, Princeton University.
   1989.   *Following the Milky Way.* Ames: Iowa University Press.
Ferme, Mariane.
   1994.   "What 'Alhaji Airplane' Saw in Mecca, and What Happened
             When He Came Home: Ritual Transformation in a Mende Com-
             munity (Sierra Leone)." In *Syncretism/Anti-syncretism: The Pol-
             itics of Religious Synthesis,* ed. R. Shaw and C. Stewart, 27–44.
             London: Routledge.
Fernandez, James.
   1965.   "Symbolic Consensus in a Fang Reformative Cult." *American An-
             thropologist* 67: 902–29.
Fernández, Jorge.
   1996.   "Ser peregrino, ser hospitalero." *Peregrino* 49: 10–11.
Ford, Richard.
   1855.   *A Handbook for Travellers in Spain.* Pt. 2. 3d ed. London: John
             Murray.
Foster, Carolyn.
   1994.   "Arduous Journeys to Inner Destinations." *San Francisco Chron-
             icle Review,* 1 May, 6.
Foucault, Michel.
   1984.   *The Foucault Reader.* Ed. P. Rabinow. New York: Pantheon.
French, R. M. trans.
   1974.   *The Way of a Pilgrim and The Pilgrim Continues His Way.* New
             York: Ballantine.
Frey, Nancy L.
   1996.   "Landscapes of Discovery: The Camino de Santiago and Its Re-
             animation, Meanings, and Reincorporation." Ph.D. disserta-
             tion, University of California, Berkeley.
Frijns, Frans.
   1995.   *Niet zomaar een weg overwegingen langs de Camino de Santi-
             ago.* With an essay by Dirk Aerts. Brugge: Vlaams genootschap
             van Santiago de Compostela.
Garáte Córdoba, José María.
   1971.   *La huella militar en el camino de Santiago.* Madrid: Publicaciones
             españolas.
García Azpillaga, Pedro.
   1995.   "50 años peregrinando." *Peregrino* 43–44: 27

1996.   "Mi primera peregrinación." *Estafeta Jacobea* 34: 21.
García Costoya, Carlos.
    1993.   *El Camino de Santiago. Año Santo 1993.* Madrid: ABL.
García Mercadal, J.
    1952.   *Viajes de extranjeros por España y Portugal desde los tiempos más remotos hasta fines de siglo XVI.* Aguilar: Madrid.
García Rodríguez, Jaime.
    1992.   *La peregrinación a Santiago en 1991.* Oficina de Acogida del Peregrino. Santiago: SAMI Cathedral.
    1995.   "Prólogo." In *Guía para una peregrinación a Compostela,* J. C. Rodríguez Fernández, 6–9. Logroño, Spain: ARACS.
    1996.   "Párrocos del Camino, III Jornadas de Pastoral." *Compostela* 9: 13–14.
Geary, Patrick.
    1986.   "Sacred Commodities: The Circulation of Medieval Relics." In *The Social Life of Things: Commodities in Cultural Perspective,* ed. A. Appadurai, 169–91. Cambridge: Cambridge University Press.
Geertz, Clifford.
    1973.   *The Interpretation of Cultures.* New York: Basic Books.
Gergen, David.
    1996.   "A Pilgrimage for Spirituality." *U.S. News & World Report,* 23 December, 80.
Gitlitz, David.
    1997.   22 años en Camino. *Peregrino* 52: 10–11.
Goicoechea Arrondo, Eusebio.
    1971.   *Rutas Jacobeas. Historia, arte, caminos.* León: Everest.
Gold, Ann Grodzins.
    1988.   *Fruitful Journeys: The Ways of Rajasthani Pilgrims.* Berkeley: University of California Press.
Gottlieb, Alma.
    1982.   "Americans' Vacations." *Annals of Tourism Research* 9: 165–87.
Graburn, Nelson H. H.
    1983.   "The Anthropology of Tourism." *Annals of Tourism Research* 10: 9–33.
    1989.   "Tourism: The Sacred Journey." In *Hosts and Guests: The Anthropology of Tourism,* 2d ed., ed. V. Smith, 21–36. Philadelphia: University of Pennsylvania Press.
    1995.   "Tourism, Modernity, Nostalgia." In *The Future of Anthropology: Its Relevance to the Contemporary World,* ed. A. S. Ahmed and C. N. Shore, 158–78. London: Athlone.
Graham, Paul, Carlos Paternina, and Adrian Wright.
    1989.   *Santiago de Compostela: A Journey to Help the Hospices.* Henham, Essex: Adrian Wright.
Guerra Campos, José.
    1982.   *Exploraciones arqueológicas en torno al sepulcro del Apóstol Santiago.* Santiago de Compostela: SAMI Cathedral.

Guijarro Camacho, Miguel Angel.
1996.   "Aquel peregrino francés." *Peregrino* 49: 12.
Gurruchaga, Juan.
1993.   "¿Existe la casualidad?" *Actividades Jacobeas. Asociación de Amigos de los Caminos de Santiago de Guipúzcoa* 11: 4–7.
Haab, Barbara.
1992.   "Weg und Wanderlung." In *Symbolik von Weg und Reise,* ed. P. Michel, 137–62. Bern: Verlag Peter Lang.
1993.   "Opiniones." *Actividades Jacobeas. Asociación de Amigos de los Caminos de Santiago de Guipúzcoa* 11: 25–26.
1996.   "The Way as an Inward Journey: An Anthropological Enquiry into the Spirituality of Present-Day Pilgrims to Santiago." Pts. 1 and 2. Trans. H. Nelson. *Confraternity of St. James Bulletin* 55: 16–32; 56: 17–36.
d'Haenens, Albert.
1988.   "Cultural Routes and Collective Memories." *A Future for Our Past* (Council of Europe) 32: 4–5.
Hanbury-Tenison, Robin.
1990.   *Spanish Pilgrimage: A Canter to St. James.* London: Hutchinson.
Harbsmeier, Michael.
1986.   "Pilgrim's Space: The Centre Out There in Comparative Perspective." *Temenos* 22: 57–77.
Henderson, Phinella, ed.
1994.   *A Pilgrim Anthology.* London: Confraternity of St. James.
Herrero Pérez, Nieves.
1994.   "Camiño de Santiago, ¿Ritual secular?" *Irimia* 13 (424): 8–10.
Hirsch, Eric.
1995.   "Introduction. Landscape: Between Place and Space." In *The Anthropology of Landscape: Perspectives on Place and Space,* ed. E. Hirsch and M. O'Hanlon, 1–30. Oxford: Clarendon Press.
Hirsch, Eric, and Michael O'Hanlon, eds.
1995.   *The Anthropology of Landscape: Perspectives on Place and Space.* Oxford: Clarendon Press.
Hitt, Jack.
1994.   *Off the Road.* New York: Simon and Schuster.
Hogarth, James, trans.
1992.   *The Pilgrim's Guide: A 12th-Century Guide for the Pilgrim to St. James of Compostella.* London: Confraternity of St. James.
Hoinacki, Lee.
1996.   *El Camino: Walking to Santiago de Compostela.* University Park: Pennsylvania State University Press.
Hooper, John.
1987.   *The Spaniards: A Portrait of the New Spain.* New York: Penguin Books.
Horne, Donald.
1984.   *The Great Museum: Re-Presentation of History.* London: Pluto Press.

Horner, Alice E.
1993. "Personally Negotiated Authenticities in Cameroonian Tourists Arts." Paper presented to the International Seminar "New Directions of Tourism, with Special Reference to Authenticity and Commoditization." Convened by Shuzo Ishimori and Nelson Graburn, National Museum of Ethnology, Osaka, Japan.

Houdijk, Cootie, and Jan Houdijk.
1990. *Naar de ware Jacob. Dagboek van een voettocht naar Santiago de Compostela.* Santiago de Compostela—Bibliotheek 4. Hague: Vitgeverij Conserve.

Huidobro y Serna, Luciano.
1949–57. *Las peregrinaciones jacobeas.* 3 vols. Madrid: Publicaciones del Instituto de España.

Iriarte, Antxon.
1993a. "¿Andando o en Bici?" *Actividades Jacobeas. Asociación de Amigos de los Caminos de Santiago de Guipúzcoa* 11: 8–11.
1993b. "Peregrinación en autobús." *Actividades Jacobeas. Asociación de Amigos de los Caminos de Santiago de Guipúzcoa* 14: 4–8.

Jacobsen, Jens Kristian S.
1997. "The Making of an Attraction: The Case of North Cape." *Annals of Tourism Research* 24(2): 341–56.

James, William.
[1902] 1985. *The Varieties of Religious Experience.* Cambridge, Mass.: Harvard University Press.

Janin, Louis.
1994. "Hospitalero en Hornillos del Camino." In *Hospitaleros en el Camino de Santiago. Informes y Experiencias. Dossier 1994,* 9–11. [Santo Domingo de la Calzada, Spain]: Oficina del Peregrino.

Kendall, Alan.
1970. *Medieval Pilgrims.* New York: Putnam.

King, Georgiana Goddard.
1920. *The Way of Saint James.* Hispanic Notes and Monographs, Peninsula Ser. 1. 3 vols. Hispanic Society of America. New York: G. P. Putnam's Sons.

Kondo, Dorinne K.
1990. *Crafting Selves: Power, Gender, and Discourses of Identity in a Japanese Workplace.* Chicago: University of Chicago Press.

Krötzl, Christian.
1989. "Pilgrims to Santiago and Their Routes in Scandinavia." *The Santiago de Compostela Routes: Architectural Heritage Reports and Studies,* no. 16, 64–69. Strasbourg: Council of Europe.

Kruyer, Ann.
1996. "The Jato Experience." *Confraternity of St. James Bulletin* 57: 23–27.

Küchler, Susan.
1993. "Landscape as Memory: The Mapping of Process and Its Repre-

sentation in a Melanesian Society." In *Landscape: Politics and Perspectives,* ed. B. Bender, 85–106. Oxford: Berg.

Künig von Vach, Hermann.
1989.   *Un guide du pèlerin vers Saint-Jacques de Compostelle. Le Wall-fahrtsbuch d'Hermann Kunig (1495).* Trans. L. Marquet. Verviers: Imprim-Express.

La Coste-Messelière, René de.
1965.   "Les chemins de Saint-Jacques." In *Pèlerins et Chemins de Saint-Jacques en France et en Europe du Xe siècle à nos jours,* ed. R. de La Coste-Messelière, 41–58. Paris: Tournon.

Ladner, Gerhart B.
1967.   "*Homo Viator:* Mediaeval Ideas on Alienation and Order." *Speculum: A Journal of Mediaeval Studies* 42: 233–59.

Laffi, Domenico.
1997.   *A Journey to the West: The Diary of a Seventeenth Century Pilgrim from Bologna to Santiago de Compostela.* Trans. J. Hall. Leiden, The Netherlands: Primavera Pers.

La Fray, Jean.
1997.   "El camino interior de un peregrino francés." *Compostela* 11: 9–10.

Lamers, Henny.
1987.   *Daboek van een pelgrim naar Santiago de Compostela.* Utrecht: H. J. Lamers.

Lanfant, Marie-Françoise, and Nelson H. H. Graburn.
1992.   "International Tourism Reconsidered." In *Tourism Alternatives: Potentials and Problems in the Development of Tourism,* ed. V. Smith and W. Eadington, 88–112. Philadelphia: University of Pennsylvania Press.

Lavie, Smadar, Kirin Narayan, and Renato Rosaldo.
1993.   "Introduction: Creativity in Anthropology." In *Creativity/Anthropology,* ed. S. Lavie, K. Narayan, and R. Rosaldo, 1–8. Ithaca: Cornell University Press.

Lea, Henry Charles.
1968.   *A History of Auricular Confession and Indulgences in the Latin Church. Vol. 2.* New York: Greenwood Press.

Lodge, David.
1995.   *Therapy.* New York: Penguin.

Longrigg, David.
1994.   *Reflections on the Santiago Pilgrimage, 1994.* Oxford: St. Giles' Church.

López-Barxas, Paco.
1994.   "Compostela. Por la capitalidad cultural del 2000." *Cuadernos del Camino de Santiago* 5: 10–20.

Lowenthal, David.
1985.   *The Past Is a Foreign Country.* Cambridge: Cambridge University Press.

1989.   "Nostalgia Tells It Like It Wasn't." In *The Imagined Past,* ed.
         C. Shaw and M. Chase, 18–32. Manchester: Manchester University Press.
de Lozoya, Marqués.
1969.   "De Santiago Peregrino a Santiago Matamoros." *Cuadernos Hispanoamericanos* 238–40: 399–405.
Luhrmann, T. M.
1989.   *Persuasions of the Witch's Craft: Ritual Magic in Contemporary England.* Cambridge, Mass.: Harvard University Press.
MacCannell, Dean.
[1976] 1989.   *The Tourist: A New Theory of the Leisure Class.* Rev. ed. New York: Schocken Books.
McKie, Alan, and Jean McKie.
1996.   "Returning from Pilgrimage." *Confraternity of St. James Bulletin* 58: 25.
McLuhan, Marshall.
1964.   *Understanding Media: The Extensions of Man.* New York: Signet.
Mahía, Andrés.
1993.   "Xerardo Estévez." *Cuadernos del Camino de Santiago* 1: 6–10.
Mandianes, Manuel.
1993.   *Peregrino a Santiago. Viaje al fin del mundo.* Barcelona: Ronsel.
Marcus, George E.
1995.   "Ethnography In/Of the World System: The Emergence of Multi-Sited Ethnography." *Annual Review of Anthropology* 24: 95–117.
Martínez, Luisa, and Francisco Novoa.
1993.   "Santiago en Europa." *Cuadernos del Camino de Santiago* 2: 82–85.
Marcos-Alonso, Jesús A.
1967.   "Hacia una tipología psicosocial de la identificación religiosa en el catolicismo española." In *Análisis Sociológico del Catolicismo Español,* ed. R. Duocastella, J. A. Marcos-Alonso, J. M. Díaz-Mozaz, and P. Almerich, 97–132. Barcelona: Nova Terra.
Mauss, Marcel.
[1936] 1973.   "Techniques of the Body." Trans. B. Brewster. *Economic Sociology* 2: 70–88.
Meintel, Deirdre A.
1973.   "Strangers, Homecomers and Ordinary Men." *Anthropological Quarterly* 46: 47–58.
Melczer, William, trans.
1993.   *The Pilgrim's Guide to Santiago de Compostela.* New York: Italica Press.
Merton, Thomas.
1967.   *Mystics and Zen Masters.* New York: Farrar, Straus and Giroux.
1993.   *Thoughts in Solitude.* London: Shambala.
Mieck, Ilja.
1977.   Kontinuität im Wandel. Politische und soziale Aspekte der Santiago-

Wallfahrt vom 18. Jahrhundert bis zur Gegenwart. *Geschichte und Gesellschaft* 3: 299–328.

Mitchell, Timothy.
1988. *Violence and Piety in Spanish Folklore.* Philadelphia: University of Pennsylvania Press.

Mooney, Carolyn.
1996. "Notes from Academe: Spain. Battling Blisters and Finding Saints on the Road to Santiago." *Chronicle of Higher Education,* 19 July, A47.

Moore, Sally F., and Barbara Myerhoff, eds.
1977. *Secular Ritual.* Amsterdam: Van Gorcum.

Mora, Juan, José Ignacio Tamargo, and Nacho Catalán.
1993. *El Camino de Santiago a pie . . . y en bicicleta.* 2d ed. Madrid: El Pais Aguilar.

Moralejo, A., C. Torres, and J. Feo, trans.
1992. *Liber Sancti Jacobi. "Codex Calixtinus."* Pontevedra: Xunta de Galicia.

Morán, Gregorio.
1996. *Nunca llegaré a Santiago.* Madrid: Anaya y Mario Muchnik.

Morín, Juan Pedro, and Jaime Cobreros.
[1976] 1990. *El Camino Iniciático de Santiago.* 4th ed. Barcelona: Ediciones 29.

Morinis, E. Alan.
1992. "Introduction." In *Sacred Journeys,* ed. E. A. Morinis, 1–28. Westport, Conn.: Greenwood Press.

Morris, James.
1964. *The Presence of Spain.* London: n.p.

Moser, Dietz-Rüdiger.
1985. "Die Pilgerlieder der Wallfahrt nach Santiago." In *Festschrift für Ernst Klusen zum 75. Geburtstag,* ed. G. Noll and M. Bröcker, 321–52. Bonn: Peter Wegener.

Mouriño López, Eva.
1997. *Vivir o camiño. Revivir a historia.* Vigo: Ir Indo Ediciones.

Myerhoff, Barbara.
1993. "Pilgrimage to Meron: Inner and Outer Peregrinations." In *Creativity/Anthropology,* ed. S. Lavie, K. Narayan, and R. Rosaldo, 211–22. Ithaca: Cornell University Press.

Myers, Joan.
1991. *Santiago: Saint of Two Worlds.* Albuquerque: University of New Mexico Press.

Neillands, Robin.
1985. *The Road to Compostela.* Ashbourne, Derbyshire: Moorland.

Nolan, Mary Lee, and Sidney Nolan.
1989. *Christian Pilgrimage in Modern Western Europe.* Chapel Hill: University of North Carolina Press.

Norris, Kathleen.
1996. "Religio-Tourism on the Shelves." *Hungry Mind Review* 37: 19, 55.

Noticiario Turístico.
1965.   *Camino de Santiago*. Suplemento no. 74. Madrid: Dirección General de Promoción de Turismo.
Los Obispos del "Camino de Santiago" en *España*.
1988.   "El Camino de Santiago." In *Un camino para la peregrinación cristiana. Carta pastoral.* 2d ed. Santiago de Compostela.
O'Guinn, Thomas, and Russell Belk.
1989.   "Heaven on Earth: Consumption at Heritage Village, USA." *Journal of Consumer Research* 16(2): 227–38.
O'Reilly, Sean, O'Reilly, James, and O'Reilly, Tim, eds.
1997.   *Travelers' Tales: The Road Within. True Stories of Transformation.* San Francisco: Travelers' Tales.
Oreja, Marcelino.
1988.   Editorial. *A Future for Our Past* (Council of Europe) 32: 3.
1989.   "Message from the Secretary General of the Council of Europe." In *Architectural Heritage Reports and Studies,* no. 16. Report of the Bamberg Congress. Strasbourg: Council of Europe.
Orensanz, Aurelio.
1974.   *Religiosidad popular española (1940–1965).* Madrid: Nacional.
Oursel, Raymond.
1984.   *Routes romanes. La route aux solitudes.* St. Leger Vauban: Zodiaque.
Palli, Pierre.
1994.   "Crónica de un hospitalero en Logroño." In *Hospitaleros en el Camino de Santiago. Informes y Experiencias. Dossier 1994,* 8. [Santo Domingo de la Calzada, Spain]: Oficina del Peregrino.
Passini, Jean.
1984.   *Villes médiévales du Chemin de Saint-Jacques-de-Compostelle, de Pampelune à Burgos.* Paris: Editions Recherche sur les Civilisations.
1988.   "Identification and Mapping of the 'French Route' in Spain." *A Future for Our Past* (Council of Europe) 32: 23–24.
Payne, Stanley.
1984.   *Spanish Catholicism: An Historical Overview.* Madison: University of Wisconsin Press.
"Un peregrino auténtico."
1989.   *Peregrino* 6: 10.
"La peregrinación en 1996."
1997.   *Compostela* 11: 19–25.
Peregrinación nacional de la Falange a Santiago.
1943.   La Coruña: Delegación Provincial de la Educación Popular.
Pérez-Díaz, Victor.
1990.   "The Emergence of a Democratic Spain and the 'Invention of a Democratic Tradition.'" *Estudios: Working Papers of the Juan March Institute* 1: 1–46.
1991.   "The Church and Religion in Contemporary Spain." *Estudios: Working Papers of the Juan March Institute,* 19: 1–72.

Pfaffenberger, Bryan.
    1983.   "Serious Pilgrims and Frivolous Tourists: The Chimera of Tourism in the Pilgrimages of Sri Lanka." *Annals of Tourism Research* 10: 57–74.
Piñeiro, Félix.
    1997.   *Camino de vida y muerte de un peregrino.* Santiago: Grial.
Pliego, Domingo.
    1994.   "¿Cómo debería de ser el »auténtico« peregrino?" *Estafeta Jacobea* 22: 38–39.
Plötz, Robert G.
    1989.   "Pilgrims and Pilgrimages Yesterday and Today, Around the Example of Santiago de Compostela." *The Santiago de Compostela Routes: Architectural Heritage Reports and Studies,* no. 16, 90–108. Strasbourg: Council of Europe.
    1997.   "Las cofradías de Santiago en Europa." *Compostela* 12: 4–11.
Pombo Rodríguez, Antón Anxo.
    1994.   "Fisterra y Muxía: Sendas jacobeas hacia el ocaso." In *Actas del III Congreso Internacional de Asociaciones Jacobeas.* Oviedo, Spain. 209–47.
Post, Paul.
    1994.   "The Modern Pilgrim: A Study of Contemporary Pilgrims' Accounts." *Ethnologia Europaea* 24: 85–100.
Prescott, H. F. M.
    1958.   *Once to Sinai: The Further Pilgrimage of Friar Felix Fabri.* New York: Macmillan.
Preston, James J.
    1992.   "Spiritual Magnetism: An Organizing Principle for the Study of Pilgrimage." In *Sacred Journeys,* ed. E. Morinis, 31–46. Westport, Conn.: Greenwood Press.
Quaife, Patricia, ed.
    1994.   *Pilgrim Guides to Spain. 1: The "Camino Francés" 1994.* London: Confraternity of St. James.
    1996.   "Discoveries." *Confraternity of St. James Bulletin* 58: 18–22.
Raju, Alison.
    1996.   "Winter Pilgrim." *Confraternity of St. James Bulletin* 58: 29–33.
Ramón y Ballesteros, Francisco de.
    1970.   *Oscurantismo finisterrano.* 2d ed. Santiago de Compostela: Porto y Cía.
    1976.   *Sinfonía en mar mayor: Finisterre.* Santiago de Compostela: Porto y Cía.
Ramos García, Armando.
    1980.   *España. Geográfica, física, humana y económica.* Madrid: Everest.
Redfield, James.
    1993.   *The Celestine Prophecy: An Adventure.* New York: Warner Books.
Rilke, Rainer Maria.
    1951.   *Duineser Elegien; Die Sonette an Orpheus.* Zurich: Manese Verlag.

Roa Irisarrí, Antonio.
  1995.   Letter to author, February 27.
Röckelein, Hedwig, and Gottfried Wendling.
  1989.   "Following in the Footsteps of the Santiago Pilgrims in the Up-
             per Rhineland." *The Santiago de Compostela Routes: Architec-
             tural Heritage Reports and Studies,* no. 16, 33–36. Strasbourg:
             Council of Europe.
Rodríguez Fernández, José Carlos.
  1995.   *Guía para una peregrinación a Compostela.* Logroño, Spain: Aso-
             ciación Riojana de Amigos del Camino de Santiago.
Rodríguez Tero, Agustín.
  1997.   "Peregrinar a Santiago y sus valores. El Camino solo y en grupo."
             Compostela 11: 6–8.
Romero Pose, Eugenio.
  1989.   *El Camino de Santiago Camino de Europa.* Madrid: Encuentro.
  1993.   "Apuntes para la teología de la peregrinación." *Lumieira* 8(22):
             11–26.
Roseman, Sharon.
  1996.   "Santiago de Compostela in the Year 2000: From Religious Cen-
             tre to European City of Culture." Paper presented at the annual
             meeting of the Canadian Anthropological Society, St. Catharines,
             Ontario, May 25–28.
Sallnow, Michael.
  1981.   "Communitas Reconsidered: The Sociology of Andean Pilgrim-
             age." *Man* 16: 163–82.
Sánchez-Agustino, José Luís.
  1993.   *La traslación del Apóstol. Historia, tradiciones y leyendas.*
             Brétema: Vigo.
Schaad, Evelyn.
  1994.   "Una experiencia de hospitalera en Belorado." In *Hospitaleros
             en el Camino de Santiago Informes y Experiencias. Dossier
             1994, 56–58.* [Santo Domingo de la Calzada, Spain]: Oficina del
             Peregrino.
Schieffelin, Edward L.
  1993.   "Performance and the Cultural Construction of Reality: A New
             Guinea Example." In *Creativity/Anthropology,* ed. S. Lavie,
             K. Narayan, and R. Rosaldo, 270–95. Ithaca: Cornell University
             Press.
Schutz, Alfred.
  1945.   "The Homecomer." *American Journal of Sociology* 50: 369–76.
Selby, Betina.
  1994.   *Pilgrim's Road: A Journey to Santiago de Compostela.* London:
             Little, Brown.
Shaw, Christopher, and Malcolm Chase.
  1989.   "The Dimensions of Nostalgia." In *The Imagined Past,* ed.
             C. Shaw and M. Chase, 1–17. Manchester: Manchester Univer-
             sity Press.

Shore, Cris, and Annabel Black.

1992.   "The European Communities and the Construction of Europe." *Anthropology Today* 8(3): 10–11.

Smith, Valene.

1992.   "The Quest in Guest." *Annals of Tourism Research* 19(1): 1–17.

Sobieski, Jacobo.

1878.   "Viaje desde el mes de Marzo hasta Julio de 1611." Trans. F. Rozansky. In *Viajes de extranjeros por España y Portugal en los siglos XV, XVI y XVII,* ed. Javier Liske, 233–67. Madrid: Medina.

Soria y Puig, Arturo.

1993.   *El Camino de Santiago. Vías, estaciones y señales.* 2d ed. Madrid: Ministero de Obras Públicas y Transportes.

Stafford, William.

1989.   "'This Once Happy Country': Nostalgia for Pre-modern Society." In *The Imagined Past,* ed. C. Shaw and M. Chase, 33–46. Manchester: Manchester University Press.

Stanton, Edward F.

1994.   *Road of Stars to Santiago.* Lexington: University of Kentucky Press.

Starkie, Walter.

1957.   *The Road to Santiago: Pilgrims of St. James.* Berkeley: University of California Press.

Stolcke, Verena.

1995.   "Talking Culture: New Boundaries, New Rhetorics of Exclusion in Europe." *Current Anthropology* 36(1): 1–24.

Storrs, Constance.

1994.   *Jacobean Pilgrims from England to St. James of Compostella.* Santiago de Compostela: Xunta de Galicia.

Stromberg, Peter.

1981.   "Consensus and Variation in the Interpretation of Religious Symbolism: A Swedish Example." *American Ethnologist* 8: 544–59.

Suárez Bautista, Joaquin.

1987.   Al peregrino del Camino de Santiago/To the Pilgrim on the Way to Santiago," trans. M. Burke Guerrero. *Confraternity of St. James Bulletin* 23: 7–9.

Sullivan, Lawrence E.

1990.   "Body Works: Knowledge of the Body in the Study of Religion." *History of Religions* 30(1): 86–99.

Sumption, Jonathan.

1975.   *Pilgrimage: An Image of Medieval Religion.* London: Faber and Faber.

"Sur les chemins de Compostelle à l'âge de la 'gazolina.'"

1962.   *Eclair,* November 8.

Swinnen, E.

1983.   Letter in author's possession, 6 June.

Tandeau, Leonard de.
    1997.   "Vivir para los peregrinos." Trans. I. Melchor. *Peregrino* 52: 12.
Taylor, Frank.
    1996.   "Pasos hasta la Compostela." *Estafeta Jacobea* 34: 11–12.
Teas, Jane.
    1988.   "'I'm Studying Monkeys; What Do You Do?' Youth Travelers in Nepal." *Kroeber Anthropological Society Papers* 67–68: 35–41.
Testimonios.
    1994.   *Actividades Jacobeas y Caminos del Espíritu. Asociación de Amigos de los Caminos de Santiago de Guipúzcoa* 18: 13–16.
Theilman, John.
    1987.   "Medieval Pilgrims and the Origins of Tourism." *Journal of Popular Culture* 20(4): 93–102.
Thoreau, Henry David.
    1952.   *Walden; or Life in the Woods. On the Duty of Civil Disobedience.* New York: Rinehart.
Tilley, Christopher.
    1994.   *A Phenomenology of Landscape: Places, Paths and Monuments.* Oxford: Berg.
Torres, Fray Juan Antonio.
    1996.   *Tu solus peregrino. Viaje interior por el Camino de Santiago.* Silos, Spain: Monasterio de Silos.
Tuan, Yi-Fu.
    1977.   *Space and Place: The Perspective of Experience.* Minneapolis: University of Minnesota Press.
Turner, Victor.
    1967.   "Betwixt and Between: The Liminal Period in Rites of Passage." In *The Forest of Symbols,* 93–111. Ithaca: Cornell University Press.
    1969.   *The Ritual Process: Structure and Anti-Structure.* Ithaca: Cornell University Press.
    1992.   "Death and the Dead in the Pilgrimage Process." In *Blazing the Trail,* ed. E. Turner, 29–47. Tucson: University of Arizona Press.
Turner, Victor, and Edith Turner.
    1978.   *Image and Pilgrimage in Christian Culture: Anthropological Perspectives.* New York: Columbia University Press.
Uli Ballaz, Alejandro.
    1990.   *¿Te vienes a Santiago?* Zaragoza: Octavio y Felez.
Uría Maqua, Juan.
    1993.   "Patronazgo de Santiago." *Cuadernos del Camino de Santiago* 2: 34–38.
Valiña, Elías.
    1986.   "Editorial." *Boletín del Camino de Santiago* 9: 132.
    1992.   *El Camino de Santiago. Guía del Peregrino a Compostela.* Vigo: Galaxia.
Van Gennep, Arnold.
    [1909] 1960.   *The Rites of Passage.* Trans. M. B. Vizedom and G. L. Caffee. Chicago: University of Chicago Press.

Vázquez de Parga, Luis, José María LaCarra, and Juan Uría Ríu.
   [1948] 1993. *Las peregrinaciones a Santiago de Compostela.* 3 vols. Pamplona: Iberdrola.
Victor.
   1994.   "Lágrimas de peregrino." *Peregrino* 37–38: 10–11.
Villares Barrio, Manuel.
   1971.   *Ritual del Peregrino. Peregrinación nacional de la Organización Juvenil Española a Santiago de Compostela.* [Madrid]: Delegación Nacional de la Juventud.
Vogel, Cyril.
   1963.   Le pèlerinage pénitential. In *Pellegrinággi e culto dei santi in Europa fino alla,* 37–94. Todi: Centro di Studi Sulla Spiritualita Medievale.
Vuijsje, Herman.
   1990.   *Pelgrim zonder God.* Amsterdam: Utigeverij Contact.
Warcollier, Jean.
   1965.   "Les confréries des pelerins de Saint Jacques." In *Pelerins et Chemins de Saint-Jacques en France et en Europe du Xe siècle a nos jours,* ed. R. de La Coste-Messeliere, 85–89. Paris: Tournon.
Ward, Benedicta.
   1982.   *Miracles and the Medieval Mind.* Philadelphia: University of Pennsylvania Press.
Wey, William.
   1992.   "An English Pilgrim to Compostela." Trans. J. Hogarth. *Medieval World* 5: 15–19.
Whitehill, Karen.
   1990.   *A Walk across Holy Ground.* Wheaton, Ill.: Tyndale House.
Winchester, Simon.
   1994.   "The Long, Sweet Road to Santiago de Compostela." *Smithsonian* 24(11): 64–75.
Zimdars-Swartz, Sandra.
   1991.   *Encountering Mary: From La Salette to Medjugorje.* Princeton: Princeton University Press.

INDEX

Boldface page numbers refer to illustrations and their captions.

modern pilgrims (*continued*)
"refuge pilgrims," 100; religious affil-
iations, 4, 8, 18, 21–22, 29–36, 72;
repeat, 19, 47, 48, 75, 211–14, 226;
return, 102, 179; "rules," 51; and sacrifice, 22, 63–65, 109; "serial," 211–
12; setting off, 52–55; signs of, 55–
63, 64; Spanish, 29, 32–33, 36–37,
50, 141, 148, 184, 211–12, 245,
259n15; as spiritual messengers, 66,
128; starting point, 53–54, 68–69;
statistics kept on, 28–30, 127, 159–
60, 258n14, 259n15; values, 27; views
of authenticity, 128–30. *See also* associations; authenticity; credential, pilgrim's; goal; home; motives; pilgrimages; social element; space; time;
transport
money. *See* economics
Monte del Gozo, 149–52, 269n14;
amusement park project, 253; bus
groups walking from, 23; as end, 140,
155; Hermitage of San Marcos, 35;
refuges, 150, 151
Monte Irago, 23–26, 24–25, 35. *See also*
Cruz de Ferro
Moors, 11, 227–28. *See also* Santiago
Matamoros/Moorslayer
Morán, Gregorio, 147
Morín, Juan Pedro, 34
Morinis, E. Alan, 178, 262n2, 271n4,
273n18
motives, 21–49, 52, 258n10, 262n2;
Angela's divisions, 30–31; and
authenticity, 128, 129, 159–61, 228;
evolving, 44–45, 138, 232; layered,
44–46, 48–49; Marina's, 72; of medieval pilgrims, 14; multiple, 27, 28–
29; nature appreciation, 37, 38, 221,
258n14; penitential, 13, 14, 42–44,
261–62n39; religious, 21–33, 55, 67,
127, 129, 155–61, 187–88, 228,
258n14; spiritual, 27–34, 159–60,
258n14; suffering soul, 45. *See also*
goal
mountaineering, associations, 242
mountains, space division and, 75
Mountains of Mercury, 23
Mouriño López, Eva, 274n1
movement, 72–81, 267–68n42; as art,
86, 132–33; and authenticity, 128–33;
cessation of, 164–65; choice of, 49;
internal, 47; meanings of, 218–23;
polemics of, 17–19, 27. *See also* inner
journey; physical activity; travel
Muslim occupation: of Jerusalem, 13;
of Spain (Moors), 11, 227–28. *See*

also Islam; Santiago Matamoros/
Moorslayer
Muxía, 170–71
Myerhoff, Barbara, 271n3
Mystery of Compostela (Charpentier),
244
mystical experiences, 81, 223. *See also*
miracles; spirituality

names, pilgrim nicknames, 92
Napoleon, 41
narratives: ending with goal, 177–78;
memoirs, 204; retelling experiences,
186–87, 199, 206, 272n13; of return,
181. *See also* books; diaries; letters;
magazine articles; newspaper articles
National Catholicism, 238, 243, 246–47
National Coordinator of Associations,
246
National Highway 120, 241–42
nationalism: associations fostering, 209;
Spanish, 238
National Social Security Institute, Spain,
22
nature appreciation: as pilgrim motive,
37, 38, 221, 258n14; and reanimation,
241, 244; sense of union, 81; and
technology, 132. *See also* landscapes;
senses
Navarre, 5–6; Alto del Perdón, 103;
cyclist pedaling through wheat, 119;
Friends, 128, 246, 264n28; languages,
88; medieval, 12; Nuestra Señora de la
Trinidad de Arre, 43; villager-pilgrim
interactions, 64–66; walking pilgrims,
19, 39, 40, 64–65. *See also* Estella
Navarro, Javier, 28
Neillands, Rob, 52
Neria, 171
New Age movements, 34, 244
newspaper articles: pilgrims inspired
by, 51; Santiago, 206
New World Movement, 244
nicknames, among pilgrims, 92
Norway, pilgrim associations, 207
nostalgia, 41–42, 175–76, 221–22,
261nn33,35. *See also* history
Noya, 34, 170
Nuestra Señora de la Trinidad de Arre,
43
Nunca Llegaré a Santiago (Morán), 147

occupation: pilgrim, 29, 258–59n15. *See
also* careers
Oikoten, 42
Opus Dei, 249
Order of Santiago, 260n27

Compositor:	Integrated Composition Systems
Text:	10/13 Sabon
Display:	Sabon
Printer and Binder:	Malloy Lithographing, Inc.